DIVIDED LOYALTIES

For David Bell, Sr.

Edited by MARTIN KOLINSKY

assisted by David Scott Bell

DIVIDED LOYALTIES

British regional assertion
and European integration

Manchester University Press

Published by Manchester University Press
Oxford Road, Manchester M13 9PL

British Library cataloguing-in-publication data

Divided loyalties.
    1. European Economic Community – Great Britain. 2. Decentralisation in government – Great Britain. 3. Great Britain – Politics and government, 1964–
    I. Kolinsky, Martin. II. Bell, David Scott.
    354'.4'082   JN329.D43

    ISBN 0–7190–0694–5

Computerised Phototypesetting by
G.C. Typeset Ltd., Bolton, Greater Manchester

Printed in Great Britain
by Unwin Brothers Limited
The Gresham Press, Old Woking, Surrey

CONTENTS

THE CONTRIBUTORS

Denis Balsom Research officer in the Department of Political Science, University College of Wales, Aberystwyth

David Scott Bell Research Fellow, Centre for Contemporary European Studies, University of Sussex

Hugh Berrington Professor of Politics, University of Newcastle upon Tyne

Peter Byrd Lecturer in Politics, University of Warwick

Byron Criddle Lecturer in Politics, University of Aberdeen

John R. Greenwood Lecturer in Government, Leicester Polytechnic

Martin Kolinsky Senior Lecturer in Political Science, University of Birmingham

Peter J. Madgwick Reader in Political Science, University College of Wales, Aberystwyth

Edward P. Moxon-Browne Lecturer in Political Science, Queen's University of Belfast

Gordon Smith Senior Lecturer in Government, London School of Economics and Political Science

Helen Wallace Lecturer in European Studies, University of Manchester Institute of Science and Technology

David J. Wilson Senior Lecturer in Politics, Leicester Polytechnic

PREFACE

A new political and constitutional environment has emerged in Great Britain during the 1970s. Parallel with growing involvement in the European Community, the rise to prominence of Scottish and Welsh nationalism intensified pressures for devolving power to sub-state levels. Are these two aspects of a basic underlying process leading to the disintegration of the classical nation-state? Or are they two different processes which may actually result in a strengthening of the role of central government? This could occur through its co-ordination of policies and close monitoring of developments at European and regional levels. The purpose of this book is to consider the impact of the changing circumstances on Westminster and Whitehall, and the attitudes and responses of the political parties.

A few comments on terminology are necessary. The term 'region' has different usages: as a geographical reference; as a unit of administration (e.g. the upper tier of local government in Scotland, Regional Hospital Boards, etc); as a sub-national political unit, comparable to provinces or *Länder*; as a territory within which there is a strong political and cultural self-awareness. The latter may be described as 'regional nationalism' or 'sub-state nationalism'.

The particular meaning is usually given by the context. However, the *ambiguity* in the phrase 'regional assertion' is of a different order because the political implications of territorially based movements are uncertain. Does nationalism lead necessarily to independence and separatism? Is it possible to delegate some powers of central government without undermining the cohesion and sovereignty of the unitary state? Is federalism, in which sovereignty is transferred on some matters but not on others, a viable half-way house between separatism and devolution? The national identities of Scotland and Wales may make it preferable to think of them as countries in some respects. But their whole relationship with England in the polity and society of the United Kingdom has to be considered also, as Richard Rose has done in his discussion of the United Kingdom as a 'multi-national' state.[1] The rise of nationalist parties in Scotland and Wales, however, has undermined the broad consensus about the nature of the relationships with central government and has sharply posed the constitutional issue. The fundamental uncertainty is that the constitutional form of a multi-national state may vary from the unitary, with different degrees of decentralisation and devolution, to the confederal.[2] Beyond that lies separatism. The development of these problems and the conjunction with the process of European integration are the basic concerns of this volume.

The book is the result of a collaborative effort which was made possible by a grant from the Nuffield Foundation. The editors wish to express their gratitude to the contributors for their tremendous co-operation during the initial stages in 1975, the workshop discussions in March 1976, and subsequently in the preparation of the chapters. The project benefited greatly from the advice and constructive criticisms of Dr William Paterson, and from the help of Dr Wyn Grant and Dr Frank Wooldridge. Pertinent comments on specific matters were made by Andrew Orridge, Dr Eva Kolinsky, John Fitzmaurice and Len Tivey. They do not, of course, necessarily agree with the views expressed in the book, nor are they responsible for any errors or omissions. A great deal of friendly assistance was provided by Mr Bert Howes, University of Birmingham library; Mr Bill Osgood, who had to cope with frequent photocopying 'emergencies'; and Miss Marjorie Davies, whose typing and secretarial aid were splendid. Eva greatly helped to keep it all in perspective, and led the way to Solla Sollew.

M.K.

NOTES

1 University of Strathclyde, Survey Research Centre, Occasional Paper No. 6, 1970.
2 See *Royal Commission on the Constitution 1969–1973* (Kilbrandon Report), Cmnd.5460, October, 1973, Vol. 1, pp. 134, 165.

MARTIN KOLINSKY

1 Introduction

Of the many changes in British political life since the 1960s the two of greatest constitutional significance have been participation in the European Community and the question of devolution. By the time the issue of membership had passed the purgatory of 'renegotiation', the question of devolution was gaining in importance. Was it a coincidence that the forceful emergence of regional identity/sub-state nationalism[1] occurred during the transition to Europe? Is it a paradox that pressures on the highly centralised unitary state for constitutional change intensified when Britain began to participate in the tortuous process of transnational integration?

On the level of day-to-day political activity, the issues did not seem to be related, although they were intertwined in the politics of Scotland and Wales. Both emerged on the national level as discrete sequences of events, affecting different groups of people, interests, and departments of government. On Labour's return to power in February 1974 both issues grew in urgency. The conflict within the Labour Party over the terms of accession to the Common Market had not abated, and the question of membership was reopened. Then, too, the nationalist parties became prominent for the first time: the Scottish National Party (SNP) and in Wales the Plaid Cymru. The future of the two major parties in Scotland was at stake, but the more immediate issue was that of Europe. The process of renegotiation was an extraordinary test of the political skills of the Labour leadership, which juggled a divided party and faced incredulous partners in the Community. The uncertainties were eventually resolved in the June 1975 referendum, with a massive endorsement of the government's position. The decisive result of 67 per cent in favour (in Scotland 58 per cent, in Wales 65 per cent) was a surprise at the time, though the forces in battle during the campaign were uneven. Both the government and the well endowed European Movement (drawing on the Conservatives, Liberals, a section of the Labour Party, the CBI and the EC Commission) supported acceptance of the renegotiated terms.[2]

The October 1974 election confirmed the growing electoral strength of the SNP. Its share of the vote in Scotland increased by more than a third (200,000 voters) to reach over 30 per cent. The SNP overtook the Conservatives as the second party in Scotland in share of votes, but won eleven seats as compared with sixteen for the Conservatives. Labour remained in the lead with forty-one seats and 36·2 per cent of the votes. It represented a very minor victory, with the recapture of a seat lost in the February election, and the loss of a mere half per cent of votes. But the decline in the share of votes from the 1966 peak of nearly 50 per cent could not be ignored, especially as the SNP continued to do consistently well in local and regional elections. The movement was poised to threaten Labour's dominance in the industrial belt.[3] Although the Plaid Cymru challenge in Wales was much less dramatic, the political pressures for constitutional change were intensifying. The report of the Royal Commission on the Constitution (Kilbrandon),[4] which had been appointed in 1969 in response to the stirrings of nationalism, was published in October 1973. This brought forward the issue of devolution, but the political agendas were crowded in the closing months of the Heath government (the Yom Kippur war, the energy crisis, the three-day week, the miners' strike) and after the February 1974 elections. Although the issue was overshadowed by renegotiation and the quarrels over Community membership, it was mentioned in the Queen's Speech of 12 March 1974. Subsequently Lord Crowther-Hunt, co-author of the Memorandum of Dissent to the Kilbrandon Report, was appointed special constitutional adviser to the government, and a Constitution Unit was established in the Cabinet Office. At irregular intervals, with rumours of behind-the-scenes wrangling and unhappy compromises, a number of government documents were issued: fuel to a sporadic, passionate, repetitious debate.

INTERACTION OF THE TWO ISSUES

Although devolution and European integration have remained separate political issues, the interaction between them has become more pronounced. It was most noticeable in the negotiations over direct elections to the European Parliament, where the question of representation of the constituent parts of the United Kingdom was affected by nationalist arguments that Scotland and Wales should have parity of representation with the small states – Denmark and Ireland. Another aspect, more fundamental, was that each issue tended to reinforce and enhance the role of central government, as was underlined by the changes in the Cabinet Office. It is not without irony that the questions of devolving and transferring powers to new political authorities stimulated further concentration in the executive-administrative core of central government. It sought a new grip on things as it was called upon to preside over modifications in the scope and patterns of its authority. This is much more than administrative co-ordination and control; the management of policies are affected as well. On a range of EC issues – fishing, energy, agriculture, transport and regional policies – the 'national' interest and the regional implications are carefully weighed and defined. The Cabinet and the civil service are acutely aware of the flashpoints in the reactions of anti-Marketeers, nationalists, and aggrieved interests which could align with them.

The interaction of the two issues derives from the changing position of the traditional nation-state in the post-war situation of military and economic interdependence. This has exposed domestic economies to a growing degree of internationalisation, but it was more belatedly recognised in Britain than in France and Western Germany. The inner reserve of sovereignty which British governments tried to maintain after the second world war and during the 1950s proved to be increasingly illusory – the aspiration for a place among the super-powers through a 'special relationship' with the United States; the hopes placed in the Commonwealth, a highly diversified organisation too loosely structured to carry much weight in international economic and political affairs; and rather despairingly the establishment of a (peripheral) Free Trade Area in Europe (EFTA), which was eventually abandoned. In the 1950s Britain had declined to join the supranational organisations which were based on the recognition of interdependence: the European Coal and Steel Community (ECSC), the proposed European Defence Community (EDC), the Common Market and Euratom. However, this attitude was revised in the 1960s when first the Conservative government (under Harold Macmillan) and then the Labour government (under Harold Wilson) made unsuccessful bids to join. The tradition of detachment from Europe was brought to an end, though a marriage[5] could not be arranged until President de Gaulle had left the scene. The adaptations and changes required by membership of a formal organisation with unique juridical and political practices and obligations were not faced until the 1970s. Then the uniqueness of Britain – its legal system, parliamentary practices, patterns of trade, and international connections – had to be brought into co-ordination with the European Community.

Membership of the European Community has accelerated the erosion of the traditional division between foreign and domestic affairs, adding a European dimension to many fields of activity in the Ministry of Agriculture, Fisheries and Food, the Departments of Trade, Industry, and the Environment, the Scottish, Welsh and Northern Ireland Offices, and the Treasury. And conversely membership has brought the Foreign and Commonwealth Office into a new relationship with the Home departments. At the same time, over a whole range of policies, concerning resources, prices, technology, law, and administrative and economic organisation, the place of decision-making has partially shifted from Whitehall-Westminster to hover uncertainly over the Channel. The change was strikingly symbolised in the controversy over milk surpluses which a leader in *The Times* (15 April 1976) commented on under the heading: 'Skimmed milk and sovereignty'. Although the focus of power remains in the Cabinet, power itself has acquired an elusive quality as new circuits of consultation and policy-making are added. The doctrine of ministerial responsibility is difficult to maintain when decisions taken in the Council of Ministers are known to be compromises based on a package deal. These changes, both actual and potential, experienced as well as anticipated, have brought into question the old fixed certainty of the authority of central government.

As Helen Wallace shows in her chapter on 'Problems of government and administration', the role of central government is challenged by claims that some policies should be managed at the international level, and others by devolved regional government. These pressures have elicited defensive reactions from Ministers and officials, who have sought to protect their traditional powers. Although attitudes towards Community membership and the devolution issue contrast significantly, in both respects there has been a marked preference for administrative devices that adapt rather than alter the framework of government. Rather than contemplate a bold recasting in accordance with a lessening of the work of Westminster and Whitehall, the prevailing tendency is to reinforce the role of central government. The drift to the centre is made apparent by the enlargement of the Cabinet Office and the development of its functions of departmental co-ordination, policy analysis, oversight and regulation of issues.

The drive for cohesion in spanning the range of activities, however, leaves unresolved the growing problem of the 'over-extension' of central government and the weakening of its capacity to deal satisfactorily with critical areas of political change. Since many Community issues have regional and local implications, the problem of integrating competing regional interests is becoming acute, especially as failure to satisfy can intensify nationalist or regional assertion. Moreover the increasing self-awareness of regions stimulates desires for more direct access to Community decision-making. The interaction of the two issues raises constitutional problems which may be only temporarily and imperfectly contained by administrative adjustments within the traditional unitary state.

However, political agreement on the direction of change has proved extremely difficult to attain, because of the very sharp divisions of opinion within the major parties. The reactions of the Labour Party are examined in Peter Byrd's chapter. Despite a long-standing commitment to the idea of Scottish home rule, the party has been suspicious about devolving power from the centre. The firm attachment of Wales and Scotland to the Union, and the allegiance of those two areas to the Labour Party, were fundamental to Labour's hopes of exercising power at Westminster. In foreign policy the party espoused the ideals of 'internationalism', but was sceptical about the development of regional supranational institutions which might threaten both wider forms of international co-operation – such as the United Nations and the Commonwealth – and the exercise of power at the national level by a Labour government. The issue of joining the European Community raised both these problems, and seriously divided the party. The management of the two issues, clearly related to each other in terms of Labour's aspirations to control the *state*, is particularly interesting because it reveals differences of policy within the different institutions of the Labour Party, and between the idealism of Labour aspirations and the pragmatism of Labour policies. The conflict, in turn, has precipitated a fundamental debate about the distribution of power within the party and the continued relevance of its traditional socialist dogma.

The attitudes in the Conservative and Liberal parties are discussed by John Greenwood and David Wilson. Divisions over membership of the Community were manifest in the Conservative

Party, though they did not become as serious and as tenacious as in the Labour Party. Whereas European integration was consistent with the outlook of the Liberal Party, it represented a certain break from traditional Conservative principles, particularly as it implied accepting unaccustomed constraints in international and domestic affairs and a downgrading of Commonwealth (Empire) connections. Several factors account for the relative ease of transition to a Community orientation, including declining trade with the Commonwealth as opposed to the sparkling economic success of the Common Market, and the unwelcome diplomatic demands of the new Commonwealth (Third World) countries as opposed to the attraction of a new European idealism. The latter, with its Churchillian antecedents, has been strongly encouraged by the party leadership since Macmillan's conversion in the early 1960s. The firm commitment of Conservative leaderships was an important political element, as was the prevailing attitude of the business community in hopeful expectation of economic rewards in Europe.

There are further contrasts in party attitudes towards devolution. The principles of decentralisation and representative regional government form an essential part of the Liberal Party programme, with its stress on a federal structure of government, whereas the Conservative Party is deeply attached to its Unionist traditions. However, electoral pressures in Scotland have not allowed the Conservatives, any more than the Labour Party, to rest at ease on the *status quo*. The Conservative leadership recognised the importance of Scottish nationalism in the late 1960s, but it did not become a major issue within the party until it became clear that the Labour government would introduce legislation on devolution. As the strength of the anti-devolutionists in the Conservative Party became more apparent during 1976, reinforced by the strong emphasis of the CBI on the economic unity of the UK, and by the unbending hostility of the Scottish CBI, Mrs Thatcher's policy became increasingly ambiguous. Although both opposition parties voted against the guillotine motion on the Scotland and Wales Bill in February 1977, there was a striking contrast between the Liberal Party's desire to strengthen the powers of the Scottish Assembly, and the probability that the Conservative commitment to an Assembly would become 'inoperative', if at all possible.

The relationship of the two issues therefore appears in a different light in each party. The federalist perspective of the Liberals enables them to advocate a reallocation of the powers of the unitary state to regional and European authorities. Given the deeply ingrained opposition to federalism, such a combination of changes is attractive to only a small minority in the other parties. Economically motivated Europeanism is hostile to devolution or any form of political decentralisation which might impinge on the economic unity of the country and make the formulation of objectives in the Common Market more uncertain. This runs parallel to a more political concept of European integration which is concerned with the problems of Western European stability and security, and which at the same time seeks to exercise British influence abroad in terms of the traditional centralised authority of the nation-state. These aspirations predominate in the Conservative party and strongly influence the leadership of the Labour party. The resultant consensus about the preferred nature of European integration is a British form of Gaullism, expressed in the ideological formulas of each party. But there are tendencies which point in the direction of some modification to this narrowly focused 'pragmatism': nationalism in Scotland and Wales has created a new sense of competing regional interests, and this is reinforced by a more explicit awareness of within-nation differences in the Community context. These tendencies have caused some internal divisions within the Conservative Party, and may lead to policy adjustments over time.

A review of changes in Britain is presented in Hugh Berrington's chapter 'Dangerous corner?' He examines the trends of 'minor partyism' in the post-war period, noting that only the most recent wave, primarily arising from Scottish and Welsh nationalism, has posed a threat to the established political institutions. The effect of nationalism will be to stimulate competition among the regions, most notably in the north of England. Although an 'English backlash' is unlikely to create break-away regional or splinter parties, more pronounced pressures may be expected to result in 'a rather undignified kind of pork-barrel regional politics, conducted to a large extent behind the scenes at Westminster'. A further possible effect is that, since regional politics of this nature cuts across the issues of class and economic control to some extent, ideological polarisation, particularly within the Labour Party, will tend to diminish.

The problems posed in the management of political change arising from this issue and the process of European integration impinge on established constitutional practices. Several aspects are considered, including the question of referenda, the blurring of conventions regarding the relationship between government and Parliament, and the issue of proportional representation. Berrington brings into the discussion of these problems a perspective on the strains to which democratic regimes are subjected.

CENTRALISATION AND THE PROBLEMS OF IDENTITY

Although the two issues interact with increasing intensity, there are striking contrasts between them. The origins of the European movements lie in the anti-Fascist Resistance of the second world war, and are unrelated to the problems of the Welsh language and the Scottish economy. The ideology of European integration, in one variation or another, is most strongly held among economic, administrative and political elites, few of whom are enthusiastic about sub-state nationalism. In some respects the two sets of ideologies are diametrically opposed: to transcend nationalism – to assert it; to enlarge the scale of economic and political co-operation – to transfer power to a smaller, more tangible political entity. The differences may be juxtaposed to exaggerate the contrasts: the plans for a Common Transport Policy – the demand for road signs in Welsh; the frantic hopes for a Common Energy Policy – the claim that offshore oil is Scottish; the vital historical reference points which recall the dreadful experiences of Nazism (in EEC jargon, 'The European civil war') – the treasured memory of Bannockburn.

The differences to a certain extent sum up in a contrast between bureaucratic elitism and emotional populism. They are underlined by the apparent paradox, often mentioned in discussions and debates,[6] that, while powers of decision-making are being transferred from Westminster to Brussels, devolutionists seek to weaken Westminister further by transferring powers to Edinburgh and Cardiff. These contrasts are overly dramatic. The shift away from a single pattern of political integration in the nation-state is not a paradox: it derives from the growing interdependence of states and the consequent effects within national structures, which together give rise to more complex patterns of political relations. Both devolution and European integration involve the central government in new processes of decision-making and in new opportunities for policy formation. There are also new opportunities for asserting identity, as will be discussed later in this section.

Despite the differences and contrasts between the two issues, there is a common focus: a questioning of the validity of the overwhelming concentration of powers in central government. It is not a theoretical and abstract questioning, but pragmatic and realistic perspectives of change which emerge from various historical tendencies.

The union of Wales and England (the Tudor Acts of 1536 and 1542) and of Scotland and England (the Union of Parliaments in 1707) provided the political framework for the far-reaching economic integration which the industrial revolution and Empire trade created. These developments resulted in an increasing centralisation of political power in London during the nineteenth century. The counter-pressures, such as the National Association for the Vindication of Scottish Rights in 1853, the Scottish Home Rule Association of 1886, and Cymru Fydd (New Wales) in 1887, were significant enough to lead to some measures of decentralisation. The office of Secretary for Scotland was established in 1885, and its chief executive was accorded the status of a Principal Secretary of State in 1926. The Scottish Grand Committee was established in Parliament in 1894 to consider Scottish legislation. The vital added stimulus behind these changes was the struggle over Home Rule for Ireland. In Wales, separate educational institutions were established in the last quarter of the nineteenth century, and the disestablishment of the Church of England in Wales, long sought, finally occurred after the first world war. Administrative decentralisation, narrower in the range of functions than in Scotland, did not follow until the second world war and after. However, the basic trend was that of increasing centralisation, and it accelerated in the twentieth century. World wars, economic crises, nationalisation, and the provision of health and welfare programmes multiplied the functions of central government. The vast expansion of the role of the state intensified the problems of exercising democratic control and has raised serious questions about the effectiveness of traditional parliamentary practices. An aspect of this broad problem is the constitutional structure of the United Kingdom and the nature of political identity in the constituent parts.

Historically, to the extent that union with England was economically successful and politically coherent, a British dimension was added to and partly merged with Scottish and Welsh identities. A balance was established between a sense of separateness and a common British identity in the experiences of war and, more generally, through pride in the Empire. Underlying and cementing the political relation were ties of marriage, social bonds, culture and language. But these ties exist with other English-speaking countries as well, and do not preclude a different order of political relationship. The declining importance of the Commonwealth, the transition to an uncertain European involvement, and the prolonged economic crisis have all contributed to a devaluation of the wider British identity. The stress in Scotland and Wales on national identity has brought the underlying paradox of dual identity into the forefront of public concern.[7] The paradox lies in the entanglement of the two identities such that neither can unambiguously stand on its own, yet the balance between them has become difficult to maintain. The rise of sub-state nationalism has undermined the political homogeneity of the unitary state, and has questioned the centralising processes of assimilation. But independence is a risk which minimises the depth of the connection with British society.[8] The problem intensified after the two elections in 1974 because the SNP, having become a serious political factor, indicated that it would interpret winning a majority of Scottish seats as a mandate to open negotiations for independence. Its highly optimistic views about the prospects for an independent Scotland, which are in marked contrast with most other analyses,[9] are of course sustained by the vision of oil revenues. Oil is a significant factor in the situation, but it is not the cause of it. Both Welsh and Scottish nationalism predate the discovery of offshore oil, though the major SNP electoral gains of 1974 occurred afterwards. There is little doubt that a majority of people in Scotland, while desiring constitutional change, do not want separation.[10] Nevertheless the political outcome is unforeseeable.

The question of whether or not it may be possible to find a solution to the problem posed by nationalism short of separation, either in some form of devolution or of federalism, may take years to determine. But it is worth noting that there are points of difference which distinguish Scots and Welsh nationalisms from similar movements elsewhere. The dimensions of ethnic/language conflict are more pronounced in Belgium and in Canada; the central government has reacted in a markedly more repressive manner in France and in Spain. This is not to deny the importance of the linguistic and cultural dimension in Wales, nor the sense of economic frustration in Scotland. But the question of the Welsh language is for Wales alone; it does not impinge directly on relations with the rest of Great Britain, as is the case of the language conflicts in Belgium and in Canada. Moreover language is not an issue at all in Scotland. Therefore the cultural/linguistic aspects of regional nationalism in the British situation are more readily separable from the central political and economic issues than elsewhere. This fact is reinforced because British identity was traditionally multiple, embracing sets of dual loyalties. The stress has been on the form of the state as unitary – and unlike France it has not been necessary to buttress it with cultural uniformity. Nor has there been a development of relatively closed socio-political 'pillars' as in Holland.[11] It could be claimed, with considerable justification, that the traditions of cultural, religious and ethnic pluralism are distinguishing achievements of the United Kingdom. There is, then, a difference of degree which exists in the recognition of Welsh cultural identity and the corresponding non-recognition of Breton or Basque identities.

These differences are obscured by the glib theory of internal colonialism',[12] which implies a parallel with national liberation movements seeking to throw off the bonds of subjugation. Both Scotland and Wales shared in the industrial development of Britain, and their economic difficulties are not separable from those of other regions. These include the decline of traditional industries on which their former prosperity was based, and the problems of attracting new industry and achieving growth.[13] Moreover, as geographically contiguous parts of the United Kingdom, their relationship with central government developed in a vastly different manner from that of a colony.[14] There was, first of all, a long-standing basic consensus about the value of the unitary structure which enabled the Scots to act as partners in the running of the Empire. The unitary structure was moreover sufficiently flexible to include a separate Scottish legal system and Scottish Church. There was also recognition of the problems of political representation of the constituent parts in Parliament and later at Cabinet level. Briefly, then, in terms of the long-standing acceptance of the unitary state, the extent of political homogeneity, or compatibility, and the expression of cultural distinctiveness, as well as the closely bound economic and social relationships, the analogy of colonial exploitation is misleading. This conclusion suggests, further, that the possibilities for compromise in the redefinition of the terms of the relationship may be greater than in France, Spain or Canada.

It is possible to analyse sub-state nationalism in terms other than its cultural-historical reference points and symbolism. It may be seen as a form of regional assertion, a reaction to bureaucratic overcentralisation and stifling of democratic potential. The matter may be put in terms of enhancing democracy by placing control of affairs in the hands of the people who live closest to the problems. The argument can be made to seem compelling: regional assemblies would reduce the overloading of central government, would return power to the people, would co-ordinate and rationalise the activities of *ad hoc* bodies, and would strengthen both national and regional economic planning.[15] This raises the prospect of English regional Assemblies. Although the boundaries of English regions are uncertain,[16] the case for directly elected regional assemblies or indirectly elected councils has been presented several times.[17] But it is clearly a marginal issue in so far as there have not been politically significant movements demanding their establishment. There is also the point, perceptively made by Peter Pulzer, that, because social class differences are nation-wide in England, 'class is itself a factor making for national unity'. He stated: 'As a result, the major political issues which divide opinion are felt equally strongly throughout the country. What affects voters in Dorset also affects voters in Northumberland.'[18] However, this may change in some respects: in the three northern regions and the south-west there is acute awareness of relative deprivation, and the reactions to proposals for devolved Assemblies in Scotland and Wales may stimulate desires for decentralisation, if not full-fledged legislative devolution.

In addition, increased awareness of internal differences is likely to follow the process of European integration. The reasons are (i) the continued internationalisation of domestic policies, and (ii) the new opportunities for identification. First, the elaboration of common European policies, and the less ambitious attempts to co-ordinate policies, stimulate a greater sense of comparability. This increases awareness of regional differences within and between nations. Secondly, there is a tendency towards pluralism or even fragmentation in the Community. The trilateral relations of West Germany, France and Great Britain form a basis for centralisation which, however, is tentative and ambiguous because of self-interest and because of the context of association with the half-dozen other states. Alignments shift and cross-cut in the changing flux of issues, so that it can be a liberating game for the smaller members. The Community structure provides an opportunity for reasserting and re-evaluating national identity (as in the case of Ireland), and setting it in a richer, more diversified context. The development of an Irish-

European sentiment is a possibility which can have appeal in Scotland and in Wales. These tendencies could also develop into pressures for a pronounced and viable English regionalism.

The transition to Europe opens the way to a recasting of identity on different levels, though the uncertainties of the integration process and the disillusionments of the epoch make it precarious.

TRENDS IN WESTERN EUROPE

The conjunction of pressures for change, which have been magnified in Britain in recent years, are trends running through Western European politics as a whole. There are regional/nationalist issues of varying intensity in France (Corsica, Brittany, Alsace), Belgium (the Flemish–Walloon problem), Italy, and Spain (the Basque country and Catalonia). More generally there are serious economic discrepancies among the regions. A comparative survey[19] has shown that whereas geographical differences in prosperity are relatively decreasing in the United States, it was not true of the European Community over the period 1960–70. The first Annual Report of the European Regional Development Fund (July 1976) confirmed the trend. Given the difficult economic situation characterised by inflation, declining investment and rising unemployment, the gap in *per capita* incomes among member states has widened dramatically, and the discrepancies between the more prosperous areas and the poorer regions has intensified. The report of the comparative survey emphasised the need for Community regional policy because the economic direction is 'towards regions which are the most interesting from the industrial point of view', and this in itself carries 'a danger that the regional prosperity discrepancies may be accentuated'. It estimated that at the present level of aids, including national aids, the Community could not narrow the range of discrepancy to that currently prevailing in the United States until the year 2025. It concluded that in order to achieve the goal of levelling out regional differences more quickly a massive transfer of resources from the well-off regions, via the European budget, is required. However, the report does not attempt to delve into the political problems of significantly expanding the budget in this direction.

One of the main arguments advanced in favour of developing a European regional policy is that a more even spread of income, employment and social opportunities is essential for the cohesion and integration of the Community. In other respects too the nature of European integration remains problematic. The wide differences in national economic performance have made the hopes of economic and monetary union by 1980 unreal. Unrestrained self-interest during the oil crisis following the Yom Kippur war seemed to threaten the very foundations of the Community. Less dramatically but persistently the formulation of Community policies is made extremely difficult by national reservations arising from domestic pressures. The European Commission, a supranational institution, has been dominated by the Council of Ministers and COREPER, representatives of the national civil services at Brussels who prepare the agendas for the Council of Ministers. The Commission has been further overshadowed by regular summit meetings of heads of government. The lack of political will was so manifest in the years 1973–75 and the sense of stagnation so profound that the Community seemed moribund.

On the other hand, the Community's capacity to survive crises has been proved many times over. Although the Commission is not in a strong position, it has been able to project the need for common policies and for closer political co-operation. The European Court of Justice is constantly elaborating on the basic legal framework of the Treaties. The Community is regarded as a force in its own right in world trade, and to a limited extent in international relations. Its development is erratic, the goals unclear, but the pull beyond the boundaries of the nation-states to some form of 'Europeanism' is strong. The underlying economic thrust is massive, and it has been accompanied by an ideological force of some attraction. At the same time the regional problems and manifestations of sub-state nationalism have intensified, so that the nation-state in Western Europe appears to be under pressure from two opposing tendencies.

A 'EUROPE OF REGIONS'?

An intriguing possibility is the ultimate convergence of these tendencies in the form of a 'Europe of Regions'.[20] This is essentially a federalist concept which could seem attractive from the perspective of regionalist movements. But it is difficult to imagine a positive response from central governments. Would an independent government in Edinburgh, for example, endorse the separate representation of the Shetland Isle in Brussels? The partial exception to the rule excluding sub-state representation in Brussels is the German *Länder* observer who attends meetings of the Council of Ministers and COREPER, and who reports to the *Länder* governments. His role is to convey information, not to participate in decision-making.[21] In the United Kingdom, the White Paper on devolution (Cmnd 6348, November 1975, para. 87) specifically excluded the possibility that devolved Assemblies could have direct relations of their own with Brussels, as do the Scotland and Wales Bills. Although some informal contacts exist,[22] it may be expected that any tendency to loosen central government control of decision-making in the Community context will be doggedly resisted.[23] The government's position has been that Scotland's advantage lies in being a constituent part of a large and influential state.

The nationalists, however, have created a dilemma by pressing the view that Scotland is best served by representing itself. It would gain a place, and a veto, at the Council of Ministers; it could be directly represented in the Commission and at the European Court of Justice; and it would have a greater number of members of the European Parliament, equal to Denmark. There is little evidence so far to suggest that British Ministers and representatives have failed to deliver on matters vital to Scotland at the EC, notably hill farming, regional aids, and energy. Scottish interests have been fully considered in these areas for two basic reasons: the heightened political sensitivity of the Scottish connection; and the fact that the Scottish Office is a repository of high-calibre expertise in those areas, so that it represents an important administrative resource for the central government in its EC negotiations. There are limits, however, since Scottish interests within the UK have to be related to the other regions. There is no guarantee that the government will always be willing or able to press the Scottish case with full heart. This would be particularly so if a fundamental divergence of views should arise, as may be the case over oil revenues, prices and the rate of depletion. Nevertheless the option of independence and equal representation with the small states of the Community has drawbacks as well. A small state benefits principally when its interests coincide with some of the others, as in the case of Irish agriculture and the Common Agricultural Policy. But Scotland has much less to gain from CAP, and as an industrialised country would have to face the rigours of competition and non-oil trade deficits on its own. The economic prospects of an independent Scotland, especially after oil depletion, are the subject of controversy among Scottish economists. Whatever one's views about how far oil revenues are likely to go in creating new industrial prospects, the small size of the Scottish home market and the consequent heavy dependence on external trade must raise the nagging problem that an 'independent' economic policy would be narrowly circumscribed by external factors.[24] In that perspective it is by no means certain that the formal status of a small state would provide as much influence and protection for Scotland in the ceaseless EC negotiations as remaining within the UK. The viability of an independent Scotland is not in question, though the political options which will influence its relative degree of prosperity or poverty are at issue.

A 'Europe of Regions' may appear an ideal solution to some, but it is not a serious prospect. The Commission is not in a position to risk a confrontation with central governments, even if it was unreservedly enthusiastic about the idea. But the logic inherent in the Commission's situation tends to preclude such a development: the 'politics of concertation'[25] is complicated enough as it is, and with the prospect of further enlargement of the Community to include Greece, Portugal and Spain, overloading could seriously impede the flow of decision-making. Moreover the Community's impetus is to the larger scale; its visions are continental. So while the Commission may seek to have some leverage against national governments by attracting the support of the regions, it can have no interest in risking the balkanisation and fragmentation of the Community.

THE MEDIATING ROLE OF THE STATE

Nevertheless the 'reactivation of the principle of political territory' (in Gordon Smith's phrase) has vigorously brought into question the concentration of powers in central government and the consequent arthritic effects on regional cultures and democracy. The movement from 'below' coincides with the growing interdependence within the Community to produce two contrary effects. One is to diminish the traditional authority and pre-eminence of the state. The other, perhaps paradoxically, has reinforced it as a medium through which the two emerging spheres necessarily function. The co-ordinating role of the central government in regional economic planning and tax sharing would be enhanced in a system of devolution. Similarly in the European Community the state does much more than function as an agent of supranational authority; it is crucial to the initiation, co-ordination and development of policies.

Both the federalist idea of the nation-state diminishing in significance, and the more general 'Europeanist' view that the state will eventually become a middle tier of government (a kind of county council) overlook the mediating and co-ordinating roles of the state. The same is true of the anti-Market fear that European union would reduce member states to the level of provinces. This is to minimise the enormous administrative capacities which have developed over a long period of time, and the extent to which the states are meaningful expressions of political territory. In short it is to misjudge the contemporary nature of the state. This is not altogether surprising because the viability of the traditional nation-state in Western Europe has come into question from several sources. After both world wars there were strong reactions against aggressive nationalism, and concomitant desires for international co-operation. The League of Nations and its successor the United Nations were established as international agencies and forums, as was the Council of Europe. But the ideology of transnational integration aimed at a different type of political organisation: a union of states, a relinquishment of sovereignties; not a forum for public declaration. The need for integration was felt strongly in Europe because of the problem of the post-war role of Germany and the development of the Cold War. It was strengthened by the growing interdependence of the military and economic spheres. The establishment of the European Coal and Steel Community and the Common Market were relatively successful innovations, with a measure of supranational autonomy, opening the prospect for the development of common policies and orientations in many fields of activity. The recent world-wide economic changes, symbolised and accelerated by the 1973 oil crisis, have reinforced the need for integration, though the politics of seeking competitive advantage with Third World suppliers of resources, as well as the vast economic discrepancies among the Nine, have made bold steps towards further integration extremely difficult to realise.

Another source of questioning the viability of the traditional nation-state arose from the internal environment. The vast expansion in the role of the state in economic and social activities, which is analysed in Gordon Smith's chapter as the 'logic of overextension', has roused a mounting volume of criticism. At one level, political pressures for cuts in public expenditure express non-socialist resentments at the erosion of traditional distinctions between private opportunities (education, property, etc) and public obligations and regulation. It is the old cry against state 'interference', perhaps more deeply felt than ever, with bitterness against the civil service becoming more notable in recent years. On another level, the criticism of overcentralisation and the attack on bureaucracy are a demand for democratic participation and strengthening of grass-roots democracy. Whereas defenders of the concept of the unitary state may see in administrative decentralisation a means of efficient management, the nationalist movements have given vivid expression to a more radical association of political territory and democracy. The notion of *devolution* is an attempt to compromise between 'managerial' and 'participatory' motivations,[26] which seem to stand in contradiction.

These internal and external changes impel new adaptations of the state. But it would be a wild exaggeration to see in them a coming eclipse of the nation-state, much less its withering away. The crisis of oil and inflation which followed the Yom Kippur war of 1973 underlined the fragility of transnational integration. The Community floundered in *sauve-qui-peut* national self-seeking, and there was serious doubt for a time about its chances of survival. The 'dangerous corner' of renegotiation, referendum, energy crisis and inflation *could* have been destructive. It was not, but it is interesting to note that the only significant (potentially at least) transfer of national sovereignty in response to the crisis was the setting up of the Kissinger-inspired International Energy Agency. This underlines the limitations of European integration, even in economic terms. It suggests that if there are to be various types of supranational organisations (some including the USA) in response to different issues, then the transfer of sovereign powers from the nation-state may be much more conditional and controlled than has been assumed hitherto.

The Community, nevertheless, is the focus of European integration, and after the traumatic years of 1973–75 a new realism about its relations with the member states had developed.[27] There is a clear recognition that the Community is capable of developing policies which co-ordinate and supplement national policies but do not replace them. The Community is therefore caught up in its own pluralism and tendencies towards fragmentation while its impetus is towards integration and centralisation.

Within this uncertain, shifting context there is a danger that democracy could become impoverished. The problem is not that it is likely to be destroyed by dictatorial closure, but that the role of parliaments will become even more marginal than at present. The chapter on 'Changing contexts of parliamentary activity' emphasises that although more parliamentary bodies are in the offing, democratic control could diminish rather than increase. The introduction of direct elections to the European Parliament poses the question of future relations with Westminster. It is important in two respects: (a) because enlargement to 410 full-time members will increase the legitimacy and potential of the European Assembly as a Parliament-in-the-making, even though there may not be an immediate prospect of augmenting its formal powers; and (b) because of the implications in the United Kingdom itself of eighty-one MEPs representing regional interests directly in European forums. In addition, the prospect of devolved Assemblies poses a further set of problems which impinge on the role of Parliament. These include the definition and exercise of the powers of the Secretaries of State for Scotland and Wales, the lack of mechanisms for administrative co-ordination and legislative implementation such as exist in full-fledged federal systems, and the possibility of reproducing on the regional level the same imbalance of executive legislative relations found at national level. These considerations indicate some of the difficulties in developing the degree of inter-parliamentary co-ordination necessary to sustain control over the multiple legislative and policy processes. Against this, the central government is in a strategic position to co-ordinate policies and to monitor developments. The drift to the centre is a prevailing response to the increasing differentiation, and overlapping, of levels of decision-making.

The viability of the European Parliament in isolation from national parliaments may be seriously doubted. The introduction of a complex political structure at the European level necessarily entails the development of complex arrangements for maintaining and strengthening democratic practices. It is an illusion to think that European, national, and regional parliaments can become effective within their own spheres by transfers of powers without considering the question of their mutual links.[28] There is a danger of gaps appearing because the transfer of power from one level does not necessarily result in a gain of competence at another. Power can easily slip away to the co-ordinators in the confusion of authority. 'Lost sovereignty'[29] would reinforce the prevalent bureaucratic tendencies of 'la "dictature" transitoire des exécutifs'.[30] Therefore a fundamental reconsideration of the potential role of national parliaments in the Community is in order. Radically new ideas for restructuring institutional relations are not required. It would be sufficient to draw the existing representative channels into a closer relationship with Community decision-making. If this end could be achieved in practical political terms, it would help overcome the crisis of legitimacy, and could provide in the future a framework in which regional assemblies could function effectively.

The conjuncture of integrative tendencies on the European scale and aspirations for regional control may at first seem contradictory. But the shift from concentrated unitary authority to more complex patterns is a result of the enormous changes in the position and potential of Europe since the second world war. The old world of the traditional United Kingdom has passed, and new forms of government and representation are emerging. An examination of the process is the purpose of this book.

NOTES

1 See preface for a discussion of these terms.
2 The opposition within the Labour Party was very strong, and the pro-Market position of the Prime Minister and Foreign Secretary was rejected by a two-to-one majority (3,724,000 votes to 1,986,000) at the special Labour Party conference, April 1975. But in the country at large the anti-Market organisations were of bantam-weight stature financially, with few outstanding personalities in their service.
3 See Byron Criddle's chapter on Scotland, and Dean H. Jaensch, 'The Scottish vote, 1974: a re-aligning party system?', *Political Studies*, September 1976. For Wales, see the chapter by Peter J. Madgwick and Denis Balsom, and their article 'Changes in party competition in elections: the Welsh case and the British context', *Parliamentary Affairs*, winter 1974–75.
4 Vol. I, 1973, Cmnd 5460; vol. II, Memorandum of Dissent, Cmnd 5460–1, by Lord Crowther-Hunt and Professor A. T. Peacock.
5 F. S. Northedge, *Descent from Power: British Foreign Policy, 1945–73*, Allen & Unwin, 1974, pp. 142–43.
6 For example, Ian Mikardo, speaking for the NEC recommendation to reject the principle of direct elections to the European Parliament at the Labour Party conference, September 1976, said, 'That was worse than riding two horses at the same time: it was riding the same horse in opposite directions at the same time.'
7 T. C. Smout, 'The historical separateness of the Scots', *New Society*, 1 July 1976.

8   See the SNP statement, 'The context of independence', July 1976.

9   See Gavin McCrone, *Scotland's Future: the Économics of Nationalism*, Blackwell, 1969; Kilbrandon Report, ch. 12; 'Labour's analysis of the economics of separation', the Scottish Council of the Labour Party, January 1976; the Smallwood–Mackay debate in M. G. Clarke and H. M. Drucker, *Our Changing Scotland*, EUSPB, 1976, pp. 98–107; Michael Fry, 'The fallacies in SNP economics', *The Scotsman*, 18 December 1976.

10 See the ORC Poll, *The Scotsman*, 26 October 1976.

11 See Arend Lijphart, *The Politcs of Accommodation*, University of California Press, 1968.

12 See Michael Hechter, *Internal Colonialism: the Celtic Fringe in British National Development, 1536–1966* Routledge & Kegan Paul, 1975. For critical comments see Cornelius O'Leary, 'Celtic nationalism: a study in diversity', IPSA Congress, August 1976, pp. 32–39.

13 Kilbrandon Report, p. 140; also pp. 178–9 re republic expenditure per head in the four countries of the UK. Britain's energetic regional policies over the last decade have been based on restraining developments in the south-east and West Midlands in order to encourage investment particularly in Scotland and Wales. See Gavin McCrone, *Regional Policy in Britain*, Allen & Unwin, 1969; Ross McKay, 'The northern region in the context of Europe', Windermere conference, 24 September 1976 (NEDC–Cumbria CC–UACES).

14 Ireland may be seen as an exception in some respects because 'centralised and effective administration and much of the impetus towards pluralist democracy came in one way or another from Ireland's lengthy period under the British Crown' (Andrew Orridge, 'Political change in Ireland: a study of Fianna Fail', Ph.D. thesis, University of Manchester, 1977, ch. 1, p. 34). His concept is not internal colonialism but a pattern of modernisation which he refers to as 'hegemonic modernisation'.

15 See Kilbrandon Report, chs 8, 9, 27; Memorandum of Dissent, especially ch. II, pp. 82–3; Derek Senior, 'Regional devolution and local government', in Craven (ed.), especially p. 144; and Craven, 'Introduction'.

16 See Peter Hall, 'The geographical puzzle of the regions', *New Society*, 1 July 1976; Kilbrandon Report, ch. 7; Senior's chapter in Craven (ed.), pp. 163–5.

17 Memorandum of Dissent; Royal Commission on Local Government in England, 1966–69 (Redcliffe, Maud), Cmnd 4040, vol. 1, ch. X; Senior, in Craven (ed.). See also Isserlis, in Craven (ed.), pp. 188–90, for a statement of a minimalist position advocating administrative decentralisation with elective regional consultative bodies.

18 Peter G. J. Pulzer, *Political Representation and Elections in Britain*, Allen & Unwin, 1972 (rev. edn), p. 46. See also pp. 118–20.

19 'Slender European budget for vast regional discrepancies', Kredietbank of Belgium, weekly bulletin, 28 February 1975.

20 For a discussion of the notion of a 'Europe of Regions' in relation to the

Kilbrandon Report see R. A. W. Rhodes, 'Anaemia in the extremities and apoplexy at the centre', *New Europe*, winter 1973–74. See also Desmond Banks, 'Liberals and a federal Europe', *ibid*.

21 See Chistopher J. Hull, 'The federal dimension of the making of European policy in West Germany, ASGP–UACES conference at LSE, May 1976.

22 See the following three chapters; also James G. Kellas, 'The effect of membership of the European Community on representative institutions in Scotland', a report for the Hansard Society, 1976.

23 The view expressed by Isserlis in Craven (ed.), p. 175, may be widely shared in central government: '. . . the probability of continuing growth in the extent of Britain's exposure to international influences and obligations will call not for less but for more integrated direction and management of the country's public business . . .'.

24 Kilbrandon Report, pp. 146–9.

25 See Ghita Ionescu, *Centripetal Politics*, Hart-Davis MacGibbon, 1975.

26 James Cornford (ed.), *The Failure of the State*, Croom Helm, 1975, 'Introduction'.

27 Antony Crosland, Secretary of State for Foreign and Commonwealth Affairs, speech to the European Parliament at the beginning of the UK presidency of the EC, *The Times*, 14 January 1977.

28 See the discussion of the 'interlocking principle' in the Memorandum of Dissent, pp., xv, xvii, 57, 116.

29 Luxemburgensis, 'The emergence of a European sovereignty', in Ghita Ionescu (ed.), 'Between sovereignty and integration', Croom Helm, 1974, pp. 131–4.

30 Charles-Albert Morand, 'Le contrôle démocratique dans les communautés Européennes', Liège, VIIIème Colloque sur les CE, March 1976, p. 9; Antonio Papisca, 'Moyens d'expression du citoyen dans un système socio-politique en formation', Colloque sur le Citoyen et l'Union Européenne, Turin, October 1976, p. 12.

EDWARD P. MOXON-BROWNE

2 Northern Ireland

In the context of the debate on devolution Northern Ireland stands in marked contrast to both Scotland and Wales. It is the only part of the United Kingdom to have had an extended period of devolved government. That experiment lasted for over fifty years. In spite of the present uncertainty in Northern Ireland, it is widely assumed that the province will eventually return to some kind of devolution in the future. By coincidence, therefore, three parts of the United Kingdom are expecting increased participation in the control of their own destinies. But there the similarity ends, since Northern Ireland would be returning to something familiar while Scotland and Wales would be embarking on something totally new. The British government has kept its options open:

The unity of the United Kingdom does not mean uniform treatment for all its parts. This White Paper is about devolution to Scotland and Wales, and its proposals are related to their circumstances. As the White Paper of September 1974 made clear, Northern Ireland is in a different category. Its history and geography distinguish it from other parts of the United Kingdom, as does the presence of two separate communities. Its problems are not those of Scotland or Wales, and therefore do not necessarily require the same treatment.[1]

Nevertheless the fact that Northern Ireland experienced over half a century of devolution is a factor in politics there today; and the basic questions are 'when' and 'how' rather than 'whether'; the debate itself can be carried on in the light of what went before, whereas in Scotland and Wales the arguments must be more hypothetical. Finally, and most obviously to outsiders, Northern Ireland has suffered civil disorder since 1968 on a scale unknown in the rest of the United Kingdom. One by-product of this violence is that it distracts local politicians from national issues which, nonetheless, help to shape events in the province. The timing of the general election in February 1974, for example, or the decision to hold a national referendum in June 1975, were viewed by local politicans as intruding awkwardly into regional politics; and both polls had unintended repercussions. Above all, violence itself produces conflicting results, since it makes politicians less willing to compromise while, at the same time, making it more urgent that they do so.

In retrospect, the most important development for Northern Ireland in the early 1970s may prove to be the entry of the United Kingdom into the EEC. In Northern Ireland the consequences of that event do not loom large in the public mind. This is not to say, however, that the EEC plays no part in politics in Northern Ireland. On the contrary, both consciously and unconsciously, politicians react to the implications of the EEC and are, in turn, influenced by it. The problem is to extricate the EEC from among a number of factors which mould politics in Northern Ireland and, in particular, to determine its effect on efforts being made there to achieve a constitutional settlement.

From the time of the Government of Ireland Act, 1920, until the enactment of the Northern Ireland (Temporary Provisions) Act, 1972, Northern Ireland enjoyed devolution within the United Kingdom to an extent far greater than anything envisaged currently for either Scotland or Wales. The 1920 Act was intended to apply to the whole of Ireland, and it was only when the southern government failed to implement certain provisions (e.g. the machinery for a Council of Ireland) that modifications became necessary in the application of the Act to Northern Ireland. Although, in theory and in law, the Northern Ireland Parliament was given power to legislate over a wide variety of matters, this freedom was in fact restricted by the reality that the area of expenditure over which Stormont had control exceeded the extent to which Stormont could levy adequate taxation. From 1945 the balance was made up by the British government, and this led naturally to both governments being in continual discussion over matters of public expenditure. Greater freedom prevailed, however, in fields where expenditure was minimal; in regulatory matters, and in security matters. The border increasingly assumed an international status as the Eire government distanced itself from the intentions of the 1920 Act. In turn, sporadic violence from the IRA in the 1920s, the 1950s and after 1968 resulted in security legislation peculiar to Northern Ireland being passed to combat terrorism. In particular the Civil Authorities (Special Powers) Act (Northern Ireland), 1922, provided for internment without trial. Later the creation of the exclusively Protestant paramilitary Ulster Special Constabulary was to become a source of grievance among the minority community. The concentration of power in the hands of one party between 1921 and 1969 led to complacency among Unionists themselves and, among the opposition, a diminishing sense of responsibility. In such an atmosphere it was easy for allegations of discrimination to thrive, in the area of local government generally, and specifically in the allocation of housing. By 1968, owing partly to factors mentioned above which Catholics were now less ready to accept, civil disorder had begun to break out in several places in Northern Ireland. The report of the Scarman Tribunal attributed these disorders not to any premeditated campaign but to a 'complex political, social and economic situation'. Although the disorders arose from small beginnings, 'the communal tensions were such that, once begun, they [the disorders] could not be controlled'. The forces of law and order were increasingly unable to cope with these disturbances and consequently the British government found itself drawn into Northern Ireland affairs to a greater extent than hitherto. In August 1969 all security operations were placed under the General Officer Commanding (Northern Ireland). At the same time the 'Downing Street declaration' reiterated the majority's right to remain within the United Kingdom as long as it wished, but also emphasised the implementation of various measures in Northern Ireland aimed at eliminating grievances of the minority community. The army's increasing strength in Northern Ireland reflected the growing gravity of the situation there. From about 3,000 in the summer of 1969 troop strength grew to 13,000 by the following summer and reached a peak of 21,000 in the summer of 1972. Neither the presence of the army nor the use of detention without trial between 1972 and 1975 made an appreciable impact on the level of violence, although, in the absence of such measures, there could have been a greater escalation of terrorism. The withdrawal of the Social Democratic and Labour Party from Stormont, and the introduction of internment in late 1971, led eventually to the transfer of responsibility for security in the province to the British government. Thereupon the Northern Ireland government resigned. The British Parliament enacted the Northern Ireland (Temporary Provisions) Act in March 1972, which effectively vested in the Secretary of State for Northern Ireland the powers formerly exercised by the Northern Ireland government. Henceforth, as previously, twelve MPs represented Northern Ireland at Westminster. 'Direct rule'

continued until 31 December 1973, when, by the Northern Ireland
Constitution Act, 1973, certain legislative and executive functions
were devolved to a Northern Ireland Assembly elected by
proportional representation. The Northern Ireland Executive took
office on 1 January 1974. Following the UWC strike in May, the
Executive resigned and the Assembly was prorogued. The
Executive's functions reverted to the Secretary of State. He and his
junior Ministers (Stanley Orme, Lord Donalson, Roland Moyle and
Dennis Concannon) became answerable to Parliament at
Westminster for the government of Northern Ireland. The junior
Ministers were each placed in charge of several departments, while
Mr Rees retained control of the crucial areas of constitutional
development, law and order, and security. In July 1974 Mr Rees
published a White Paper proposing a Northern Ireland Convention,
to be given the task of considering what provision for the government
of the province was likely to command the most widespread
acceptance there. The Convention elections were held on 1 May
1975. The Convention submitted a report in December 1975, but the
British government asked the Convention to consider further some
aspects of the report, in particular those relating to the participation
of the minority parties in government. This second phase ended in
February 1976, without any major breakthrough.

THE EEC AND NORTHERN IRELAND

As part of the United Kingdom, Northern Ireland experienced
changes on entering the EEC which were fundamentally no different
from those experienced by the country as a whole. In one sense, of
course, the impact was less, since Northern Ireland already enjoyed
conditions of free trade within the United Kingdom and, to an
increasing extent, with the Irish Republic. In another sense, the
impact was to become more noticeable, since the Northern Ireland
economy differs in important respects from that of the mainland.
Both the burdens and the privileges of membership have affected
Northern Ireland more markedly than they have the remainder of
the United Kingdom.

In November 1971 the government of Northern Ireland had issued
a White Paper, *Northern Ireland and the European Communities* (Cmnd
563), in which the implications of membership for Northern Ireland
were set out. The principal theme of the White Paper (and its

slender dimensions) made one point clear: the Northern Ireland government did not expect the province to be affected by membership in any way distinct from the rest of the country. The only important respect in which the terms of entry had taken account of Northern Ireland's special needs was in the matter of employment. To enable Northern Ireland to continue the operation of the Safeguarding of Employment Act (Northern Ireland), 1947, which instituted a system of permits for those seeking employment in the province, the EEC 'agreed to grant to the United Kingdom for a period of five years a derogation from the Community's secondary legislation in the field of the free movement of labour in respect of Northern Ireland'.[2]

Despite the generally optimistic tone of the White Paper and its echoing of sentiments already expressed by the British government in its own account of the entry negotiations (*The United Kingdom and the European Communities*, Cmnd 4715), there were hints of problems peculiar to Northern Ireland. Three will be mentioned here. Firstly, while it was realised that the lowering of tariffs between the United Kingdom and the Six would open up new opportunities for Northern Ireland exporters, it was also realised that the British market, which absorbs about 60 per cent of Northern Ireland exports, would now be open to imports from the Continent competing on equal terms. Secondly, whereas previously foreign investors might have selected Northern Ireland as a point of access to the United Kingdom and, by extension, EFTA markets, the relative attractions of the province within an extended customs union might be considerably reduced. Thirdly, while a fairly rosy prospect for beef, pork and dairy farmers was envisaged under the application of the Common Agricultural Policy, it was pointed out that the greater dependence of Northern Ireland on imported feedstuffs (85 per cent) as compared with Britain (35 per cent) could lead to a proportionately heavier burden of costs falling on the Northern Ireland farmer than on his British counterpart. The relatively greater efficiency of the latter was, in any case, reflected in the fact that Northern Ireland farms are generally half the size of British ones.

The impact of EEC membership did not become a topic of public discussion until the end of 1974, when the Labour government embarked on its 'renegotiation' of the entry terms for the United Kingdom as a whole. The public interest which that process aroused in Britain extended to Northern Ireland, but it was not until the new terms had been finalised, and the referendum announced, that political parties took up positions on the various issues involved. Thus we turn next to the referendum in Northern Ireland.

THE REFERENDUM

The decision of the British government to hold a referendum on 5 June 1975 to test public reaction to the renegotiated terms of EEC entry did not create quite the same impact in Northern Ireland as it did in the rest of the United Kingdom. The referendum itself was not an innovation for the Northern Ireland electorate, since the device had been used in March 1973 in an attempt to dispose of the border as an issue in Northern Ireland politics. Secondly, the EEC was not, and never had been, a very live issue in Northern Ireland, since it was realised that the province could not influence either the conditions of membership or the outcome of the national result to any great extent. Thirdly, and most important, local politics continued to predominate both in the public consciousness and in the media. This was especially the case in the spring of 1975, when both the Convention elections on 1 May, and later the sessions of the Convention itself, captured all the public attention as well as the headlines. Just as the general election of February 1974 had been held for 'British' reasons on issues which hardly concerned Ulster; just as that election had had the unintended consequences in local politics of revealing widespread opposition to power-sharing; so, also, the Common Market referendum seemed irrelevant and distracting beside the immeasurably greater problem of drafting a constitution for the province. Yet, despite the heavy responsibility thrust on them by the terms of the Northern Ireland Act, 1974, politicians in Northern Ireland found themselves required by their electorate to pronounce upon the merits or otherwise of the United Kingdom's remaining within the EEC. This was an issue which had received neither study nor interest hitherto; and thus, at a time when parties had to campaign for the Convention elections, they also had to brief themselves on the implications of EEC membership. The task was a daunting one, since the politicians found themselves faced by an issue which could not be assessed simply in the context of a divided community. Almost any other issue could be logically viewed through lenses tinted with sectarian hostility; but not the EEC. Thus the politicians were faced with an issue which could not easily arouse tribal passions, and yet it required a reaction from a community traditionally divided along sectarian lines. The result was deliberate obfuscation. Both the issues and the reactions to the issues were deliberately clouded to make them more manageable, with the result that truth was distorted and a potentially elevated and unifying theme (i.e. co-operation in Europe) rendered mundane and divisive. The political parties were not, of course, the only groups which sought to guide the electorate in the run-up to the referendum. A number of non-political organisations, some permanent and some formed specially for the purpose, gave clear guidance to their adherents as to how they should vote on the day. Unlike the political parties, these groups were not constrained by the sectarian cleavage which lies at the heart of Ulster politics. On the other hand, they probably carried less weight with the voters than did the political parties, since the latter were able, in some cases, to capitalise on the affective ties of religion. This last point is not, of course, peculiar to the referendum. It is one of the features of Ulster politics that religious and political leaders often play convergent roles; and the path from pulpit to ballot box is short and straight. The existence, however, of non-political interest groups, campaigning on either side of the Common Market issue, meant that an individual might be subjected to conflicting advice and, in the event, be forced to decide whether his role as farmer, for example, outweighed his role as follower of a particular political party.

During the month prior to the referendum it was widely predicted that Northern Ireland would vote by a slim majority against the EEC. A poll taken among the seventy-eight members of the Northern Ireland Convention a month before polling day revealed that forty of them would vote 'no' and thirty would vote 'yes', with eight undecided. If the members of the Convention were an accurate reflection of Northern Ireland views on the EEC, then there would be a majority in favour of leaving. The poll showed that there was a strong correlation between power-sharing and the EEC. The fact that of the forty-seven Loyalists in the Convention thirty-eight were opposed to the EEC showed the extent to which, by May 1975, the EEC issue was becoming resolved along sectarian lines. There were, however, a number of factors which made it increasingly easy for Loyalists to adopt an anti-EEC stance. Firstly, there was the justifiable fear that the EEC represented a threat to national sovereignty. Already smarting from the loss of a regional parliament in Belfast, Loyalists deplored the remoteness of decision-making which 'direct rule' implied. How much worse it would be, they

argued, for economic decisions to be taken in Brussels. Coupled to
this fear was the corollary realisation that the border would become
less important in Irish politics the greater the degree of
harmonisation between member states of the EEC. Secondly,
Loyalists resented the 'meddling' (as they saw it) by European
organisations in Northern Ireland's internal affairs, aided and
abetted, so it sometimes seemed, by the Irish government. The long-
drawn-out case before the European Court of Human Rights
concerning the treatment of detainees in Northern Ireland, and the
discussion of the Northern Ireland problem in the European
Parliament, were perceived as examples of interference and
suggested that Northern Ireland was, in some way, less a part of the
United Kingdom than other regions, since the British government
was hardly likely to tolerate such discussions in respect of other
domestic matters. Thirdly, the more the Irish government expressed
enthusiasm about the EEC the more the Loyalists suspected that the
EEC was a strategy for achieving a united Ireland by stealth. These
suspicions were deepened in the period before the referendum, when
the Irish government made it clear that Ireland would remain in the
EEC whatever the outcome of the British poll. The prospect of the
Community's external tariff barrier running between the two parts
of Ireland (if the United Kingdom withdrew from the EEC) helped
to rally moderate opinion around the pro-Market cause. Nor did the
fact that Ireland (by virtue of its presidency of the Council of
Ministers) was the focus of much Community activity in the spring
of 1975 do anything to allay Loyalist fears.

It can be appreciated from what has been said that there is no
direct ideological link between being in favour of both power-sharing
and the EEC. The correlation of the two at the time of the
referendum was due to the need to render the EEC issue more
assimilable by redefining it in sectarian terms. Indirectly, however,
there is a link in that the two viewpoints imply similar attitudes
towards the border. Power-sharing would involve Catholics in a
government of Northern Ireland, and this would imply acceptance,
albeit a tacit acceptance, of an 'Irish dimension' in Northern Ireland
politics. Co-operation within an EEC framework obviously
facilitates both the 'Irish dimension' and the cross-border co-
operation which would go with it. The 'power-sharing' parties thus
favour continued membership of the EEC for exactly the same
reasons the Loyalists oppose it. Broadly speaking, to favour power-
sharing in Northern Ireland government is to believe that national

sovereignty *stricto sensu* is obsolete, since to include two divergent political aspirations in one government makes sense only if neither aspiration is absolute. In the context of an emerging European sovereignty a dual allegiance in Northern Ireland government will pose less of a threat to political stability. The more that power is relinquished to Brussels by London and Dublin the less it will matter that residual loyalties in Northern Ireland remain bifurcated.

Bearing in mind the broad distinctions between parties in favour of power-sharing and those against, we look now at the attitudes promulgated by the spokesmen of the principal parties in Northern Ireland during the referendum campaign. Predictably, perhaps, the Rev. Ian Paisley emphasised the Roman Catholic character of the EEC. He claimed that the Pope had referred to the Virgin Mary as the 'Madonna of the Common Market' and pointed to the majority of Catholics inhabiting the original six countries of the EEC, implying that this had left an indelible impression on the Community's economic and social policies. He also objected to the loss of sovereignty involved in EEC membership. Other charges against the EEC were that it had been disastrous for agriculture in Northern Ireland and that it encouraged an 'Irish dimension' which intruded into Britain's legal system. A 'no' vote in Northern Ireland, Paisley claimed, would not lead to independence but it would strengthen the case for some kind of devolved government in the province. Enoch Powell, also a United Ulster Unionist Council member of the Convention and appointed UUUC spokesman on EEC affairs, attracted much attention in his South Down constituency. His principal theme was sovereignty and its diminution in the EEC.

Both the Unionist Party of Northern Ireland and the Alliance Party urged their followers to vote for remaining within the EEC. Here the arguments rested principally on the link with Britain, and the need to attract investment from abroad. In addition the prospect of a continental market for Northern Ireland exports was also stressed. No party was more enthusiastic about the EEC, however, than the Social Democratic and Labour Party. After a number of visits to Brussels and a 'teach-in' in County Donegal, the SDLP executive decided to declare the party in favour of the United Kingdom remaining in the EEC. Individuals were permitted to dissent (as Fitt and Devlin did) but they agreed not to campaign openly against EEC membership. There were political and economic issues which made the EEC especially appealing to the

SDLP. Firstly, the cause of Irish unity would be irreparably harmed if Northern Ireland left the EEC along with the United Kingdom. Secondly, the various funds of the EEC promised to alleviate the serious problem of unemployment which falls more heavily on Catholics. Thirdly, although the life of the small farmer has never been a comfortable one, EEC membership would give the agricultural lobby a chance to influence the CAP in favour of the small farmers, many of whom are Catholic. In particular, farmers in Eire would be competing with Northern Ireland farmers, and the former would have all the advantages of improvement grants if the latter were to be excluded from the CAP. Fourthly, the various schemes for cross-border co-operation were more likely to succeed under EEC auspices, since the Community to some extent depoliticises them. Outside the EEC, such schemes would be fraught with danger in the context of Northern Ireland politics.

Finally, an articulate opposition to the Common Market was mounted by the Republican Clubs. Their principal grievances were agriculture, jobs, and loss of sovereignty. They argued that Ireland (north and south) should be outside the EEC so that it could better determine its own economic priorities. In addition, they argued that the CAP was aimed at phasing out the small farmer and that unemployment had risen since the United Kingdom joined the EEC. The high price of food hit the lower-income groups the hardest. Lastly, the challenge of foreign firms selling goods in Ireland constituted an unfair attack on the jobs and livelihood of those who worked in Irish firms and who required precisely the tariff protection that the EEC was designed to eliminate.

The Ulster Farmers' Union declared itself officially in favour of the United Kingdom remaining in the EEC and its leaders urged farmers to vote in favour of the EEC on referendum day. The UFU represents the more prosperous farmers in Northern Ireland, who, for historical reasons, tend to be Protestant, and for whom the CAP represents less of a threat than for the smallholder. Nonetheless, divisions of opinion about the EEC did emerge among Northern Ireland farmers and these divisions were directly related to the fortunes of various sectors in agriculture during the first two years of membership. Pig farmers were notably less enthusiastic about the EEC than their colleagues in beef or dairy production. Other unions in Northern Ireland were less well informed about the implications of EEC membership, and most of them adopted a formal stance against remaining in the EEC. This, however, did not prevent prominent trade unionists, in a personal capacity, from campaigning in favour of the EEC; just as one or two prominent political leaders (notably Fitt and Craig) took positions on the EEC that were diametrically opposed to their parties'. These inconsistencies reflected the difficulty that politicians experienced in trying to fit the square peg of EEC membership into the round hole of Ulster politics!

The principal umbrella organisation campaigning against EEC membership was the Northern Ireland branch of the 'Get Britain Out of the EEC' movement. This consisted principally of Loyalist politicians who, under the chairmanship of Official Unionist Neil Oliver, launched their campaign in the Europa Hotel only three weeks before polling day. Among the issues the campaign used to win influence were ones which might appeal to Loyalist sentiments: the Roman Catholic character of the EEC; the threat of 'direct rule' from Brussels; and 'power-sharing' with European institutions. At the Europa Hotel, Mr Oliver told his listeners that they 'rejected power-sharing and a Council of Ireland, so indeed we will reject power-sharing and a Council of Europe'.

The principal organisations in favour of remaining in the EEC were the Northern Ireland branch of the Labour Committee for Europe and the Northern Ireland branch of the Keep Britain in Europe Campaign. The former group tended to emphasise the social and economic benefits accruing from membership – especially in relation to employment – and, in more general terms, the beneficial effect of the EEC in diluting nationalism. The latter organisation focused on businessmen, who, as a group, were likely to benefit most from EEC membership. But the campaign also delivered leaflets on food prices to thousands of homes, and on jobs to workers.

In the few days prior to the referendum the newspapers in Northern Ireland carried official government notices informing the electorate of the referendum, of the question to be asked, and of the times the polling booths would be open. The political parties placed advertisements during the last few days to capture the attention of the waverers and the disinterested. The messages put over in these last few days became increasingly crude and sectarian, and became increasingly confined to the papers read exclusively in each community – the *Irish News* (for the Catholics) and the *News Letter* (for the Protestants). The non-sectarian *Belfast Telegraph* was relatively free of party propaganda but carried one or two detailed analyses of the arguments for and against membership. On the eve of polling day it urged people to vote – one way or the other. The principal papers carried, in addition, correspondence columns where readers' arguments for and against were aired; but the volume of correspondence never outweighed the perpetual and predominant concern with the local crisis.

The fifth of June was one of the most peaceful polling days that Northern Ireland had known for years. The lack of violence may have been a reflection of the general indifference to the issue, an indifference that was certainly reflected in the low turn-out – 48 per cent and the third lowest in the United Kingdom. Commentators agreed that the public were weary with the issue and with going to the polls – the seventh time in just over two years. Only two days before the poll a triple murder on the border had captured widespread sympathy and concern, and the media focused on this, and on the dilatory sparring in the Convention, to the detriment of the Common Market issue. The result of the referendum in Northern Ireland revealed, unexpectedly, a narrow margin in favour of remaining in the EEC – 259,251 votes to 237,911 – and the margin might, arguably, have been closer had not 10,000 British troops also cast their votes in the Northern Ireland poll.[1]

THE IMPACT OF AID FROM THE EEC

Membership of the EEC has given Northern Ireland access to the various funds which the Commission has at its disposal. The following account of aid received by Northern Ireland is not intended to be exhaustive. On the contrary, selected examples of projects assisted by the EEC serve to illustrate a general argument – that the aims of the EEC and the aims of the British government happen to coincide. The Community's aim is to raise the level of prosperity in its disadvantaged regions, which lie, for the most part, on the periphery; while the aim of the British government is twofold: to redress the balance of economic opportunity in favour of the outer areas of Northern Ireland, which have been traditionally neglected; and to enhance the viability of Northern Ireland as a 'self-sufficient' economic unit. EEC grants should be viewed as 'topping up' the cost of projects already set in train by the government. Consequently the amount of EEC support for a scheme is probably less important than the type of scheme chosen for assistance and its geographical location. Unsurprisingly, EEC grants tend to be directed towards areas which are relatively speaking the most deprived. Thus under the CAP, for example, grants have gone to food-processing plants at Annalong, Co. Down, Dungannon, Co. Tyronne; and the major part of a grant for new fishing vessels to Bilkeel, Co. Down. Owing to the high rate of unemployment in Northern Ireland, considerable grants from the Social Fund for the resettlement and retraining of workers have been allocated. Unemployment 'black spots' like Dungannon, Omagh, Strabane and Newry feature prominently in these grants. As an area that qualifies for aid, by almost any criteria, Northern Ireland has received more from the Regional Fund than any other part of the EEC. Although the fund became 'operational' only in January 1975, the province was quicker off the mark than many other disadvantaged areas in claiming Brussels aid. This success can be largely attributed to the fact that Stormont had well prepared bids already drafted by the time the fund was set up. By the spring of 1976 Northern Ireland had been allocated about £10 million from the Regional Fund – a sizable proportion of the UK total, and more than the Irish Republic, despite having half its population. One of the more significant grants made recently was to Courtaulds in Co. Londonderry. The *Irish Times* commented:

. . . the project commands particular favour inside Mr Thomson's Regional Development Directorate in having a cross-Border connotation of the kind Brussels is anxious to promote. One of its main sources of supply for fibres will be the polyester filament yarn plant which Courtaulds is building in parallel at Letterkenny twenty miles away in Co. Donegal.

Offering together about 3000 jobs in the economically deprived north-west of this island and likely to promote cross-Border labour mobility, Courtaulds twin factories are seen in Brussels to be a more impressive example of planned cross-Border development than the Commission has itself managed to promote in the Dutch province of Limburg and neighbouring parts of Belgium and Germany.[3]

Finally, mention should be made of the one loan made by the European Investment Bank to Northern Ireland. A five-year loan of £2½ million at 10½ per cent interest was made (in 1975) to Short Bros & Harland, especially for the development of their SD3–30 wide-body commuter aircraft. The grant was reckoned to have safeguarded several thousand jobs for the foreseeable future.

In the long term the financial aid given by the EEC to the regions according to criteria agreed by all nine member states could reduce the dependence of Northern Ireland on the British government. If the amounts from the various funds (mentioned above) are added together, one has a significant flow of capital being allocated according to Community criteria. This is all the more remarkable when one considers the complementary amounts being given by the British Exchequer. The trend will continue to be towards treating Northern Ireland as an economic unit and less as an appendage of the British economy. The shift in emphasis away from the Belfast area to the outlying parts of the province can be understood only in this light. The projects supported by the Community aim at alleviating the serious unemployment problem in the small towns farthest from Belfast and, at the same time, helping to erode the worst effects of the border, which, almost by definition, runs through countryside considered to be of economically peripheral importance to both the British and Irish governments. These developments may have more than economic significance. One motive behind the British government's eagerness to co-sponsor projects with the Community in these remote areas may be its own political intentions for Northern Ireland. London may become increasingly willing to allow Brussels a free hand in designating the pattern of development in Northern Ireland in order to accelerate both the need and the desire for some devolution of power or even, in some circumstances, for autonomy where a government in Belfast could make its own decisions about allocating grants from the EEC.

The continuing controversy about whether the British intend to 'pull out' of Ulster economically or politically is a product of these trends. The decisions, for example, to exclude Harland & Wolff from the nationalised shipbuilding industry in Britain and to exclude Short Bros & Harland from the nationalised aircraft industry are perceived in some quarters as evidence of just such a 'pull out'. While both these decisions and the decision to suspend the British Rail ferry between Belfast and Heysham can be defended on purely economic grounds, the suspicion remains. It is clearly in the British government's interest to allow something of these suspicions to linger, since it is the strongest card, perhaps the only card, the British government can play in compelling the political parties in Northern Ireland to reach agreement on a constitution for the province. In public statements Mr Orme has, however, denied the 'pull out' allegations but in a way which still leaves room for doubt. To say that the British government is 'fully involved' in the economic life of the provice is not to say how, or for what reasons. Certainly the *extent* of involvement is unprecedented, but the strategy may now be different. All the indications are that the British government is adopting a strategy for Northern Ireland's economy which might be termed as 'Ulsterisation', i.e. to make it as self-sufficient as possible. It is not difficult to see political pressures in England building up in the future which would reinforce the government's desire to be much less involved in Northern Ireland affairs. The triple burden of a political, military and economic commitment will simply become too heavy in the late 1970s.

For all these reasons, if for no others, it seems very likely that Northern Ireland will achieve a form of devolved government more complete than anything contemplated for Scotland or Wales. The province has already had experience of devolution, and that makes devolution a natural minimal demand in any constitutional negotiations. But the economic arguments would be enough in themselves, since the financial relationship between London and Belfast is so unfavourable to the former. Neither Scotland nor Wales is potentially such a drain on the Exchequer. However, devolution may prove to be only a stepping stone towards autonomy, and autonomy (if it could be made economically viable) would suit the British government even better.

This trend towards self-determination in Northern Ireland will be further accentuated by two other factors in an EEC context – both of them involving differences of perspective between Northern Ireland and the rest of the United Kingdom. Firstly, it would be in Northern Ireland's interest to ensure that the limits on industrial aid are enforced over as much of the EEC as possible (excepting only the periphery), whereas the United Kingdom will want to moderate these restrictions. Likewise, whereas Northern Ireland stands to gain by a limited interpretation of the 'development areas', the United Kingdom would prefer a fairly flexible definition. Secondly, under the Common Agricultural Policy, it will suit Northern Ireland if farm prices are kept high, since Ulster is a net exporter of agricultural produce, and one in ten workers is on the land. In Britain, on the other hand, high foods prices are a politically sensitive issue, and a larger proportion of food is imported than anywhere else in Europe. These divergences of interest are likely to increase the more the Community involves itself in economic and regional planning. In political terms such a tension could have important repercussions on the choice of options open to Northern Ireland in the future. The degree of devolution or, *in extremis*, the type of autonomy sought could well be moulded by these kinds of considerations; and so the EEC is likely to continue playing an oblique but incisive role in Northern Ireland politics.

LOCAL GOVERNMENT AND THE EEC

The local government system merits some consideration at this juncture, since it constitutes a point of contact between the EEC and its grass roots. Since 1973 local government has been based on twenty-six districts. The new district councils have three main roles: responsibility for a range of local services; a representative role whereby they nominate members to various regional boards; and a consultative role whereby they can express views on major projects that are likely to affect their areas. Regional services, requiring larger areas for the sake of efficiency, include planning, roads and traffic management, education, libraries, and social services. The new local government structure in Northern Ireland is not a monument to democracy, since the elective councils in the districts have been stripped of all major powers, and the regional boards are appointed by the relevant government departments, but the new system has been widely accepted as providing fair administration for all. The procedure for council meetings and the formation of sub-committees are not unusual but it is worthy of mention (in the EEC context) that two or more councils may form joint committees 'for any purpose relating to a statutory function in which there is a common interest'.

The interest of the EEC Commission in fostering cross-border development was widely appreciated in Ireland long before specific projects were either discussed or suggested. In general, this was due to an understandable reluctance on the part of the British government to act precipitately in an area where Loyalist sensitivities might be aroused, especially while the delicate process of finding a constitutional settlement for Northern Ireland was under way. In the period prior to the referendum, moreover, the British government was anxious to avoid blatantly deriving benefits from membership. After the referendum, however, local councils took the initiative. The Fermanagh council was stung into action by the total neglect of the county in the first *tranche* of Regional Fund aid in the summer of 1975. The council chairman, Tom Daly, was reported in the press as having said, 'We in Fermanagh are going to have to put up a hell of a fight to get EEC aid for our area. If we don't put up a strong and determined fight, we are going to get nothing. Nobody else is going to do anything for us.'[4] Realising that the best strategy lay in a cross-border approach, Fermanagh and Donegal councils have now been meeting on a regular basis with a view to submitting a joint proposal for aid to Brussels. The EEC Commission responds warmly to these moves and visits have been exchanged between Commission officials and councillors from Northern Ireland. Despite the fact that any grants made must have the approval of the national governments concerned, these links between local government and Brussels do constitute an important new point at which pressure can be exerted, since the publicity attached to the tentative projects makes it politically awkward for the national government to resist what are reasonable demands from deprived areas.

In one case, cross-border discussion has borne fruit. In November 1975 it was announced that the British and Irish governments had lodged an application for a cross-border study to be carried out by the EEC in the Derry–Donegal region. The terms of reference for the study will allow consideration of roads, railways, ports, airports and telecommunications. The EEC finances half the cost of the study, with the other half shared equally between the two governments. Other specific projects which have been discussed on a cross-border basis are the extension of the St Angelo airfield at Enniskillen and the feasibility of constructing a bridge near Warrenpoint to facilitate tourist and industrial traffic between Eire and Northern Ireland. Unsurprisingly most of these cross-border talks are inspired by councils on which the SDLP are well represented, and the precarious balance of *de facto* power-sharing which operates in these councils is constantly under threat from a Loyalist backlash. To date the only indication of such a backlash has come in mid-Ulster, where the Unionist Constituency Association condemned cross-border talks as a 'cynical exercise' in propaganda for the SDLP. The extent of the cross-border discussions so far is a reflection of the almost infinite possibilities that the EEC offers; but the objections of Loyalist opinion to such talks is an indication of how 'supping with the devil' requires a long spoon.

The significance of these cross-border contacts is not widely appreciated inside Northern Ireland, but the implications for politics in the province are likely to be permanent. Firstly, these contacts constitute a modest 'Irish dimension' in local government, something which has been found to be unworkable at the regional level, although it has to be admitted that the substance of the contacts is not as ambitious as that for which a Council of Ireland would have provided. Indeed, in one sense, these contacts merely continue a long tradition of cross-border co-operation stretching back to the

1920s but never extending beyond the most uncontroversial topics; yet, in another sense, they are a quite revolutionary development in that they use the EEC as a means to outflank central government, which finds itself the object of converging pressure from above and below. Secondly, cross-border conversations entail a maximalist interpretation of the district council's statutory powers to form joint committees with other councils in areas of mutual interest. Although these areas were tightly circumscribed so as to reduce any possibility of sectarianism emerging in local government, the tension between power-sharing parties and the UUUC has been revived but not to the extent of paralysing local government except, for a short time, in Fermanagh. Thirdly, cross-border schemes, when they bear fruit, will bring aid to regions which are among the most deprived in the EEC. In this respect the district councils will be helping to fulfil the 'grand design' of the EEC's regional policy by revitalising the peripheral areas of the Community and, at the same time, playing a part in the new British strategy of creating a more balanced economy in the province. Lastly, in an international context, the EEC is providing a politically neutral 'umbrella' under which these discussions can take place. Owing to the Commission's interest in assisting border areas of the Community, the district councils are able to capitalise on this interest by formulating schemes which will attract Community funding. The issue is depoliticised and both national governments are able to participate in the projects under the cloak of EEC membership, and to minimise the risks of a Loyalist backlash. The mere existence of the EEC thus enables a process which is both economic and political to go forward in a way that would be inconceivable if either part, or both parts, of Ireland were outside the Community.

CONCLUSION: THE IMPLICATIONS OF MORE 'DIRECT RULE'

With the failure of the Convention, Northern Ireland faces continuing 'direct rule' from Westminster. In one sense, it is a case of 'back to the drawing board', since, as far as a constitutional settlement is concerned, things are back where they were in 1972 when Stormont was suspended. In other respects, however, enough has changed to make the political map more complex, and more hazardous, to read than it was four years ago. The years of violence, and of internment, of 'direct rule' and STV, and of a five-month experiment with power-sharing, give cause for both hope and anxiety. On the one hand, the monolith of Unionism has fragmented beyond repair but, on the other, the emergence of a more extreme form of Unionism under the banner of the UUUC appears to hold a commanding position on one side, at least, of the political spectrum. Thus, while moderate Unionists have drifted hopefully towards the UPNI and Alliance, the more numerous hard-liners have entrenched themselves in the camp of West and Paisley. The impasse in Northern Ireland politics is due simply to the fact that there are barely enough voters willing to support a constitutional agreement that is acceptable to the British government. The violence of the last few years may well have made many people more willing to compromise; but it has also made others even more intransigent.

The continuation of 'direct rule' is not likely to satisfy anyone, but it represents an alternative to greater bloodshed.[5] Pressure for some kind of devolution is likely to continue during 'direct rule', since its blatantly undemocratic character offends both the sense and sensibilities of local politicians. The inability of public representatives to gain access to civil servants at Stormont, and the allegedly arbitrary and ignorant decision-making emanating therefrom, are not likely to endear the 'British link' to Ulster hearts.

On the British side this sense of alienation is likely to be reciprocated. Mr Wilson's 'spongers' speech in May 1974, ill judged and ill timed though it was, reflected both the exasperation and the bitterness of the British taxpayer at the government's apparently infinite financial and military commitments to Northern Ireland. In fact the burden of maintaining (or even attaining) parity between Northern Ireland and the rest of the United Kingdom in the field of social welfare, for example, is likely to become intolerable by the end of the decade, especially in view of the wide-ranging cuts in public expenditure forecast for the late 1970s. If the costs of military commitments and compensation for damage continue to rise, Northern Ireland is going to become a disproportionately expensive part of the United Kingdom to maintain. Conversely, as the total amount of public expenditure contracts in the next five years, so the marginal advantages to Northern Ireland of being part of the United Kingdom will diminish. Politically, moreover, Northern Ireland affairs are an unwelcome addition to the legislative programme at Westminster. There are three ways in which legislation can be passed for Northern Ireland: first, by simply providing that a British Act shall apply in Northern Ireland; secondly, by passing special Northern Ireland

Acts through the full Westminster procedures; and, third, by using Orders in Council. Each of these methods has drawbacks from the British point of view; none gives the Northern Ireland politicians much chance of criticism or amendment. The problem is compounded by the fact that Northern Ireland is under-represented in the House of Commons and the time available for Northern Ireland is so scarce that most of it is absorbed by the most pressing matters of security and constitutional issues. Social and economic problems, on the other hand, receive scant attention.[6]

The violence and the sectarian politics of Northern Ireland deny it the sympathy in Britain that its problems require for solution. The well intentioned attempts of the British government to find such a solution by being both flexible and impartial are seen as evidence of ineptitude and inconsistency. Above all, the government's strategy of giving first one, then the other side a little of what it wants has succeeded in winning it a few short-term allies at the expense of alienating large sections on both sides on whose co-operation any long-term settlement must ultimately depend.

The role of the EEC in Northern Ireland politics has, if anything, delineated more clearly the divisions which bedevil politics there. The EEC has come to be identified with Irish unity and remote government. The recipients of EEC aid live predominantly in Catholic areas; and the cross-border discussions (encouraged by the EEC) are perceived by Loyalists as a deliberate affront. In more general terms, Loyalists feel that the more remote decision-making becomes the less likely it is that their predicament will find a sympathetic response. If 'direct rule' from London is resented, how much more so is rule from Brussels. For much the same reasons Loyalists are deeply suspicious of attempts to 'Europeanise' the Northern Ireland problem. Above all, the explicit aim of the EEC is to render national frontiers superfluous, and for Loyalists the frontier of Northern Ireland has special significance: it is the outward and visible sign of their inward and spiritual creed.

The lack of representation for Northern Ireland in the Community institutions underlines the feeling (in other spheres) that the province is neglected. The omission of Belfast as a site for an EEC information office, when Edinburgh and Cardiff have theirs, has not gone unnoticed. The absence of informal pressure groups on EEC matters either at Stormont or in Brussels is a result of the political malaise that 'direct rule' fosters: Northern Ireland is administered bureaucratically, not democratically, by civil servants.

So there are a number of factors, internal and external, which will maintain the pressure in favour of devolved government for Northern Ireland. Indeed, the danger now is not that this pressure will prove ineffectual, but that it may become so overwhelming that Northern Ireland will find itself heading down the devolutionary road towards some kind of independence.[7] This is not the place to weigh up the merits of such an outcome except to note that the existence of the EEC does provide an encouraging framework for such an evolution. Be that as it may, it now looks as if the sense of community on which the integrity of any political system depends is under strain in various parts of the United Kingdom; and probably nowhere more acutely than in Northern Ireland.

NOTES

1 *Our Changing Democracy: Devolution to Scotland and Wales*, London, HMSO (Cmnd 6348), p. 2.
2 *Northern Ireland and the European Communities*, Belfast, HMSO (Cmnd 563), p. 6.
3 *Irish Times*, 17 December 1975.
4 *Belfast Telegraph*, 8 November 1975.
5 In a poll, published by the *Belfast Telegraph* on 19 March 1976, 'direct rule' was the most popular option among several suggested. Seventy-four per cent of those polled supported direct rule, and even when broken down by religion, class and age, the support stood at over 70 per cent.
6 Official disquiet about the way Northern Ireland legislation is dealt with at Westminster is voiced in the *Twentieth Report from the Joint Committee on Statutory Instruments*, London, HMSO, May 1976, pp. 2–3.
7 For some discussion of the independence 'option' see David McKittrick, 'Is independence the answer?', *Irish Times*, 6 November 1976, and comment in *The Times*, 10 and 12 November 1976. See also *Sunday Times*, 21 November 1976.

BYRON CRIDDLE[1]

3   Scotland, the EEC and devolution

The politics of Scotland from the mid-1960s onwards bore eloquent testimony to the variety of ills which had come to afflict the British state in that period. Whether affording evidence of a sense of relative deprivation or of heightened aspirations, the deviant political manifestations in Scotland have had a profound impact on the British polity. It could be argued that without the Scottish National Party's capture of the safe Labour seat of Hamilton in 1967 and the destruction of Labour control in Glasgow in 1968 there would have been no Crowther–Kilbrandon Commission on the Constitution; without the election of eleven SNP MPs in 1974 no proposals for devolution; without the relatively greater Scottish hostility to the EEC less talk or practice of referenda; and without the threat of a Nationalist majority in any devolved Scottish Assembly less talk of changing the traditional electoral system.

The general elections of 1974 provided evidence enough of the degree of dislocation threatening the unity of the United Kingdom. By October the Scottish National Party had obtained the support of one in three of the Scottish voters: a level of support unequalled by any other ostensibly secessionist movement since that of the Irish Nationalists in the early years of the century. Since a party identified with 'nationalism' has had such a dramatic impact in Scotland, it is tempting to offer explanations of its success in terms of Scotland's peculiar 'national' characteristics and thus to resist the view of Scotland as merely a disaffected *region* of the United Kingdom. Certainly the 1707 Act of Union which effected the union of the Scottish and English Parliaments left the Scots, as compensation for the loss of parliamentary sovereignty, certain autonomous institutions which might be taken as the trappings of statehood, notably a distinct legal system, a Presbyterian establishment in religion, and, as they evolved, distinct educational and local government systems, comprising in sum a cluster of very prominent institutions serving to act as a focus for Scottish identity. By the end of the nineteenth century the Scottish Office had been established (1885), with a Secretary of State, of Cabinet rank (by 1926), and a Scottish Grand Committee in the House of Commons handling legislation relating to those subjects devolved administratively to the Scottish Office.[2]

All Scots are nurtured in a climate of 'Scottishness'. The school system, with its Scottish curricula and examinations, directs its middle-class children to the Scottish universities and thence to the Scottish professions. Even the civil service, which has grown up around the 1885 mini-devolution represented by the (now 10,000-strong) Scottish Office, recruits essentially from among Scottish educated graduates; and of the seventy-one Scots MPs elected to Westminster in 1974 only three were not of Scottish birth. The working class also has its 'Scottish' institutions: a *Scottish* TUC to defend 'Scottish' workers, a *Scottish* Football Association, and a *Scottish* football team. The Scottish manual worker is moreover catered for by an almost entirely indigenously produced daily press. Fleet Street dailies are read by very few (6 per cent) Scots adults, and London Sundays by only 23 per cent. The most widely circulating popular daily is the *Daily Record* (48 per cent), with most of the rest of the market (43 per cent) catered for by the *Scottish Daily Express*. There are also two highly popular Scottish Sunday papers: the *Sunday Post* (77 per cent) and *Sunday Mail* (52 per cent), both of which have aggressively Scottish personalities. Middle-class readers are catered for by *The Scotsman* (Edinburgh; 5 per cent) and the *Glasgow Herald* (6 per cent) both of which by containing much Scottish, and relatively little foreign, news have arguably a parochialising effect.[3]

None of the symbols of a separate Scottish identity thus far mentioned is, however, necessarily invested with any special political significance, but serves rather as a badge of identity in what has been termed a 'multi-national' state, where Scots are content with a bifurcated nationality, rendering them 'Scottish' for certain purposes and 'British' for others.[4] Indeed, the distinctly Scottish institutions (such as the Church and the law) have enabled this coexistence of dual identities by serving to integrate their members within a Union which has guaranteed their particular interests. Thus to identify autonomous Scottish institutions or traditions is not necessarily to identify the seedbeds of political nationalism. Nor indeed are such Scottish institutions of strong significance for all Scots. There are identifiable groups of strongly British orientation.

The upper and upper middle-class stratum, for example, albeit thin, looks primarily to London and the south and the English public schools whence it came, and depends on the Union for its social status and wealth. (The Conservative party in Scotland is closely identified with this stratum.) Many people of all classes, especially the old, invest considerable emotional capital in the British monarchy and the focal point it provides for them and their kin in the old Commonwealth. Service past or present in the armed forces, or recollection of the war, likewise reinforces a British identity. Those in the employment of British-oriented organisations (companies, unions, universities), even if organised as Scottish subsidiaries, will be constantly aware of their status as a *branch* of a British concern and may well, looking south for promotion, value the retention of an integrated structure. Peculiar ethnic factors in the west of Scotland involving the muted hostility of Catholic Scots Irish and Protestant Scots, with their rival banners of *Irish* tricolour and *British* union jack, also would seem to have awkward implications for the creation of an unfragmented sense of national identity for Scots in that important part of the country. There are moreover certain categories of Scottish voters – defined by their regional characteristics (e.g. Hebrideans, Orcadians, north-easterners, etc) or by their socio-economic position – who may value 'Britishness' in preference to too overt a political expression of Scottishness which might have as its consequence the establishment of an independent Scotland in which the particular industrial and social interests of west central Scotland would numerically dominate the whole. For such Scots British (London) rule is to be preferred to Scottish (Glasgow) rule.

Finally the degree of institutional autonomy characteristic in certain social and legal spheres is effectively lacking in the political arena, where all major institutions – the bureaucracy, the MPs, the parties (even, at present, the SNP) – despite the Scottish Office lack any real autonomous character and serve to focus the Scots' attentions upon the decision-making centres of Whitehall and Westminster. Because Scotland has for 270 years been governed from London it is British-oriented policy and politics which are purveyed by the parties – especially the two traditional major parties, Labour and Conservative, which until the 1970s had, in the lifetime of most Scottish voters, shown little interest in diminishing the force of such a British orientation. Election manifestos in both parties, as late as February 1974, have been entirely standardised in their appeal to all British voters, with Labour candidates in particular using election literature as appropriate to Battersea as to Banffshire. With any 'Scottish' dimension thus traditionally denied by the political class, it would appear that those who have voted for such British-oriented parties throughout a political lifetime should be, to an extent, insulated from the siren voices of new non-British parties.

At the same time, however, it has been argued that the seeming denial of the salience of 'Scottish' political identity built into the existing political institutions may encourage a feeling that Scottish interests are not adequately catered for at Westminster, where, for example, Scottish Bills have to wait in a long legislative queue, resulting in delays in the reforming of the law (as in the case of local government, divorce, and licensing hours). In fact, given the conservatism existing in Scotland over many social questions such as divorce and drinking regulations, the political institutions cannot carry all the blame. A more fundamental objection, however, is that 'Scottish' interests are not articulated by the British-oriented representative mediators in the Conservative and Labour parties, that such parties see Scotland in purely regional terms, and that even a rigorous defence of 'regional' interests is risky for any Scots Labour or Conservative MP who values the chances of his political survival as a member of a party in which patronage flows, effectively, from the party leadership in London and not from any branch office in Edinburgh or Glasgow.

Electoral and parliamentary strength of the parties in Scotland, 1945–74

	Cons.		Lab.		Lib.		SNP		Lab. –Cons.	Third party
	% Votes	Seats	% Votes	Seats	% Votes	Seats	% Votes	Seats	% vote	% vote
1945	41·1	27	47·6	37	5·0	2	1·2	–	88·7	6·2
1950	44·8	31	46·2	37	6·6	1	0·4	–	91·0	7·0
1951	48·6	35	47·9	35	2·7	1	0·3	–	96·5	3·0
1955	50·1	36	46·7	34	1·9	1	0·5	–	96·8	2·4
1959	47·2	31	46·7	38	4·1	1	0·8	–	93·9	4·9
1964	40·6	24	48·7	43	7·6	4	2·4	–	89·3	10·0
1966	37·7	20	49·9	46	6·8	5	5·0	–	87·6	11·8
1970	38·0	23	44·5	44	5·5	3	11·4	1	82·5	16·9
1974Feb	32·9	21	36·6	40	7·9	3	21·9	7	69·5	29·8
1974Oct.	24·7	16	36·3	41	8·3	3	30·4	11	61·0	38·7

The effectiveness of the British-oriented parties in mobilising the Scottish electorate since 1945 is demonstrated in the table. Until the late 1950s the party system in Scotland closely resembled the English, with the electorate neatly bipolarised between Conservative and Labour, and a tiny minority supporting the Liberal party. After 1959, however, the Scottish and English party systems began to diverge, with a serious decline of Conservative support. With Conservative decline went a far greater upsurge in support for third parties than was the case south of the border. Whilst about 20 per cent of the English voters voted for the English third party (the Liberals), in both 1974 elections in Scotland the two third parties (Liberals and SNP) together obtained the support of 30 per cent in February, and almost 40 per cent in October. Thus the collapse of the post-war British two-party system (by 1974 the Conservatives had lost half, and Labour one third, of their 1955 vote) has been much more dramatic in Scotland, and only the vagaries of the electoral system have enabled the Labour Party to avoid the dramatic loss of parliamentary seats sustained by the Conservatives. In effect the age of the safe (Labour or Conservative) seat appeared ended by the October 1974 election. In only twelve of Labour's forty-one seats had the party won more than 50 per cent of the votes cast; whilst the best performance of any Conservative Member was a meagre 43·6 per cent in a rural north-eastern constituency. Moreover in only sixteen seats did the two 'major' parties remain, after October 1974, as the two dominant parties; and in thirty-five of Labour's forty-one seats the (often very close) runner-up was a third-party candidate (thirty-three SNP; two Lib.). It looked as if the traditional Lab.–Con. duopoly was at best at an advanced stage of decomposition.

Whilst the most common explanation for the rapid rise of support for a nationalist party is to suggest that 'nationalism' is the motive, and independence for the 'nation' the objective, opinion poll data thus far suggest that only about half those who vote SNP want independence, with the rest opting for federation or rather weaker forms of devolution.[5] Half those who support the SNP want 'more for Scotland' but not the full nationalist goal of a Scottish state. The SNP, indeed, had in the elections of 1974 sought to appeal to the Scots voters less by offering them national .fulfilment through independence than by pointing to the higher living standards which would flow from more local Scottish decision-making. Whether or not the SNP voter consciously makes the connection between economic prosperity, or lack of it, and the need for local Scottish decision-making, it would appear that the rise and fall of nationalist support was, initially at any rate, closely related to the recession–boom cycle of the British economy, with the periods of depression, austerity and freeze (the 1930s, late 1940s, late 1960s and early 1970s) being identified as years of SNP growth. The increasing intensity of SNP support since the 1960s, on this analysis, correlated with the rapid run-down of antiquated heavy industries (with new industries insufficiently compensatory), levels of unemployment (rising both absolutely and relatively in comparison with English levels), and intense urban decay in west central Scotland – all of which served to deepen the impression (increasingly highlighted by the penetration of mass communications) of Scotland as a relatively deprived part of the United Kingdom, and for which political blame attached collectively to the governing Conservative and Labour parties.[6] An alternative explanation, however (to that of relative deprivation), and one which began to gain currency in the 1970s, was one predicated on the view that the Scots economy was in fact showing signs of much greater health than the English; that unemployment levels were evening out (albeit as the result of a relative worsening of unemployment in England rather than an improvement in Scotland); that in areas of economic growth (new towns, 'oil boom' areas) perception of a more hopeful future found expression in rising aspirations and confidence (quite absent from the deprived communities of declining Clydeside) which in turn was reflected in support for a party freed from identification with the 'old' and focused upon the 'new' – the SNP.[7] There was evidence to suggest that *both* heightened perceptions of relative deprivation *and* the growth of rising aspirations assisted SNP advance. The party had, after all, by 1974 managed to appeal, albeit with different rates of success, to both instincts: 'See how bad things are (Hamilton, Govan) and yet how good they might become (Cumbernauld and East Kilbride)'.[8] For Labour, however, a party more staunchly proletarian than its southern equivalent, *relative deprivation* was easier to combat than were *rising aspirations*. The former could in normal times hopefully be alleviated by traditional methods of increasing public expenditure to reduce urban blight and unemployment levels. The latter was more problematic: Glaswegians could be rehoused in clean new towns, but how could the social and economic aspirations apparently unleashed by such a move be met by a party so rooted in the mythology and folk lore of red Clydeside, run by relatively old men wedded to a belief in municipalised housing and hostile to owner-occupation as a symbol of class betrayal. In the relatively classless ambiance of the new towns and suburbs Labour seemed lost, whilst the SNP, identifying with the desire for home ownership (at a time when across Scotland the owner-occupied housing sector was growing more rapidly than for a decade), polled significantly well among mortgagees.[9] If Labour was ill equipped to cope with social mobility and heightened aspirations, so also was a Conservative party of anglicised persona, identified in the minds of disaffected working-class and aspiring lower middle-class voters with the English establishment on which much of the blame for the relative deprivation and thwarted ambitions of Scots was being laid. By contrast, the SNP has drawn its leading activists from the aspirant non-anglicised middle class, a class for whom Scotland within the United Kingdom has neither provided the security of a trade union movement nor the status of the professions. To one observer it is an aggrieved group:

These Nationalists are seldom either from the working class or are at the top of their profession: clerks, shop-keepers, apprentices, they suspect and resist the cosmopolitanism and confidence they associate with their stereotype of the Englishman. Not very successful they neither possess the assurance of the skilled worker and trade unionist, nor do they see themselves reaching the head office (which may be in London) or becoming manager (which may require a wider outlook), and they vent their distaste and sense of inferiority on those who do not suffer these limitations.[10]

It may be that the frustrations of certain middle-class groups are articulated by the SNP in the way suggested, but it is nevertheless wrong to see the party, despite the persona of its leadership, as anything other than an aggregative electoral machine with support equally strong in all occupational groups.[11] Above all it appeals strongly to the *young* of all classes, and in the light of what is known about the moulding of electoral loyalties by the way an individual casts his earliest votes, the British-oriented parties have most cause to worry that young Scots were given *two* opportunities in 1974 to vote for the SNP.[12]

The realignment of voters in the *rural periphery* of Scotland requires additional consideration. Scotland's geographically extensive and politically important rural periphery comprises nineteen of the seventy-one Scottish constitutencies and 25 per cent of the total electorate. It is, moreover, in the rural periphery, and not the urban industrial heartland, that the SNP has had its greatest electoral successes: eight of the party's eleven MPs represent such constituencies. The rural periphery is characterised by rural, small-town settlement patterns, the absence of all but the most small-scale manufacturing industry, the importance of primary industry (farming and fishing), a high incidence of self-employment and a low incidence of trade unionism. In many ways this periphery has been left behind, even untouched, by industrialism and is in the process of losing much of the sparse infrastructure industrialism brought to it, such as public (especially rail) transport and chain-store retailing. It is peripheral not only in the sense of being hundreds of miles from London – and indeed most of it two hundred miles from Edinburgh – but peripheral in a cultural and social sense. Its norms and values are peripheral to those of the larger society; kinship and acquaintance count for more than class; party politics have traditionally been seen as disruptive of community harmony. Politically speaking, the rural periphery was never properly integrated into the politics of an increasingly large-scale, collectivist, centralised industrial society in the sense that it never adopted the Labour–Conservative bipolarisation, essentially attuned to the major interests in *urban* society. A 'third party' tradition persisted, and the Liberals, the traditional party of rural anti-Conservatism, benefited from such a tradition, polling well in the rural periphery up till the second world war; and as the national economy got into deeper and deeper difficulties in the late 1950s and early 1960s it was the Liberals who picked up the disaffected voters in the rural constituencies where Labour's identification with class conflict and trade unionism rendered that party an alien urban force. Somewhere between 1966 and 1970 the Liberals were replaced in the periphery as grievance articulators by a more aggressive third party – the SNP – which has shown itself able to do what the rather more sedate middle-class Liberals failed to do – to mobilise the unorganised working-class voters in the small towns, whose hostility to the Labour Party outdid their rejection of the Conservatives. To effect this takeover, the SNP projects itself as an overtly populist force in such rural small-town constituencies; exploiting residual anti-lairdism; defending the self-employed from the collectivist jaws of big business, big labour and big government; damning class-polarised politics as needlessly divisive, extolling the virtue of *les petits gens*; painting a vision of a co-operative, small-scale, familiar society. On such a basis an anti-Conservative populist coalition was assembled by the SNP, and the Conservatives were swept out of all but a handful of their rural seats in 1974.

In both urban and rural contexts the SNP obviously benefits enormously, at a time of collapsed confidence in the traditional governing parties *qua* governing parties (Labour and Conservative), from its denial of class politics and, a concomitant of this denial, its ideological heterogeneity. The speeches of SNP leaders and candidates are littered with references to the need for *centrism* in politics and a rejection of the salience of 'left' and 'right'.[13] The party's ambition is to be as voter-oriented and as 'catch-all' as possible, to which end all ideological baggage is avoided in order to exploit an electoral climate favourable to third parties. That the SNP and not the Liberals have been the beneficiaries owes much to the discovery of North Sea oil, which has had the most damaging impact on the credibility of the *British* parties. It not only gives flesh to the nationalists' clever slogan 'Poor British – rich Scots'; it also lets the SNP off the awkward hook of deciding how existing Scottish resources are to be allocated, by allowing it to promise prosperity for all out of vast *new* resources. In this way the party can continue to mobilise both the rural periphery and the industrial heartland by lambasting the failed unionist establishment without facing the contradictions within its electorate.

For the SNP a happy conjunction of circumstances has put it at the centre of the British political stage, albeit with a tiny share of the overall British electorate. Behind the 'Scottish dimension' which it formally represents lies a complex welter of forces which have served to diminish the appeal of the traditional parties and enhances its own. Assuming that the party at leadership level is a *bona fide* anti-system party, it has been the intention here to suggest that there may well be considerable disjunction between leaders and voters. But just as it is academic to distinguish between 'socialist' leaders and 'Labour' voters, so is it idle to pretend that the SNP does not exist to destroy the United Kingdom.

THE EEC REFERENDUM

If the elections of 1974 transformed Scottish politics and threatened irrevocably to alter the relationship between the constituent parts of the United Kingdom, the EEC referendum could only assist the centrifugal forces that were at work. In the light of poll data[14] the possibility of a negative majority in Scotland could not be discounted, given both higher levels of anti-EEC feeling in Scotland, and greater enthusiasm among anti-Marketeers for the referendum. The SNP was being provided with yet another opportunity to take to the hustings, this time to stimulate a massive composite 'No' to London and Brussels, and the effectiveness of the major parties as sustainers of the Union was likely to be reduced by internal divisions over the EEC question.

Whilst the danger for the Scots Conservatives (and Liberals) was slight, it was clear that the Labour Party would be more seriously divided in Scotland than in the rest of the United Kingdom. In the Commons vote (9 April) approving the renegotiated terms, of the Scots Labour MPs who voted, twenty (57 per cent) opposed and fifteen approved the terms: the division reflecting slightly greater hostility to the renegotiated terms than that in the PLP as a whole, where the split was 145 (51 per cent) against the terms, to 137 for them. By polling day itself the Scots PLP alignment was twenty-four (anti) to seventeen (pro), with most of the professional middle-class (and relatively more right-wing) MPs in the 'pro' lobby, and all but two of the party's eleven former manual worker MPs favouring withdrawal from the EEC. Of the fourteen Scots Labour MPs in ministerial posts, eight were opposed to continued British membership, the most prominent and potentially the most embarrassing being William Ross, the Secretary of State. In the event Ross distanced himself entirely from the six other 'anti' Cabinet Ministers, kept well out of the limelight throughout the campaign, as if conscious of his debt of loyalty to a Prime Minister who had made his time at the Scottish Office the longest ever, and anxious, no doubt, to avoid any identification with the Nationalist presence in the No campaign.

Of the 'anti' MPs who did campaign the most prominent was Buchan, a former Scottish Office Minister, who resigned in October 1974 and in March 1975 set up SLAM (Scottish Labour Against the Market). Buchan's leadership of the Labour anti-Marketeers owed much to his being one of the more fluent of the relatively low-calibre Scots Labour group, and, through his close involvement with the Tribune Group, very much a UK-oriented ideological socialist who was contemptuous of nationalist politics and the need to accommodate them (even if he had led demands from Scotland for a regional rather than a national count so as to deny the SNP yet another grievance). Apart from Buchan and his few colleagues, however, there can be no doubt that the Labour machine in west central Scotland (and elsewhere, save in the odd constitutency where the MP had decided to campaign) went discreetly into neutral for the duration of the campaign.

On the other side, Labour's pro-Marketeer MPs were scarcely less coy about campaigning (Mackintosh and Dickson Mabon being the most vocal), and the prominence as active campaigners in the 'Labour Campaign for Europe' of a number of *former* Labour MPs (Douglas, Lawson, Miss Herbison and Hannan – Labour campaign organiser) and George Thomson, Labour MP for Dundee prior to becoming an EEC Commissioner, suggested that those with nothing to lose politically were more prepared to bear the brunt of campaigning than those preoccupied with constituencies and careers.

In the Conservative Party – where a benign pro-EEC consensus reigned – there were few problems. Of the sixteen Conservative MPs, only two campaigned for a No vote, one of whom was Teddy Taylor of Glasgow, the party's only effective politician on Clydeside. His isolation was so complete that he decided to campaign against his party's line alongside the leader of the SNP's No campaign, Margo MacDonald, and Labour's Jim Sillars, in a curious trio. Apart from such minor diversions, the Conservatives provided solid if unobtrusive back-up for the Yes campaign. The same was true of the somewhat depleted Liberals, whose three MPs mirrored the committedly pro-European posture of their party, despite the real threat within their peripheral constituencies posed by the SNP. Perhaps for this reason Grimond confined his activities to the national campaign.

The SNP's referendum posture was tactical to the point of being, in retrospect, confusing. Whilst the eleven MPs voted in unison against acceptance of the renegotiated terms, the party's slogan – 'Common Market NO on anybody else's terms' – was one temporising enough to allow those in the party (thought to include at least five of the party's eleven MPs) who positively favoured membership of the EEC for an *independent* Scotland to coexist with those (including at least 75 per cent of the party members) who were, like Donald Stewart, the parliamentary leader, opposed to the EEC *per se*. Of the nationalist figures who campaigned, the most visible were Winifred Ewing, the party's parliamentary spokesman on European affairs; Margo MacDonald (briefly MP for Govan 1973–74), who was in official charge of the SNP campaign; and the effective populist orator Douglas Henderson, the party's

Westminster whip, who also featured in the British campaign as a vice-president of the National Referendum Campaign. Henderson and Ewing both represented fishing constituencies, where the party had in 1970 established a bridgehead by deliberately exploiting fears about the EEC, whilst Margo MacDonald was part of what might be called the SNP's 'southern strategy'. Having mopped up much of the rural periphery in 1974, it was now eager to tackle the real obstacle to continued success: Labour's hold over industrial Scotland, where its failure to turn votes into seats was what stood between the SNP as a Scottish interest party and the SNP as a party 'with a mandate for independence'. Margo MacDonald, the only SNP leader with working-class credentials, was thus significantly placed at the head of the party's campaign, to appeal to the industrial working-class electorate who were already being wooed by a 'Save Scottish Steel' campaign. The party was also engaged in an attempt to undermine the position of Grimond in Shetland, and to that end were campaigning for a 'Fifty-mile fishing limit NOW'. That one of the party's national anti-EEC leaflets openly sported a membership application form confirmed that the referendum was being used for a recruiting drive.

The referendum umbrellas

The Yes and No organisations in Scotland both took on a 'Scottish' aspect: the Marketeers operating under the 'Scotland in Europe' banner, and their opponents with the rather more 'branch office' title of 'Get Britain Out – National Referendum Campaign (Scotland)'. 'Scotland in Europe' had a well financed and well staffed organisation under a Conservative organiser (Hardie) and a Liberal secretary (Fraser). The chairmanship and vice-chairmanship of the organisation were filled by two Labour politicians – J. Dickson Mabon, MP, and Dick Douglas (former MP). In all appointments to committees – both centrally and in twenty-eight local organisations – party political balance (Con.–Lab.–Lib.) was sought throughout. Most of the places singled out as special target areas were SNP-occupied parliamentary seats: Argyll, Galloway, Moray and Nairn, and those in Tayside. Abundant supplies of Scottish-oriented ('Scotland says Yes to Europe') leaflets (on oil, food prices, jobs, fishing) were available to supplement the more than adequate quantities of London and Community-produced literature.

Given the need to penetrate the proletarian redoubt of Clydeside,

the potentially most important element in 'Scotland in Europe' was
that of the Labour pro-Marketeers. Yet without any strong *trade
union* contacts outside the GMWU the 'Labour Campaign for
Europe' was not able to get past what William Hannan, its
organiser, described as communist shop stewards, when seeking to
campaign in the shipyards and factories; though 'Labour Campaign
for Europe' posters were ubiquitous in the industrial areas, and out
of eighteen prominently deployed Yes campaign speakers no fewer
than ten were from the Labour party. There was no evidence that
the pro-EEC coalition suffered any stresses: nor indeed should it
have, given the breadth of its support within Scotland from the CBI,
SNFU and the Church, and the whole weight of the British political
establishment behind it.

'Get Britain Out – National Referendum Campaign (Scotland)',
on the other hand, was a far more ramshackle coalition, not only in
relation to its rival but also in comparison with its English
equivalent, whose leaders were (Wedgwood Benn excepted) at least
sufficiently lacking in open antipathy to share common platforms
and press conferences. The Scottish Nos came in at least five
varieties: (i) SLAM ('Scottish Labour Against the Market') –
basically the two left-wingers Norman and Janey Buchan; (ii) the
STUC – with specific AUEW, TGWU and NUM support, and trade
councils; (iii) the SNP; (iv) the Sillars–Taylor–MacDonald all-party
trio; (v) dissident Tories (SCATOR), sundry anti-Marketeer
industrialists. Unlike the Scottish pro-Marketeers the No campaign
(except, obviously, for the SNP) was virtually entirely reliant on
London-produced literature; some locally produced leaflets were
used: one each by SLAM and SCATOR and two by the STUC,
which gave the printed campaign a Scottish focus but in no way
matched the material available to 'Scotland in Europe'. From the
establishment of 'NRC (Scotland)' it was dominated by left-wing
element of the political and industrial wings of the Labour
movement on Clydeside, its most prominent officeholders being two
AUEW organisers, Ferry and Laird, and Jim Sillars. Stewart, the
SNP party leader, and Clark-Hutchison, the Conservative MP, were
also on the letter head, though other right-wing personnel came and
went rapidly, unable to work easily with the Clydeside left.
Particularly ironic, given such left-wing dominance of the No
campaign, was the fact that the best audience of the No campaign
was that obtained (700) by Enoch Powell at Arbroath.

The campaign outside the industrial belt was conducted by the

non-trade unionist part of the alliance, namely a curious group of
independent operators, of generally rightist hue: on Tayside, a fish
merchant; in Grampian, a right-wing ex-army officer; and in many
other peripheral areas (Highlands and Islands) normally SNP
activists. Disregarding the transpectrum heterogeneity of the
'cartel', even at the socialist end of the organisation mutual
suspicions and antagonisms raged. Relations between the Buchans
and Sillars were bad, stemming from their disagreement over
devolution (Sillars being a maximalist, and Buchan at that time
more or less anti-devolution). Sillars was perceived to be building an
independent career for himself in Scottish politics, and using the
referendum as a launching pad. His campaigning style was
aggressively independent. At one point he observed that those
urging a Yes vote were 'the same people who, for the past fifteen
years, have between them *in different governments* made such an
appalling mess of the economy and foreign policy'.[15] Moreover the
SNP was resented for its 'No – on anybody else's terms', thought to
be a confusing, and therefore vote-losing, slogan. Thus the No
campaign as a whole was a thoroughly fragmented effort, co-
ordinated activity being made impossible by severe personal and
political incompatibilities, themselves the reflection of the growing
fragmentation of Scottish politics.

Of the *issues* in the Scottish campaign, some were not dissimilar to
those in England, merely more intensely stressed, while others were
peculiar to Scotland. Most prominent in the first category, and the
most constant theme of the campaign, was the *jobs* issue: would the
EEC mean more jobs and investment, or, on the contrary, fewer jobs
as the steel and car industries contracted, with jobs and investment
sucked into the 'golden triangle'? Would Scots have to 'emigrate' not
merely to the English Midlands, as had been traditional, but to the
Ruhr?[16] What significance did the EEC have for the government's
regional policies, most particularly the Scottish Development Agency
which was about to be established? Did Community regional aid
represent positive help, or was it no more than the return of part of
Britain's 'membership subscription'? Finally, *food prices*. Had the
EEC put Britain (Scotland) on a prices ratchet which still had some
way to go? Did the EEC offer the benefit of safe food supplies? In
sum these issues reflected preoccupation with Scotland's traditional
ills.

Issues more particular to Scotland were oil, fishing and Norway.
The key to Scotland's new-found self-confidence is the discovery of

oil. Academics have been publishing books (one on the eve of the referendum)[17] showing how the oil, if used solely, or mainly, in Scotland, could mean the abolition of VAT and even of income tax. What implications had the feared EEC energy policy for such a fantasy: would Scotland forfeit all the hoped-for gains? Secondly, *fishing*. Was this declining industry to face unbridled EEC member state competition right up to the Scottish shores by 1982? Or was it benefiting from generous EEC grants for boat-building? Both oil and fishing issues led naturally on to *Norway*. Had not Norway, a small country with similar oil and fishing industries, said No and gone on to get a better deal out of the oil companies and to enjoy a higher living standards? Or was it in fact suffering from inflation and exclusion from the European market? These three issues, exclusively in the case of the last one, were raised largely by the SNP, and behind the debate around all these issues there loomed another question also identified with the SNP: *devolution*. The debate on devolution rumbled on through the referendum, surfacing towards the end in the form of the question: did membership of the EEC render more difficult the establishment of a Scottish Assembly (as argued by the anti-EEC Scottish Office Minister in charge of devolution, Harry Ewing), or was it perfectly feasible (as argued by Lord Home)?[18] Did not EEC membership strengthen the SNP's separatist case for independent Scottish representation at Brussels in order to prevent an indifferent, unresponsive and distant British power centre being replaced by a very much more insensitive and distant European one? In this way Scotland's self-perception as the periphery of the periphery was reflected in much of the campaigning.

The media

All the Scottish national papers were pro-Market, including *The Scotsman*. Its leader on polling day was, even so, rather temporisingly headed 'Reasons for not voting No'. The popular press worked hard to counter the anti-EEC trade union lobby, with the *Daily Record* throwing the headline 'AYE–Answer Yes to Europe' across its polling day edition. In the press as a whole, the pro-Marketeers' warning about the loss of Scottish jobs if Britain left the Market was more prominent than the counter-argument that if Britain stayed in the job loss would be worse.

The broadcasting media, and particularly television, provided, in addition to the London-produced broadcasts on behalf of the two campaigns (some of which contained snatches angled at the Scottish voter), time for screening locally produced debates and gave time for one broadcast each for *Scotland in Europe* and *NRC Scotland*. Nevertheless the overall impact probably represented the most Britishising agent in the Scottish campaign, serving to erode some of its peculiarities.

The result

The result in Scotland (58 per cent Yes, 42 per cent No) indeed confirmed the failure of the No cartel to render the periphery of the periphery as electorally distinct as had been expected. Admittedly, taking the results region by region from south to north, the No vote increased with latitude, though the No majorities in Western Isles and Shetland, involving as they did such miniscule electorates, were of little significance. More interesting was the fact that neither industrial Strathclyde (with half the country's population), nor the regions of SNP strength (Central, Tayside, Grampian and Highland) produced results significantly different from the Scottish mean. Nor was the Scottish turn-out (61 per cent) all that different from the English (65 per cent).

The relative similarity of the Scottish and English results suggests that unifying forces were at work countermanding the separatist tendency. The unifying agent was, most probably, the British Labour Party, whose voters, when it came to the day, followed their leaders into the Yes lobby. Certainly a great change came over the Scottish Labour voter between April 1974, when 61 per cent were opposed to British membership of the EEC, and May 1975, when only 27 per cent were of that opinion and 50 per cent favoured the *status quo*. Poll data[19] also revealed, however, that, whilst reconciled to the EEC, 70 per cent of Scots wanted to have independent representation at Brussels – a strong SNP theme, and one also taken up by Jim Sillars immediately after the referendum. Demands for an independent Scottish voice in all the institutions of the EEC were, as they had to be, rejected by the government. Even a request from Buchan and the Liberal, Steel, for a Scottish office in Brussels (the Commission had opened an office in Edinburgh after the referendum) was rejected by Secretary of State Ross, who argued that Scots interests would be protected well enough by Scots interest groups and by Scottish Office officials. Ross revealed that such officials had attended to support the permanent UK delegation in Brussels on ninety-four occasions in the year ending 31 May 1975, and that an EEC hill-farming directive had issued from a committee in which a Scottish Office Minister had led the British team.

Scottish representation in the Strasbourg Assembly after the referendum numbered five: W. Hamilton and Dalyell for Labour (both pro-Marketeers); Fletcher and Corrie for the Conservatives; and Mrs Ewing (who replaced the Liberal, Johnston). The latter proceeded to 'defend Scottish interests', leaving aside broader questions of whether an independent Scotland would remain in the Community; that, she announced at a press conference in March 1976, would be put to another referendum after a Scottish government had renegotiated the terms. Through Mrs Ewing the SNP sought to keep the spotlight on the distinctly Scottish concerns of energy, fishing and farming – though the other four Scottish representatives made sure she did not get all the limelight. For example, on oil, Dalyell brushed in July 1975 with Commissioner Simonet about extraction rates and price guarantees. On fishing limits policy Scottish fishermen's organisations opened a campaign in March 1976 to resist the introduction of a 200 mile limit common to all EEC member states and demand instead an exclusive 100 mile limit for British boats. The government appeared committed to negotiate for an exclusive fifty-mile limit up the east coast (a figure thought irresponsibly extravagant when advocated by the SNP during the referendum). When a Commons committee in July 1976 recommended a Scottish representation of eight in the proposed eighty-one-seat United Kingdom delegation to the first directly elected European Assembly, the SNP immediately sought parity with Denmark (a country of similar population size), with Henderson asking, 'If Denmark has sixteen seats, does that mean one Dane is worth two Scotsmen?' – a characteristic remark, made with one eye cocked as ever on the opinion polls.

The future shape of Scotland's relations with the EEC depended, obviously enough, on the outcome of the debate concerning Scotland's relations with England; but what the debate in Scotland over Britain's renegotiated terms had done was simultaneously to assist the separatist case by highlighting the peculiarities of the Scottish situation, whilst seriously dividing the most important organisational bulwark of the Union – the Labour party – on whose enduring strength and self-confidence effective resistance to the radical demands of the SNP now depended.

DEVOLUTION

Within Scotland, as the EEC issue faded, the devolution debate resumed its place at the centre of the stage. Quite apart from the fundamental doubt concerning whether the strength of a secessionist movement unleashed by the force of economic discontents could be attenuated by purely institutional reforms, the nature of the devolutionary response remained very much to be determined. As far as the electorate was concerned, poll data consistently in the post-1974 period confirmed that no more than a fifth of Scots voters wanted independence. The vast majority favoured the retention of the Union in some form, with federalism the most strongly supported option. This, however, appeared to be the one option, other than independence, that the government was not prepared to take up, on account of its view that federalism was incompatible with the economic unity of the United Kingdom.

For the major unionist parties, however, the prime concern was survival. For Labour nationally its continuance as a British governing party at Westminster absolutely required the saving of its Scottish seats, since at only two elections since 1945 had it won a clear majority of *English* constituencies. If devolution to a Scottish Assembly was the price Labour had to pay to keep the SNP out of its seats, then it had to be paid, and yet the scale of devolution – the extent of powers devolved – could not fail to involve the likelihood of reduced Scottish representation at Westminster – a possibility, for reasons stated, that Labour had to resist. The problem was therefore to know whether minimal devolution (the sort that could justify the retention of Scotland's seventy-one seats in London) would be sufficient to buy off a significant proportion of the SNP's voters.

A second problem facing the British Labour leadership was to impress upon their Scottish wing the urgency of the matter. One problem was the relatively rotten state of the party at grass-roots level in Scotland, where many constituency organisations had become mere empty husks presided over by aging, complacent cliques virtually answerable to no one and unexposed to new ideas; and where resistance to devolution was rationalised by reference to those parts of the socialist canon that spoke of 'internationalism' and 'working-class unity' (especially by a wartime generation who equated the nationalism which devolution was supposed to appease with black reaction). Scottish Labour's unresponsiveness was also to be explained by the hostility to devolution of Labour's arch-unionist

Secretary of State William Ross, who, with his junior Ministers, had little to gain and much to lose and gave no encouragement to the devolvers in London. One slight chink in the monolithism of Scots Labour had, however, been revealed prior to the February 1974 election when four left-wing trade unionist MPs published a pamphlet advocating a Scottish parliament. They (and John Mackintosh, MP, who was a committed devolutionist, though at the other end of Labour's spectrum) formed important nuclei around which opposition to the party's conservative leadership in Scotland could be built, but not in time, it seemed, to prevent the Scottish Council of the Labour Party Executive in June 1974 rejecting by six to five (with eighteen absentees) a recently published Kilbrandon-based government statement on devolution policy as 'constitutional tinkering which does not contribute to socialist objectives'.

Electoral necessity decreed, however, that such views could not prevail, and, led by the NEC of the party in London and the Cabinet, the Scottish party was obliged, at a special conference in August 1974, to endorse the government's devolution proposals, which were published shortly before the October election (*Democracy and Devolution: Proposals for Scotland and Wales*, HMSO, Cmnd 5732, September 1974). Labour's October election manifesto in Scotland represented an extensive concession to 'Scottishness', not least in the promise of 'a Scottish Assembly dealing with Scottish affairs with control over its own expenditure', and whilst most Labour MPs were clearly unhappy at conceding so much to the nationalist impulse the strategem appeared to succeed: Labour's vote held sufficiently for it to suffer no loss of seats.

Despite British Labour's conviction that devolution was politically unavoidable, a perceptible disinclination at the centre to act was evident. An influential group of Cabinet Ministers interpreted the EEC referendum result as showing that politics in Scotland were ceasing to be as deviant and problematic and that the Scots thus required less to be appeased than the previous elections had suggested. Similarly there were growing reservations in Whitehall as the constitutional implications of devolution came to be fully examined. For these and other reasons, notably the generalised hope in London that the Scots would grow bored with the devolution issue and with the SNP, the devolution Bill was put off until the autumn of 1976. Meanwhile a further White Paper in which the devolution Bill was ultimately to be based (*Our Changing Democracy: Devolution to Scotland and Wales*, HMSO, Cmnd 6348, November

1975) outlined the government's minimalist proposals: a Scottish Assembly of 142 members, directly elected every four years; a chief executive and Ministers drawn from the Assembly; legislative powers to cover most of those areas already the subject of administrative devolution to the Scottish Office; finance to be by way of an annual block grant, with independent taxation powers denied. The Secretary of State was to be allowed to exercise a power of veto over any Assembly enactments as well as retain his authority in certain fields; the civil service to remain undividedly British; and Scotland to retain its seventy-one seats at Westminster. Outside the Labour Party in Scotland these proposals (which reflected the government's irreconcilable objectives of giving Scots 'a decisive voice in running their own affairs' whilst doing nothing to abridge 'the vital and fundamental principle of the economic and political unity of the United Kingdom') were roundly condemned for their conflict-creating potential. Within the Labour Party they were used by Sillars as the pretext for finally breaking away to form his 'Scottish Labour Party' with another advanced devolutionist MP (Robertson) and the Labour Party's Scottish research officer. The SLP was to campaign for an assembly with 'full economic powers' (which it claimed Labour had promised), Scottish representation at Brussels, and a 'return to socialist policies' at home.[20] Labour's two other left-wing devolutionists, Eadie and Ewing, having been silenced by office, it remained to Mackintosh, on the party's right wing, to attack the minimalism of the proposals. More representative of the Scots MPs as a whole, however, was Buchan, who, like most on the party's left, could only brook devolution by seeing it as a means for entailing wider participation in decision-making, and who advocated a referendum less to stop devolution (the political inevitability of which he reluctantly accepted) than to set clear parameters beyond which it would not proceed. The suggestion drew a ready response from anti-devolutionist English Tribunite MPs such as Heffer (who had started to show much interest in political developments in Scotland), as well as from root-and-branch Scots Labour unionists such as Dalyell. Mackintosh, however, wanted no truck with 'government by opinion poll', and Judith Hart warned that a referendum on separatism/independence could not be guaranteed to produce the desired Union-endorsing response. It was left to William Ross, by now a convert to the view that 'without devolution you can say goodbye to the Labour Party in Scotland',[21] to rally the troops behind the proposals and even to advocate ceding more of his powers as Secretary of State to the proposed Assembly. A campaign – 'Devolution, not separation' – was launched in January 1976 but quickly petered out, suggesting that Labour had no stomach for a fight which exposed it to SNP-inspired taunts that to be merely an electorally motivated piecemeal and reluctant devolutionist was to deny pride in one's Scottish identity.

In effect Labour in Scotland had neither the courage to say no nor the confidence to say yes to devolution. Nor had it helped that by 1976 the maximalist case was represented on the one hand by the renegade Sillars, who had left the party hurling insults at all his former friends, accusing them of reneging not only on devolution but also on socialism, and on the other hand by the intellectual Mackintosh, whose influence in Labour's Clydeside heartland was virtually nil. Nor yet did the identity of Labour's two most vocal unionists, Dalyell and William Hamilton, encourage the traditionalist socialist centralisers of the Clyde, for both were right-wing, pro-EEC and lacking any influence in the Labour movement in Scotland. The debate, in other words, was in the hands of men peripheral to the party's Scottish establishment. In the event, impelled by perceptions of electoral necessity, and concerned to staunch the flow of trade unionists, even shop stewards, to the SNP, all but two of the Scots Labour group voted for the devolution Bill on its second reading in December 1976.

For the Conservative Party in Scotland – easily the most southward-looking of all the parties and in leadership and style the most anglicised, the devolution question was potentially very awkward. On the other hand the party had been known nationally for its capacity for pragmatic adaptation to change, and following the electoral disasters of 1974 the Scots Conservatives began to adjust to the new climate. As the English public school-educated Conservative MPs were swept aside by the SNP, they were replaced by native-born and educated Scots, and indeed by 1975 the party's Scottish front-bench team included two new MPs, Fairgrieve and Rifkind, who were from business and legal backgrounds respectively, and who projected a rather less anglicised and county persona than those who had traditionally dominated the party in Scotland. Both men, moreover, sought to align the party firmly behind proposals for devolution, to which the party had been formally committed since the late 1960s when it accepted Douglas-Home's idea of an indirectly elected Assembly.[22] Out of fear, however, after the October 1974 election, that commitment was upgraded to one envisaging a *directly* elected assembly, and it was against this that the unionist core of the party reacted during 1975. Led by Iain Sproat, MP, at least five of the sixteen Scots Tory MPs formed 'Keep Britain United', a group opposed to any devolution, on grounds of expense, bureaucracy, over-government, and fear both of rule within Scotland by Glasgow and of clashes between Westminster and a Scottish Assembly. Such unreconstructed unionists were encouraged by the election of Margaret Thatcher, who was indifferent towards devolution and argued, with some force, that the party should confront the Scots electorate not as the fourth most enthusiastic devolutionist party but as the only unapologetically unionist party in Scotland. Having set its face against such a retreat from electoral reality, however, the Scottish Conservative leadership negotiated a compromise with the national leadership which took the form of retaining the commitment to an Assembly, but envisaging it as no more than an adjunct of the House of Commons, taking second readings and committee stages of Scottish Bills, and to reject any Bill based on the Labour government's devolution proposals. A very uneasy and noisy Scottish Conservative conference in May 1976 endorsed a decision to oppose the Labour government's devolution Bill, but a serious split appeared at the second reading of the Bill in December 1976 when, after three front-bench resignations – including that of the shadow Secretary of State, Alick Buchanan-Smith – only six of the sixteen Scots Tory Members backed the official Thatcherite opposition to the Bill, whilst seven abstained and three voted with the government. The revolt, involving all but one of the party's recent past, or present, front-bench spokesmen on Scotland, was unprecedented. Moreover the gulf between the Edinburgh and London leaderships of the party was widened by a Commons speech by Buchanan-Smith in which federalism was mentioned as a preferable alternative to the government's conflict-strewn proposals.

   Other parties' reactions were less remarkable. The Liberals, long committed in Scotland to federalism,[23] criticised the devolution proposals for their minimalism and spoke out unceasingly for the need for proportional representation in any Scots Assembly. The Scottish Committee of the Communist Party, with perhaps more than half the British Communist membership concentrated in Scotland, and influential on Clydeside, likewise had long favoured a Scottish legislature with economic powers, and promoted such views through the unions in which it had prominent activists (NUM and AUEW). Whilst of somewhat restricted audience, Liberal and Communist spokesmen reinforced the maximalist push, and neither party suffered any obvious dissensions. The SNP's leadership, whilst understandably critical of the proposals, was in the main committed to a 'two-step' progress towards independence, with the Edinburgh Assembly acting as a stepping stone, coaxing the Scots away from their enduring psychological dependence on the Union. A small impatient minority, however, including the voluble MP Henderson, appeared to prefer an early election and the securing of a mandate for early independence.

Interest group reaction was more cautious. The *teaching profession* on the whole welcomed devolution, anxious as they were to resist what they held to be the increasing anglicisation of Scots education, and were annoyed that the *universities*, at their own request, were not to be devolved. The *lawyers* were looking for adequate safeguards for Scots law, especially in the European context, and welcomed devolution if it improved on what was regarded as London's indifference. *The Church*, inclining towards the Liberal position, welcomed the proposals, as did the *STUC*, which was anxious for devolution with economic teeth, and active, via its constituent unions, in the promotion of such views within the Labour Party. *The CBI in Scotland*, however, was very worried, fearing the break-up of the economic unity of the UK, excessive additional governmental interference, rule by the Glasgow left, and a retreat further from UK-standardised educational qualifications which would add to industrial recruiting problems. Like the lawyers, however, the CBI recognised the importance of the European dimension and favoured the fullest exploration of EEC regional aid opportunities. The *local authorities* were worried that an Assembly would tamper with the new two-tier system of local government set up only as recently as 1974, the regional tier of which had been attacked on grounds of needless expense and remoteness from the public. Labour-controlled regions (Strathclyde, Central) tended reluctantly and out of party loyalty to back the proposals, whilst Conservative-held regions (Grampian, Tayside) mirrored in the variety of their reactions the substantial divisions within the Tory party. The remote and oil-rich island authority of Shetland, anxious to protect lucrative deals made with the oil companies and fearing domination by Glasgow, spoke of seeking Channel Island status within the UK should an Assembly be established in Scotland.[24]

What these reactions implied was that, whilst devolution had not necessarily been embraced with universal enthusiasm, it had – with important popular press backing and with very persistent support from *The Scotsman* – come to be regarded as at least in some form inevitable. The *status quo*, continued unionist activity notwithstanding,[25] had, it seemed, ceased to be an option, even despite the collapse in February 1977 of the committee stage of the Scotland and Wales Bill. That collapse, occasioned by the government's failure to obtain a majority for a guillotine motion designed to save the Bill from a filibustering campaign conducted by mainly English opponents of devolution, highlighted the problem of transferring the debate from Scotland, where outright hostility to some kind of devolution had ceased to be regarded as credible politics, to a House of Commons dominated – front benches included – by the unsympathetic and the indifferent. In so hostile an environment the already weak and shallow commitment of the Labour Party in Scotland was put under great pressure. In the event, with the notable exceptions of the home-ruler Mackintosh and the reluctant 'realist' Buchan, Scottish Labour MPs sat quietly by as Merseyside and Tyneside representatives of Labour's English backlash joined with Conservatives to torpedo the project. All but four Scots Labour MPs did their minimal duty and backed the government's attempt to keep the Bill going, whilst all sixteen Scots Conservative Members – including the embryo federalists Buchanan-Smith and Rifkind – rallied against from a variety of motives. The eleven Nationalist MPs, keen for devolution of almost any kind, backed the government, as did the two-man Scottish Labour Party. The three Scottish Liberal Members, however, somewhat surprisingly opposed the guillotine motion, ostensibly because they favoured a more maximalist Bill involving an assembly with tax-raising powers and access to some oil revenues: a memorandum outlining such proposals was submitted to the government in March after the forging of the Lib.–Lab. pact designed to ensure survival of the, by then, minority Labour government. It was, however, clear, and not without irony, that the House of Commons, whose party composition bore testimony enough to the presence of the centrifugal strains which had come to threaten the unity of the United Kingdom, was unprepared to reconcile itself easily to legislation designed to alleviate the force of those very strains. Yet some form of reconciliation was ultimately unavoidable. The transformation of Scottish political life had been both mirrored in and intensified by the debates over relations with England and the European Community. What remained to be determined was the particular shape the reformulation of relationships was to take, as well as the date of introduction of any institutional changes, and for this the main burden of responsibility continued to rest with the Scottish voters.

NOTES

1 The author thanks Michael Dyer, with whom he has discussed some of the points raised in this chapter.

2 The departments of the Scottish Office are as follows: Agriculture and Fisheries; Development; Economic Planning; Education; Home and Health.

3 Figures taken from the National Readership Survey, 1973, cited in J. G. Kellas, *The Scottish Political System*, 1975.

4 R. Rose, *The United Kingdom as a Multi-national State*, University of Strathclyde, Occasional Paper No. 6, 1970, and *The Future of Scottish Politics*, Fraser of Allander Institute Speculative Papers, No. 3, 1975.

5 See Opinion Research Centre surveys published in *The Scotsman*, June 1975, December 1975, October 1976. These surveys showed an average of 20 per cent for complete independence; 27 per cent for federalism; 20 per cent for limited devolution to a directly elected legislature; 10 per cent for limited devolution to an unelected legislature; and 20 per cent for the *status quo*.

6 Scotland, with 11 per cent of the British population, has 97·5 per cent of the worst areas of urban deprivation – 95 per cent on Clydeside alone. See *Census Indicators of Urban Deprivation*, Working Note No. 6, Department of the Environment, February 1975 – a publication much cited by the SNP.

7 M. J. Esman, *Scottish Nationalism, North Sea Oil and the British Response*, Edinburgh University, Department of Politics, Occasional Paper No. 6. See also A. Harrison, *The Distribution of Personal Wealth in Scotland*. Fraser of Allander Institute for Research into the Scottish Economy, 1975.

8 Hamilton and Govan, scenes of past SNP by-election victories, represent the old, declining industrial areas of north Lanarkshire and Clydeside. Cumbernauld and East Kilbride are new towns where the SNP has penetrated deeply.

9 See British Election Study Data, *The Scotsman*, 15 October 1975.

10 J. Mackintosh, 'Scottish Nationalism', *Political Quarterly*, vol. 38, 1967, pp. 389–402.

11 The British Election Study data, *op. cit.*, suggest that in 1974 the SNP had the support of 37 per cent of higher managerials, 29 per cent of lower managerials, 27 per cent of skilled non-manuals, 26 per cent of other non-manuals, 33 per cent of skilled manuals, and 20 per cent of

other manuals. Worrying for the Labour Party was the confirmation provided by this survey that 26 per cent of trade unionists voted SNP in 1974.

12 The *Glasgow Herald* System Three poll of 8 March 1976 credited the SNP with 46 per cent of the 18–34 age group.

13 See the *Glasgow Herald*, 8 May 1975; *Le Nouvel Observateur*, 7–13 October 1974.

14 See P. Barker and N. Spencer, 'People and power', *New Society*, 29 May 1975.

15 *The Scotsman*, 12 May 1975.

16 James Milne (STUC) on GTV, 21 May 1975.

17 D. I. Mackay and G. A. Mackay, *The Political Economy of North Sea Oil*, Martin Robertson, 1975.

18 Lord Home: 'If we stay in the Community we are just as entitled to a Scottish assembly as Germans are entitled to their laender.' (BBC-TV, 30 May 1975.)

19 ORC, *The Scotsman*, 31 May 1975.

20 Survey data suggested that, given the chance, 28 per cent of Labour voters would vote for the SLP. (ORC, *The Scotsman*, 29 October 1976.)

21 *The Scotsman*, 16 January 1976.

22 It was in fact under previous Conservative administrations that all the substantive measures of administrative devolution to Scotland had taken place (i.e. the appointment of the first Scottish Secretary; the elevation of the post to Cabinet status, and the move of the Scottish Office to Edinburgh).

23 *Scottish Self-government*, Scottish Liberal Party, May 1976.

24 Almost half the oilfields lie in 'Shetland' waters, and it was to discredit any idea of Shetland autonomy that the SNP tabled in December 1976 a Commons motion calling on the government 'to introduce . . . as proof of their sincerity in implementing the wishes of the Shetland people . . . early legislation to give effect to Shetland's decision to leave the EEC, as expressed in the [June 1975] referendum'.

25 Anti-devolutionists formed in November 1976 a 'Scotland is British' campaign, comprising individuals from the CBI, and from various unions (UCATT, AUEW), as well as a former Conservative Minister (Lord Polwarth), former Labour MPs, and the Labour chairman of the Fife Regional Council (Sir George Sharp), who happened also to be president of the Convention of Scottish Local Authorities. Its message, proclaimed from poster sites in the larger towns, was 'Stop stampeding Scotland into devolution – Scotland is British'.

DENIS BALSOM AND P. J. MADGWICK

4   Wales, European integration and devolution

The question of European integration is not separable from the question of devolution within the United Kingdom. Both matters involve the modification of sovereignty, and the territorial distribution of power. In Wales the connection was emphasised by the coincidence of the public discussion, indeed agitation, on these questions. British membership of the EEC arose as a political issue in the early 1960s, following Macmillan's unsuccessful application. The national question first burst into public awareness when the president of Plaid Cymru, Mr Gwynfor Evans, gained the Carmarthen seat in a famous by-election in July 1966. There followed a run of by-election success for Plaid Cymru, which took no seats but almost destroyed some massive Labour majorities in South Wales. Meanwhile the SNP was launched on its way in Scotland by the victory of Hamilton in November 1967. Thus from the mid-'60s onwards, the issues of integration and devolution were to run in close parallel in the politics of the Celtic fringe. The referendum in 1975 provided not a climax exactly, but certainly another peak of excitement in a long-running serial. The question of Britain's belonging to the EEC was caught up in questions about the status of Wales itself and the condition of the Welsh economy. Counting the votes showed Wales to be little different from the rest of the UK. But the Welsh 'Yes' carried within it many notes of discord.

The referendum campaign was affected by and itself disturbed the existing patterns of Welsh politics. In particular the campaign emphasised the disarray of the Welsh Labour Party after a long period of dominance, and witnessed a new political activism of the trade unions in Wales. It also revealed the ambivalence of Plaid Cymru both in its attitude to Europe and in its uneven dual political base in rural and industrial Wales. These points may be explained more fully as follows.

(i) The dominance of the Labour Party began to erode. In 1910 Wales was dominated by the Liberal Party, which then took over half the votes and three-quarters of the seats. Twenty years later the position was transformed: Labour held twenty-five of thirty-five seats, with 44 per cent of the votes. The high point of Labour dominance was reached in 1966, when the party took two-thirds of the vote and thirty-two of thirty-six seats. Labour could hardly expect to do much better, and in fact soon began to slip from this exalted position. In the 1974 elections the Labour vote fell below 50 per cent, and the party's tally of seats to twenty-three of thirty-six. The decline reflected economic and social change, the decay and diversification of industry, and matching movements in support for the three other parties.[1]

(ii) Support for Plaid Cymru, the party of Welsh nationalism, grew. Nationalism was not a new phenomenon in Welsh politics, and had been a diffuse force in the old Liberal Party. Plaid Cymru, founded in 1926, remained a cultural elite on the margins of Welsh politics until the 1960s. Then nationalism acquired a new impulse associated with the revival of the Welsh language, the revolt of the young and the discontents of the times. Its take-off in parliamentary politics came in July 1966 with the capture of the Carmarthen seat in a by-election by Gwynfor Evans, the party's president. There followed a run of by-election successes, with dramatically high polls in Labour strongholds, but no victories. The Carmarthen seat was lost in 1970. But in 1974 the party gained three seats. It was a modest victory, but it gave the Nationalists some political influence in a narrowly balanced Parliament, and a wholly new and skilfully exploited prominence, standing and self-confidence. This was enhanced by further success in local elections. The party enjoyed a triumph far beyond the actual limits of its achievement, a popular vote stopped at 11 per cent, and just three seats, all in the Celtic, Welsh-speaking areas of west and north-west Wales. Thus Welsh Nationalists could not approach the striking success of their Scottish colleagues, but they contrived to hang on to Scottish coat tails without losing dignity.[2]

(iii) The Liberals took more of the vote than Plaid Cymru, about sixteen per cent in 1974, but, lacking territorial concentration, they held only two seats. Their position in Wales is similar to that in England. They draw support from the major parties without winning seats, and contribute to the multi-party politics which characterises one third to one half of the Welsh constituencies.

(iv) Alongside these movements in party and electoral politics, some significant changes occurred in the pattern of political forces in

Wales. In 1964 the Labour government established a Welsh Office, headed by a Secretary of State with a seat in the Cabinet. Thus Wales acquired an equivalent of the longer-standing Scottish Office, though, especially at first, with more restricted powers. This was an undramatic but highly significant step. Henceforth government in Wales had a spokesman in the Cabinet, a recognised, if minor status in the parliamentary timetable, a place in the structure of the civil service, and a role in the crucial relationships between central and lcoal government. All this is the small change of the politics of headlines and crises, but the very substance of day-to-day government.

(v) The establishment of the Welsh Office was, moreover, a stimulus to Welsh political activity. Increasingly the major interest groups pursued Welsh interests in Cardiff, and adjusted their own structure to fit a pattern of decentralised government. This is true, for example, of the NFU, the CBI and the TUC. Existing Welsh bodies – for teachers and local authorities, for example – were also more active. New forms of government stimulated areas of political activity, which in turn stimulated government.[3]

(vi) The media in Wales both responded to and encouraged the revival of Welsh political activity. The press and broadcasting have a strong Welsh orientation, a concern with Wales as a region, which is inevitably and indeed naturally, but unassertively, nationalist. Of course, the London media still outweigh the Welsh in quantity and penetration, but the Welsh media offer a continuing additional channel for the stream of news and current affairs.

There are two daily papers, the *Western Mail*, part of the Thomson group, published in Cardiff but circulating widely, and the self-styled 'national newspaper of Wales'. In the north the *Liverpool Daily Post* publishes a North Wales edition. In broadcasting, BBC Wales and Harlech television put out about twenty hours a week of their own programmes, about a half in the Welsh language. In addition there are about thirty hours of radio broadcasts. Morning and early evening news and news magazine programmes figure prominently in this output. In consequence politics is well represented and politicians have comparatively easy access to the media.

There is little quantitative or qualitative evidence by which to assess the impact of the Welsh media. Plainly by their very nature they tend to convey a sense of regional or national identity, and offer a Welsh slant to the reporting of many current events, for example economic problems and unemployment. The *Western Mail* has supported both European integration and devolution. BBC Wales is a missionary for Welsh culture. But these Welsh orientations have to compete with the London media, and against the normal resistances of the audience. It is known that many people, given the choice arising from proximity to England, opt out of Welsh programmes. On the other hand, circulation figures for the regional and local press are high.

(vii) There are two other aspects of Welsh politics which are generally significant and certainly coloured the debates on both integration and devolution – the Welsh language and the Welsh economy. The Welsh language has declined sharply since the beginning of the century, from 50 per cent of the population speaking Welsh to 21 per cent in the census of 1971.[4] The causes of this decline include (in some combination) the movement of population, secularisation, the growth of the London mass media, government inaction or hostility, and popular indifference; in sum and above all, the overwhelming impact of near-by England. In the 1960s a fight for the revival of the language began, sparked by the census figures, and exploiting the political disintegration of the times. Pressures from the Welsh elites, militant groups, and, more tardily, the political parties, brought about some advances in the position of the language in public affairs, in education and in broadcasting, and the promise of a wholly Welsh television channel. But the language issue divides Wales, more sharply perhaps than the more ambiguous character of Scottishness divides Scotland. English-speakers complain of the cost of bilingual road signs and official documents, bemoan their lost television programmes, fear for their jobs or the education of their children; and feel uncomfortable in the new ethnocentric and occasionally xenophobic atmosphere of Welsh-speaking Wales. Even Plaid Cymru treads cautiously along this political divide. In Wales, far more than in Scotland, the question of a new constitutional status raises for many people what is in fact an ethnic test which they cannot and do not wish to pass.

(viii) The Welsh economy is a persistent and acute but less divisive question. The Welsh, like the Scots, live in a depressed area. They may conclude that this is a consequence of the Union, which must be dissolved, or at least fundamentally modified, as a prelude to economic regeneration. In the absence of oil, the new dynamic they seek is political, to do with the management of the economy, and the wastefulness of imperial defence expenditure. An alternative view is that comparative depression is a matter of history, not to be blamed on the English, who have their own depressed areas. Rather the London government should be seen as a source of financial aid for Wales, giving subsidies to assist development, and support to local governments to equalise the standards of local services. Government accounts for Wales, not universally accepted as valid, support the fact of Welsh dependence. The implications for future independence are equally open to argument.

Altogether the politics of contemporary Wales offers a crowded, lively but somewhat shifting and unsteady background to the question of accession to the EEC. Integration in Europe might have seemed a soothing antidote to disintegration at home. But the pattern is not so neat; in effect there was a double challenge to the constitutional status of Wales. Hence the European issue and the referendum campaign contributed one more element to an already disturbed political system. Such disturbances may be seen as a dysfunction in a decision-making system, or a proper source of energy in a democracy.

ACTIVITIES OF VARIOUS GROUPS IN THE REFERENDUM CAMPAIGN, 1975

There were three fairly distinct groups of participants in the referendum campaign. These were (i) the two major 'umbrella' organisations operating from Welsh headquarters in Cardiff and controlling various subsidiary groups throughout the country; (ii) the political parties, whose organisational structure already existed in all parts of Wales; (iii) the Members of Parliament for the Welsh constituencies.

1. The 'umbrella' groups

(i) *'Wales in Europe'*. 'Wales in Europe' was the Welsh offshoot of the London-based 'Britain in Europe' organisation, and as such was responsible for the 'Yes' campaign throughout Wales. The organisation went out of its way to dissociate itself from any one political party, but could not wholly avoid some political ambiguity. The chairman was Will Edwards, a former Labour MP, who had been defeated in February 1974 when Plaid Cymru captured Merioneth. Other senior officials included the former secretary of the Welsh Council of Labour, and the Conservative deputy agent for Wales. No attempt was made to create a specifically Welsh dimension for the campaign, though there was some evidence, from

Ireland particularly, that this type of appeal might have been fruitful. Nor did 'Wales in Europe' attempt to operate an electoral machine in the way that a political party would fight a normal election. Little was done to canvass specific areas, and there was a reluctance, for example, to take the risk of sending an earnest pro-European Tory to canvass 'wavering' Labour supporters in safe Labour wards.

Despite the problems of mounting a campaign, 'Wales in Europe' was not lacking in confidence, even a week before polling day. It could not be certain of taking a majority in every one of the eight counties, and regarded mid-Glamorgan and Gwent as marginal. But it had little doubt that in absolute votes Wales would say Yes to Europe.

(ii) *'Wales Get Britain Out'*. 'Wales Get Britain Out', formed in February, 1975, was the campaign arm of a strange alliance of unions, Nationalists and official (as distinct from government) Labourites.

The composition of the executive committee of WGBO gives a clear indication of its general orientation. The chairman was Jack Brookes, Labour leader of South Glamorgan County Council. The secretary was George Wright, Regional Secretary of the T&GWU, and Secretary of the Wales TUC. The treasurer was Don Hayward of the NUM. The committee included Derek Driscoll, T&GWU; Bert Pearce, Welsh Communist Party; the Rev. Bill Morgan, Gwent Independent Mission; Dafydd Williams, General Secretary of Plaid Cymru; Bill Cooper, AUEW.

The committee was formed as the result of a meeting in Cardiff to which 1,600 invitations had been issued largely by the local trades councils throughout Wales. At that meeting it was decided that the 'Get Britain Out' organisation in Wales would remain distinct from its parent body in London. However, a Plaid Cymru motion that the name of the group should be 'The Get Wales Out Campaign' was rejected. The campaign was run under the auspices of the Wales TUC, and several staff members were seconded from the WTUC and the T&GWU for the duration of the campaign.

The composition of WGBO naturally led to internal political disputes. At the outset the National Front had been excluded from the organisation. The initial wrangle over the formal title of the group illustrates the conflicts likely to arise when a group of industrially oriented trade unionists have to work together with Welsh Nationalists. Right-wing Tories were also active in some parts of Cardiff, but appear to have played virtually no part in the central WGBO structure. The socio-economic complexion of Wales also presented difficulties to a campaign that was to be run primarily through the trade union organisations and local trades councils. Union membership is highly concentrated in the industrial areas of the south and north-east. It was fortunate, therefore, that in the remaining rural areas the organisation of Plaid Cymru was at its strongest.

Jack Brookes claimed that WGBO was to be '. . . all-party and non-party',[5] but this policy lapsed occasionally. For the climactic rally in Sophia Gardens, Cardiff, Tony Benn would only appear on an all-Labour platform, yet Michael Foot had appeared with nationalists at several other meetings.

Labour's big guns, supported by trade union power in the valleys and Plaid Cymru in the countryside, could still not stem the European tide. Not a single county, not even industrial mid-Glamorgan, voted 'No'. A WGBO spokesman, reviewing the campaign later, concluded rather bitterly that the coverage by the media had been heavily pro-European; the amount of money spent by Wales in Europe had probably been ten times their own budget; and only about seven of the Welsh Labour MPs had played an active part in the campaign.

On the positive side, the gains of the campaign were rather more diffuse and long-term. The newly formed Wales TUC had been able to use the campaign as a means of establishing itself, and the experience of having to mount a national campaign may well prove to be useful (if, for example, there were a referendum on the devolution issue, on which the WTUC favours a legislative assembly for Wales). Working links between the WTUC and Plaid Cymru were established and there is some co-operation on research. In the shifting currents of Welsh politics the implications of that relationship may have some consequences for the Labour Party. It might be argued further that the referendum campaign provided the left with a standard around which to rally. There were some who welcomed the chance for a section of the Labour Party to show its mettle and might not have been too disappointed had the rifts in the party proved to have been permanent.

(iii) *Wales Labour and Trade Union Committee for Europe*. This group worked in close association with Wales in Europe, and strictly was not an umbrella group, since its membership was exclusively Labour. It was, however, an *ad hoc* group, formed specifically for the referendum campaign. Hence it resembles the umbrella groups in political terms. This group was able to offer facilities to those Labour supporters who felt unable to join with other parties and were denied facilities by their own party machine. Labour pro-Europeans were thus able to avoid the accusation that they were joining a coalition with their political enemies. In particular, pro-European government Ministers were able to appear on platforms without compromising themselves.

The chairman of the Wales Labour and Trade Union Committee for Europe was Cledwyn Hughes, MP, its secretary Graham Saunders of APEX. Other important unions represented included the NUR, G&MWU, ISTC and NUPE. Tal Lloyd of the AUEW was the vice-chairman of the committee – in clear defiance of his union's position. Also on the committee were two local AUEW shop stewards recently at odds with their president, Hugh Scanlon, over the issue of postal ballots within the union. These positions illustrate the left/right, or moderate/militant, dimension which underlay the campaign. A particular stance on the Europe issue reflected, or was seen to reflect, a stance in the tangled and often bitter politics of the Labour movement in the summer of 1975.

2. The parties

The major United Kingdom parties did not alter their general campaign strategy very much for the Welsh contest. The Labour Party in Wales endeavoured to remain somewhat above the fray; individual constituency parties were able to decide whether or not to campaign. Officially, however, the party organisation could only join in on the 'anti' side. This was obviously a period of some embarrassment to the party; in consequence its Cardiff headquarters made very little direct impact upon the campaign. The Conservative Party in Wales and the Welsh Liberal Party seemed to be content to operate almost exclusively under the cover of 'Wales in Europe'. In the constituencies, some party offices were active in the campaign but chiefly as the local centres of 'Wales in Europe'. Hence the most interesting aspect of the referendum in Wales was the part played by Plaid Cymru.

In many ways the referendum campaign was a great opportunity for Plaid Cymru. Here were the other parties, Plaid Cymru's usual political opponents, making points that had been part of the rhetoric of the nationalist case for years. The key referendum issues of sovereignty, centralisation, the domination of bureaucracy have

provided basic themes in Plaid Cymru's political appeal. It was
hardly surprising, therefore, that the nationalists, in advocating a
negative response to the referendum question, took the opportunity
to remind the electorate of this paradox and of their longer-term
goals. ' "The rallying call of Labour Ministers . . . is to be self-
government and Home Rule" – says Tony Benn . . . (from the EEC
of course).'[6] 'The occasion of the referendum marks a failure of the
two-party centralist system of government.'[7]

Plaid Cymru's attitude to the referendum campaign was
determined by previous conference decisions. The issue of Europe
had long been contentious within the party. Since the application for
membership made by the Heath administration, party conferences
had consistently opposed Britain's joining the EEC whilst both
Britain and the Community retain their present constitutional form.
But it is opposition to these institutional forms and not to the
European ideal that is the basis of the Plaid Cymru view. The
nationalist sees Wales as an independent element in a common
European cultural heritage, with strong links to the other small
nations of Europe, especially those of Celtic origin. This ideal has
always been close to the heart of the party.

But, for Plaid Cymru, ideals were backed by an impressive volume
of referendum study papers.[8] The Plaid Cymru Research Group
examined all aspects of the EEC issue and drew up its conclusions.
These were not without a certain ambiguity. It was not always clear
whether the group was arguing a case related to Wales in the United
Kingdom or an independent Wales, or to conditions which might
hasten the bringing about of an independent Wales. In the research
paper on the Steel Industry Keith Bush concludes:

Having regard . . . to the very slight degree to which a small country can
influence Community policies even as a full member, it seems plain that a
form of external association with a wide measure of free trade with the
European Communities is the best prospect for the Welsh Steel industry
and for Wales.[9]

It is not clear whether the author is here referring to the British Steel
Corporation as presently constituted, the Welsh section of the
BSC [which is by no means autonomous], or to a Welsh steel
industry that might come to exist after independence. Only the first
of these alternatives really lay within the bounds of the referendum
debate as seen and presented by the majority of the participants.
Such ambiguities were inherent in Plaid Cymru's position in a

campaign which raised the fundamental issue of British national sovereignty without regard for changes within Britain itself.

For much of the day-to-day campaign Plaid Cymru co-operated fully with the WGBO organisation. Joint meetings and platforms were sponsored at which the Plaid Cymru representatives somewhat subdued their demands for self-government and concentrated upon the immediate campaign issues. But the party's vigorous nationalism could not be wholly confined within these limits. In fact Plaid Cymru fought two almost separate campaigns. One, with WGBO, followed an agenda largely determined by the WTUC. At the same time, especially in the rural and highly Welsh-speaking areas, Plaid Cymru's party organisation and local branches conducted their own campaign and speaking programmes. This second campaign was fought on an agenda framed in their own terms. Dafydd Elis Thomas was especially active in the constituencies, attending up to four meetings each evening, in general election style. Curiously, this vigorous campaign in the homelands led in effect to a defeat for Plaid Cymru. It committed itself as a party to a particular cause, and was voted down.

However, the gains for the Nationalists from the first campaign were substantial even though WGBO lost the referendum. The party stood to benefit from increasing contact with the WTUC, and from divisions within the Labour Party and the trade unions. It also stood to gain from any issue which was likely to unite sections of the Welsh electorate and which would reflect a Welsh 'national' context. Normally most of the basic tenets of the nationalist ideology divide rather than unite Wales and leave nationalists relatively isolated. The referendum campaign, although inherently divisive, offered an opportunity for a large section of the politically active community in Wales to unite around one single issue, which – with luck and skill – could be associated with the nationalist case. It was the best opportunity the nationalists had ever had to move from the margins to the mainstream of politics.

The result of the referendum clearly showed that in Plaid Cymru's strongest electoral territory, the north and the west, their campaign was less successful. By contrast the decision to align with the WTUC, at the possible expense of the rural areas, appears to have been a risk worth taking. The political future of Plaid Cymru and the prospect of an independent Wales hinge upon the closer identification of the population with recognisably Welsh issues, and electoral success in industrial South Wales. There is already some evidence that the strategy of alliance may pay dividends. The WTUC has become a fairly regular visitor to Downing Street for discussions on 'Welsh' unemployment, and 'Welsh' industrial development. National United Kingdom issues are being redefined into Welsh issues. The logical extension of this process is that the decision-making machinery must also be redesigned in a Welsh dimension. The prospect of a referendum on devolution, with the WTUC firmly committed to a legislative assembly for Wales, would be for Plaid Cymru a highly successful culmination to this strategy of alliance.

The leadership of Plaid Cymru was not wholly united in its opposition to the Common Market. There is a long established European tradition within the party, which rejects insularity along with the historical oppressor, England. The founder and father figure of this section of the party, Saunders Lewis, made a rare contribution to contemporary party affairs in a letter advocating abstention on the referendum question.[10] A more central figure, Dafydd Wigley, the member for Caernarfon, accepted the party's decision to oppose membership of the EEC and played no further part in the campaign. However, his absence was conspicuous, a positive act, and must have had some effect on the party's supporters in Gwynedd who voted so overwhelmingly to remain in Europe.

Of all parties in the campaign, Plaid Cymru had little to lose, and much to gain, no matter what the eventual decision of the referendum. The party seized its opportunities vigorously, and on balance emerged with its experience and credibility enhanced. Immediately after the result was announced the party issued a (long-prepared) statement: 'From the very beginning, we have recognised that EEC membership, whilst bad for Wales, is good for Plaid Cymru.'[11] The problem of fringe parties is how to be taken seriously. The campaign enabled Plaid Cymru to be active for once on the platforms of influence. These are still, of course, a distance away from the corridors of power.

3.   The Welsh Constituency MPs

The operations of the 'umbrella' organisation, and the non-involvement of the official party machines in the referendum campaign, undermined somewhat the normal position of the Members of Parliament. The Members were obviously under some obligation to adopt a specific position on Europe, in a way which does not arise for single issues in a complete party manifesto. In

Wales it is particularly difficult for Members of Parliament to avoid public identification, since the relative accessibility of the media makes conspicuous even a deliberately low profile.

The Conservative and Liberal Members all endorsed the case for remaining in Europe. Several of their number, however, might be called 'reluctant Marketeers'. Geraint Howells (Cardigan) described himself in these terms and his only Welsh Liberal colleague in the House, Emlyn Hooson (Montgomery), had opposed membership in 1971. This reluctance distinguishes the Welsh Liberal Party, strongest in the rural and agricultural areas, from its English counterpart, with its power base in the south-east of England and its ambitions in the suburbs. Other Westminster Liberals have always been in the van of the demand for Britain to join Europe. There was some reticence, if not reluctance, among the Welsh Conservatives too. For example, Geraint Morgan (Denbigh) had opposed membership in 1971 and abstained in the immediate pre-referendum division. He did, however, allow his name to be used on some local pro-Europe literature.

The twenty-three Welsh Labour Members offer a classic illustration of how the party was divided and at odds with itself over the issue of the Common Market. In the 1971 division, seeking approval for Mr Heath's terms of entry, committed Marketeers such as Tom Ellis (Wrexham), Ifor Davies (Gower) and Leo Abse (Pontypool) defied the whips and supported the government. Cledwyn Hughes (Anglesey) also refused to vote with his party on that occasion. The situation was strangely reversed in the 1975 division, when the fervent anti-Marketeers rejected Harold Wilson's renegotiated terms. Neil Kinnock (Bedwellty), Fred Evans (Caerphilly), Roy Hughes (Newport) and Caerwyn Roderick (Brecon and Radnor) all voted against the Cabinet's recommendation. The most distinguished 'rebel' was Michael Foot (Ebbw Vale), who played a major role in the United Kingdom campaign, 'Get Britain Out'. The other Labour 'rebels' were all junior Ministers in the Wilson administration and they took little part in the campaign, either in Wales or beyond. These were Denzil Davies (Llanelli), a Treasury Minister; Brynmor John (Pontypridd), Minister for the Royal Air Force, and Alec Jones (Rhondda), a Welsh Office Minister.

The remaining eleven Labour Members, just under half, followed the party line, rejecting the earlier Heath terms, and accepting Wilson's renegotiation. This split in the Labour Party over the EEC was to be followed by further disagreements over the government's proposals for devolution. On this issue dissent within the party hardened after the publication of the Scotland and Wales Bill. Ioan Evans (Aberdare) resigned as PPS to the Welsh Secretary of State in order to campaign actively against the Bill. The dissidents gained a significant victory in forcing the government to concede the holding of a referendum on the issue – a referendum they had hoped to win. The anti-devolutionists in the Welsh Labour Party include both pro- and anti-Europeans. Thus four of the most persistent and vigorous campaigners against devolution, Neil Kinnock, Fred Evans, Leo Abse and Donald Anderson were divided over Euope, the last two being as enthusiastic for integration as they are hostile to devolution.

Individual positions are not all sharp and consistent, and the ambiguities of official and government positions complicate the pattern. In effect, individuals could be placed in a matrix indicating their position for or against European integration and Welsh devolution.

Devolution	*Pro*	*Anti*
Integration		
Pro	1	2
Anti	3	4

These cells might be labelled: (1) Welsh Europeans; (2) British Europeans; (3) Welsh nationalists; and (4) British nationalists. The pattern is neat but it is in the nature of the issues that it is difficult to categorise individuals and groups quite so precisely. In the terms of this matrix, Plaid Cymru moved from Welsh nationalist towards Welsh European. The Liberals were Welsh Europeans, with some misgivings about the European aspect. Many Conservatives were British Europeans, but some were plainly British nationalists – or English Unionists. The Labour Party is more difficult to fit into the matrix, for it certainly included both British and Welsh nationalists as well as both kinds of European.

THE REFERENDUM RESULTS

A comparative illustration of how the voting in Wales differed from that elsewhere in the United Kingdom can be seen in the accompanying table. Electoral behaviour in Wales is complex, and many constituency contests are of a multi-party nature.[12] To add to the complexity, the four parties, and individual Members of Parliament, have shifted their position on the Common Market issue, sometimes more than once. Even so, the normal relationships between socio-economic environment and voting appear to be sustained, but in a slightly modified form. It appears that the key issues, both political (sovereignty) and economic (prosperity), were perceived in rather differing ways by the parties and by the voters. This is most clearly illustrated by the campaign of Plaid Cymru. The rural and agricultural seats held by the party (Carmarthen, Merioneth and Caernarfon), all areas with large Welsh-speaking populations, rejected the advice of the nationalists and voted conclusively to remain in Europe.

	The referendum result in Wales				
Electorate	*'Yes' vote*	*%*	*'No' vote*	*%*
Wales	869,135	64·8	472,071	35·2
England	14,918,009	68·76	812,052	31·3
Scotland	1,332,186	58·4	948,039	41·6
N. Ireland	259,251	52·1	237,911	47·9
UK	17,378,581	67·28	470,073	32·8

Partly, of course, this may be explained by inertia. But there are two factors in the politics of rural Wales which pressed towards a Yes vote. First, the agricultural community in Wales was generally pro-European; the NFU categorically endorsed continued membership, whilst the Farmers' Union of Wales, without issuing an endorsement one way or the other, appeared to be generally in favour and left the decision to individual members. Of possibly equal significance was the fact that the 'No' campaign was organised almost wholly through the trade union movement, and the counties of Dyfed, Powys and Gwynedd are particularly thin areas for the unions.

In the industrial areas the most surprising result was in mid-Glamorgan. In an area with still some of the highest Labour majorities in Britain, and a very high concentration of unionised labour, a majority 'No' vote might have been expected. Mid-Glamorgan can still be typified as a mining community, although the actual percentage of labour employed in the mines is now quite small. The painful processes of industrial reconstruction and diversification have been most deeply felt in this area. In this situation it seems likely that the pro-Marketeers' emphasis upon the benefits of the Community's Regional Development Policy, and the grants from the Coal and Steel Community, may have had some persuasive effect.

However, there is a danger that the causal relationship between voting behaviour and the voter's assessment of his own social and economic position can be overstated. The referendum vote was plainly not random political behaviour; but neither was it wholly and intimately set within the pattern of regular party loyalties. Some part of the voter's response to the referendum seems, reasonably enough, to have been specific to the issue and the campaign – thus conforming to the pure theory of the referendum, as the submission of a single issue to the arbitrament of the popular wisdom. Both sides in the campaign produced a wealth of material arguing that their particular analysis of the situation for steel or agriculture or employment was the correct one. It may well be that many voters responded to the argument in the manner of the model intelligent voter, seeking after truth; or, more likely, ducked this confusing mass of propaganda, and made the decision on more general grounds, a feel for the issue, going along with what seemed the tide of opinion, following the lead of the major figures in the government, believing that Britain was in the Common Market anyway and withdrawing would be too much trouble. Only detailed survey research could elaborate upon the voters' motivations.

REGIONAL REPRESENTATION AT WESTMINSTER AND BRUSSELS

Once the question of Community membership had been settled conclusively, the focus of attention shifted to the role Wales might play within Europe. This was seen in three perspectives: first, from within Wales, a view most salient to the nationalists; second, the view of Wales from Europe, best seen through the Commission and its representative in Cardiff; third, the view of the developing relationship between Wales and Europe perceived by the UK government and the Welsh Office.

Plaid Cymru carefully avoided the anticlimax associated with being on the losing side of a campaign by moving directly into the attack over the representation of Wales in Europe. Its initiative was

once again double-edged, urging immediate representation for
Wales in Brussels while arguing that the case for self-government
was now even stronger than before the referendum.

> The Referendum has transformed the drive for self-government for Wales in
> two ways. On the one hand, membership of the Common Market makes full
> national status an urgent necessity to get fair representation: on the other it
> demolishes the major reason hitherto advanced against it – economic
> separatism.
>   The Referendum means that plans for devolution to a Welsh Assembly
> have already become outmoded, and that the need for full National Status is
> clearer than ever. . . . Now that Wales is governed by Brussels as well as by
> London, the importance of London will diminish in the minds of the people
> of Wales.[13]

As an interim measure the party urged the establishment of a Welsh
Office Bureau in Brussels, the allocation of eight out of the United
Kingdom's thirty-six European Assembly seats to Wales on an all-
party basis, and the allocation of five of the United Kingdom's
twenty-four seats on the EEC's Social and Economic Committee to
Wales.

In a further initiative Plaid Cymru co-operated with several other
European nationalist movements to found 'The Bureau of
Unrepresented Nations'. The bureau's function is to act as a lobby
for the various nationalist groups in Brussels, and to encourage co-
operation between its members, the Bretons, the Basques, the
Alsatians and the Welsh. However, the Scottish National Party has
not joined the Bureau of Unrepresented Nations. Instead the SNP is
represented in the United Kingdom delegation to the European
Parliament by Mrs Winifred Ewing, who keeps in touch with Plaid
Cymru MPs. It is a sign of the SNP's self-confidence that it avoids
association with these fringe elements in European politics,
preferring to act as one of the major United Kingdom parties. By
contrast, Plaid Cymru is drawn towards other nationalist groups,
particularly those of Celtic origin, by its history and strong cultural
roots. Such associations make the party appear somewhat
peripheral in the total context of West European politics.

Plaid Cymru's double-edged political thrust leads to ambiguity
over certain objectives. The party wants representation within the
institutions of Europe, but does not want those institutions to
acquire any further powers. To strengthen these bodies would be
contrary to the party's policy of resistance to centralisation. Yet,
paradoxically, it is from within the Community, particularly from

the Commission, that there is support and recognition for smaller units. While the member 'nation' states hold back from further union, Plaid Cymru hesitates: which alternative constitutes the greater evil – a dependent Wales within the United Kingdom, or an independent Wales in a highly centralised Europe? Or is a decentralised Europe a possibility? The historical and political probabilities are uncertain but not discouraging.

During the referendum campaign the European Commission appeared to emphasise the opportunities for the political development of Wales within Europe. In an interview given whilst on a visit to Wales during the campaign, George Thompson, the Commissioner for Regional Policy, stated, 'It will be much easier to alter the United Kingdom constitution in favour of decentralisation in the context of the EEC than in the framework of Britain alone.'[14] A campaign document issued by the Commission, *Wales in Europe*, went further:

With regional assemblies in Wales and Scotland, Britain would be moving towards a European pattern of democracy. In the context of the European Parliament, Wales and the other countries and regions of the United Kingdom would have a common interest with the many regions of Europe and would, with them, be part of a large and powerful regional lobby, and a significant counterweight to any centralist tendencies.

In all these developments there is nothing that poses a threat to the Welsh language and culture. On the contrary, in so far as regionalism in Europe is strengthened, concern for the cultural problems of Wales will also be increased. The recognition of Wales as a nation is likely to be greater.[15]

These statements reflect the tendency within the Commission to overemphasise the political benefits of European membership. On a practical level, the Commission has established an office in Cardiff, headed by Gwyn Morgan, the former Transport House official and *chef du cabinet* to George Thompson. The role of the Cardiff office would appear to be to encourage enquiries and applications for European assistance, advise upon the availability of grants, and so on. In practice, however, the functions of the office are wider in scope and more positive. Likely applicants for schemes are sought out, advised and encouraged. Public relations gives way to lobbying when prospective applicants are referred to the Welsh Office, which must handle all formal applications, and the Cardiff Office's view is made known to the Welsh Office. When the bids eventually reach the relevant department in Brussels, Cardiff may be involved again in advising upon the allocation of the monies available.

The Commission's local representative would seem, therefore, to be engaged in a 'brokerage' and propagating role, encouraging and lubricating the flow of European funds to Wales. Wales has done comparatively well recently in the receipt of grants and aid. These informal links are thus quite productive, and the Commission seems to favour more direct relations. However, the Commission's view implies in the long run that the states or regions, local authorities, and eventually individuals, should develop a greater commitment to Europe and to the European ideals of which the Commission is the greatest exponent.

In official terms, of course, there is no formal relationship between Wales and Europe. The Welsh Office has a European Division to advise individuals and organisations within Wales, and also to assist other divisions on the European aspects of their work. All formal contact with Brussels, however, is through the relevant department in Whitehall. In practice, informal links have been established, and the Welsh Office has 'observer' status on many of the official delegations and committees. The Welsh Office is represented on the official committees of the United Kingdom delegation which meet before ministerial meetings. Some of these are of special relevance to Wales, for example the Regional Fund Management Committee and the Regional Policy Committee. In these relationships the Welsh Office sees its strength in its proximity to, and involvement with, Welsh affairs. It represents a clearly identifiable interest. In this respect Wales has a considerable advantage over other regions in England. But London remains the final arbiter in all cases.

The establishment of an elected Welsh Assembly is likely to enhance Welsh relations with Europe. Under the proposed scheme of devolution, none of the powers of the Welsh Assembly includes an extensive European dimension. But in important areas of policy, agriculture, industry, coal and steel, the Assembly might well develop into a powerful lobby both in Whitehall and in Brussels. Its elective base, skilfully exploited, could launch it into the politics of institutional pressures, at a time when the boundaries of formal sovereignty are blurred.

Wales seems to have benefited from the slight ambiguities of its present political status. The Commission, the Welsh Office and Plaid Cymru are aware of this. However, the current situation is insecure and transitional. Fundamental political change can take place only within the parameters of the new European dimension to British politics.

DEVOLUTION

The Labour government's proposals for devolution in Wales fall far short of independence.[16] The Welsh Assembly will have about seventy members, elected for a term of four years by the simple plurality system. The present parliamentary constituencies will be later divided for this purpose. The Assembly will have executive but not legislative powers in the fields of local government, health and social services, education, housing, physical planning and transport policy. Financially the Assembly will be dependent on a block grant. In Wales, unlike Scotland, there will not be a separate executive. Instead an Executive Committee composed mainly of committee 'business leaders' will co-ordinate, and allocate funds for, the work of specialist committees. (The actual working of this system could be transformed by the use of a disciplined party majority.) Ultimate sovereignty rests at Westminister, and – which could be more significant in practice – the Welsh Office and its Secretary of State would remain.

These proposals do not go nearly far enough for nationalists ('separatists') and others who would wish for the transfer of legislative authority, greater fiscal powers and powers over major economic affairs. For others, the proposals are already excessive, a needless addition to a system which, through the Welsh Office and local governments, distributes what little power is available in a democratic and effective way. Many on both sides of this division see the proposals as an unstable half-way house, likely to give rise to conflicts between Westminster and Cardiff at both political and official levels, and again with local governments. The four parties each have differing positions, and the Labour Party, both nationally and in Wales, contains within it widely divergent views.

Practical proposals for devolution have now to be considered at a time when older patterns of government have been mildly disturbed by the referendum and final accession to the EEC, and the implied acceptance of the passing of national economic sovereignty. In deciding whether the constutitonal *status quo* of the United Kingdom is 'not an option' the consideration of shifts of power already in train is quite as significant as the discovery of 'what the people of Wales think'. This is not to say that European integration leads inexorably to British devolution; only that the European dimension, and the context in which it has been developed, have profound implications for the future constitutional status of Wales.

NOTES

1 For a short account of recent political history in Wales see K. O. Morgan, 'Welsh politics', in R. Brinley Jones (ed.), *Anatomy of Wales*, Peterston-super-Ely, 1972.
2 See A. Butt Philip, *The Welsh Question*, Cardiff, 1975, for an historical account of the emergence of 'Wales' and Welsh issues in British politics.
3 On the growth of government in Wales see articles by P. J. Randall and E. Rowlands, *Public Administration*, 50, 1972.
4 For some account of the position and politics of the language see D. Ellis Evans, in R. Brinley Jones (ed.), *op. cit.*; P. J. Madgwick *et al.*, *The Politics of Rural Wales*, London, 1973; M. Stephens (ed.), *The Welsh Language Today*, Llandysul, 1973; C. Betts, *Culture in Crisis*, Upton (Wirral), 1976.
5 *Western Mail*, 15 February 1975.
6 *Welsh Nation*, 23 May 1975. (*Welsh Nation* is the English-language weekly of Plaid Cymru.)
7 *Ibid.*, 16 May 1975.
8 *Wales and the Common Market*, Plaid Cymru Research Group, 1975.
9 K. Bush, 'The Welsh steel industry and the EEC', in *Wales and the Common Market*, ch. 5, p. 6.
10 Letter to the *Western Mail*, quoted in *Welsh Nation*, 16 May 1975.
11 Plaid Cymru news release, 9 June 1975.
12 P. J. Madgwick and D. Balsom, 'Changes in party competition in elections: the Welsh case and the British context', *Parl. Affairs*, 28, winter 1974–75.
13 Plaid Cymru news release, 9 June 1975.
14 *Western Mail*, 21 May 1975.
15 *Wales in Europe* pamphlet issued by the Commission of the European Communities.
16 These proposals are contained in the *Scotland and Wales Bill*, House of Commons, November 1976; the Wales Act, November 1977.

5 Problems of government and administration

British government has been buffeted by successive changes in structure and functions since the early '60s. Ministries have been created, expanded, amalgamated, subdivided, even abolished. Government committees and Royal Commissions have pondered and reported: some of their proposals have been implemented. The Fulton Committee (1968) led to an apparently radical restructuring of the civil service, including the creation of a new Civil Service Department. The Maud Commission (1969) reconsidered the whole pattern of local government in England, while parallel enquiries took place in Scotland and Wales. The reforms which emerged introduced a two-tier system of new local authorities throughout mainland Britain which did not take into account dissenting opinions arguing the relevance of the regional dimension.[1] This was to be followed by the Layfield Committee (1975) on the financing of local government, which also touched on the financial relationship between local and central government. The late '60s saw a spate of proposals on parliamentary reform, including experiments with select committees and an abortive attempt to reform the House of Lords.

Responding to an upsurge of nationalist votes in Scottish and Welsh by-elections, the then Labour government established in 1969 a Royal Commission on the Constitution 'to examine the present functions of the central legislature and government in relation to the several countries, nations and regions of the United Kingdom . . .'.[2] Its 1973 report reflected a lack of consensus among its members on the form and scope of any devolved level of government. The new Conservative government took office in 1970 pledged to overhaul the managerial efficiency of central government, and rapidly introduced new 'super-Ministries' and a Central Policy Review Staff (CPRS) in the Cabinet Office. Meanwhile in the field of foreign policy the Plowden Report (1964) had led to an amalgamation of services and Ministries into the Foreign and Commonwealth office, and the

Duncan Report (1969) had recommended further reforms. In 1976 the CPRS was conducting another major review of the overall management of Britain's external relations.

The cumulative effect was to create a climate of continual administrative reorganisation. No clear conception of a wider strategy of constitutional change has at any point been evident. Each measure was introduced piecemeal, largely without reference to its implications for the working of government as a whole. Whether or not a period of consolidation is now desirable to enable Ministers and officials to catch up with the consequences of these various reforms, the maintenance of the *status quo* is not an option. Entry into the European Communities, eventually achieved in 1973, posed a number of new problems and imposed new burdens and constraints. Demands for devolution have not subsided, contrary to the hopes of both Labour and Conservative governments. Although so far successive governments have kept the two issues in separate compartments, both raise parallel questions about the underlying assumptions of the British constitution and the adaptive capacities of central government.

The relationship between the two issues is thus more than one of coincidence in timing. Although Community membership and devolution each present different demands for adaptation by central government and each involve different principal actors, both question the role of central government and its appropriateness as the determining level of policy-making. Accession to the European Communities reflected an eventual and almost grudging admission on the part of Ministers and officials that certain key policy problems were no longer manageable at the national level. The clamour for devolution derives from the claim for smaller units of government to respond to and express national and regional identities and aspirations. Both imply an incapacity on the part of a single centralised source of authority either to handle existing functions of government or to embrace new tasks. This is compounded by the problem of overload at the centre of British government in a period of steady increases in the functions of government and the size of the public sector. The emergence of Community membership and the slide towards devolution as new focuses of interest have coincided with continuing pressures on government in other intractable areas of policy, notably the recurrent problems of managing the economy and the running sore of Northern Ireland. Neither the Cabinet nor the central policy-making structure that underpins it is well equipped to grapple with more than a handful of critical issues at any given moment, particularly when they include calls for major political change. Historically the success of the British system has depended on what its advocates term consensus formation or what its critics would dub fudging the options. The mechanisms for resolving conflict in Whitehall are ill suited to achieving viable compromises in a situation of slender parliamentary majorities and deep internal divisions within the governing party over both priorities and objectives.

GOVERNMENTAL ATTITUDES TO CONSTITUTIONAL CHANGE

Both Community membership and devolution have been the subject of controversy within government, and this factor has militated against the adoption of coherent policies. On the contrary, in both areas the defensive response has been to opt for marginal change and to attempt to insulate both from their wider constitutional context. Policy has been reactive rather than positive, designed to contain the problems narrowly rather than to risk a more explicit re-examination of their implications. It has been recognised that both issues threaten constitutional conventions in terms of the unitary nature of the state, the doctrine of parliamentary sovereignty and the legal relationships among different tiers of government. Yet the overwhelming view within government has been to play down the ramifications of these threats. In the memorandum of dissent published in volume II of the Royal Commission on the Constitution Lord Crowther-Hunt argued for a more radical approach. He suggested that Community membership would 'remove important areas of decision still further away from the British people', 'weaken the doctrine of ministerial responsibility . . .' and 'increase even more the power of officials' (para. 106). He further indicated that it would lead to 'a major increase in the load on the central machinery of government'. In his view this was relevant to devolution in two important ways: first, it strengthened the case for devolution to lighten the load on Whitehall; second, it set 'constraints on the form and extent of devolution' (para. 112). Basically, the Crowther-Hunt case was for considering constitutional change as part of a 'seamless web', an approach which was at odds with the practice of government. Where linkages have been perceived among tiers of government they have on the whole been viewed as negative constraints on the freedom of manoeuvre still available. This has had particularly serious consequences for the devolution debate. At one end of the scale local government reorganisation has apparently already pre-empted the options for the management of certain public services, while at the other end Community membership seemed to require that certain areas of policy could not be devolved down from central government.

This defensiveness marks not simply an ostrich-like attitude to the constitutional issues but also a deeply rooted resistance to change away from the traditions of a unified and centralised system of government. At its crudest level this can be explained in terms of a predictable inclination to preserve existing powers and responsibilities at the centre and to avoid any dilution of policy-making resources. This antipathy towards the unknown has, however, been elevated to the status of doctrine that runs through the official publications and statements of government. The arcane mandarin prose of successive White Papers on both Community membership and devolution has avoided questions of principle and concentrated instead on describing the mechanical details of the projected changes in policies and structures. During the run-up to British accession to the European Communities Ministers and officials repeatedly asserted that adjustment in Whitehall would be a straightforward matter of adapting existing procedures to take on board the Community dimension. It was only a small minority of those involved in Whitehall who stated the case for a more radical recasting of policy processes.[3] Similarly the management of European policy since 1973 has been characterised by its emphasis on short-term policy interests and its avoidance of the more long-term issues implied in extending the powers and functions of the Community institutions. The Whitehall response to Europe has been to define relations between London and Brussels so as to minimise the impact on British government and to protect the status and influence of those Ministries and agencies most directly affected. Though it is perhaps rash to oversimplify in delineating the overall posture, Whitehall has taken Europe on board fairly confidently in so far as it has been generally assumed that the management of Community policy could be absorbed without too great a disturbance to central government.

Whitehall has been less sure-footed in grappling with the preparations for devolution. The attitude of Ministers and officials has been not merely ambivalent but on occasion hysterical. Part of the explanation for the difference is that, whereas accession to the Communities derived from changed perceptions within government, in the case of devolution the pressures have been pushing in on Whitehall from the outside. It is also that the implications of devolution are perceived as more obviously far-reaching and threatening in that it would overtly fragment both public powers and policy resources. The British response thus has much in common with French bureaucratic reactions to calls for greater regional autonomy, both based on traditions of highly centralised systems of government. Dispersal of powers has tended to be viewed as the dangerous edge of the slippery slope towards a disunited kingdom and as detrimental to the efficient and effective conduct of government. Thus the public documents have shied away from confronting the fundamental question of what frame of reference should form the basis of the territorial reallocation of governmental authority. The Scotland and Wales Bill published on 29 November 1976 contained no preamble on constitutional principles. During the early debates in the House of Commons Ministers reiterated that federalism was not an option but presented no alternative framework. This absence of systematic criteria has compounded the problems of identifying an approach which would be either politically or administratively viable.

Part of the explanation for this lack of clarity in response to both Community membership and devolution lies in the difficulty of determining the appropriate level at which different policy issues should be handled. The West German experience of both internal federalism and Community membership, by contrast, has followed a doctrine of *subsidiarité*. Broadly this states that problems should be tackled at the lowest level possible and that the raising and allocation of financial resources should be accommodated into a scheme that clearly differentiates among hierarchical tiers of government. This kind of doctrine is aesthetically pleasing in its apparent tidiness, and is workable in a political context where centralisation is regarded as a vice rather than a virtue. The British situation is, however, far more complex. Civil servants and Ministers are reluctant to admit the deficiencies of centralisation as such; even when they are admitted, there is no consensus as to which level of government is most suitable for any given issues.

A rough and ready acceptance has emerged that some policies have to be managed transnationally – security, international trade, parts of monetary policy; that others should be retained at the national level – economic management, nationalised industries, fiscal policy; and that yet others can more or less safely be dealt with at a more local level – housing, planning, social services. However, this leaves grey areas of policy sectors that overlap some or all of the tiers. Policies on industry, regional development, employment, agriculture and fisheries have all been raised at the Community level. Yet all concern sectors where there have been claims for a substantial influence at the devolved level of government and where there is already a degree of decentralised management in Scotland, Wales, Northern Ireland and to a lesser extent in England. Thus the now fashionable awareness of the predicament of interdependence between the national and international levels is being overlaid by a less clearly thought through interdependence between the national and the proposed devolved levels within the United Kingdom.

Community membership and devolution have both become more visible problems in recent years, since British accession in 1973 and the upsurge in SNP support in the 1974 elections. However, there is a much longer history of gradual adaptation by Whitehall to both issues. What has characterised the response in both instances has been the search for administrative devices to handle awkward political problems. In managing European policy central government has adapted rather than altered existing administrative structures, and attempted to contain the debate on policy options for Community negotiations as far as possible within the executive. The emphasis has been on building up a core of European specialists within the relevant Ministries to ensure that Britain was able to match its new partners in terms of technical knowledge and bargaining skills. This has been a cumulative process of developing experience and expertise since the mid-'60s.

The acceptance of the case for regional differentiation in the management of government policies started much earlier with the late nineteenth-century appointment of a Secretary for Scotland and the creation of an embryonic Scottish Office in London. It was not, however, until 1939 that a substantial Scottish Office emerged with a base in St Andrew's House in Edinburgh. Since the war the scope and size of the Scottish Office and of special Scottish agencies has extended to provide a considerable degree of decentralised administration in Scotland.[4] The Welsh Office is a much more recent development, established only in 1964 with rather more modest terms of reference. Even in England there has been a steady growth of the regional arms of central government offices of the Departments of the Environment, Industry and Trade. Other new agencies were created in the mid-'60s such as the Regional Economic Planning Boards and Councils, with some limited public participation.[5] This extensive deconcentration of administrative organisation was, however, tied to the maintenance of a unitary structure and was not accompanied by changes in public accountability. Westminster and Whitehall remained firmly in command. A similar pattern obtained in the distribution of financial resources within the United Kingdom. Regional economic and industrial development also became fashionable in the mid-'60s, partly for general economic objectives but partly too due to the belief of Ministers and officials in London that pumping extra financial resources would satisfy regional discontents.[6] Officials further argued that to manage this discretely through internal government policies was a more effective method of channelling resources into deprived areas than would have been possible in a more open and explicitly competitive system.

THE ROLE OF THE CENTRE OF GOVERNMENT

Paradoxically at the same time there was a drift towards the centre of British government reinforced by a protectionist reflex to conserve and consolidate the central policy-making resources of Whitehall. In part this was reflected in a series of attempts to reassert the collective role of the Cabinet as the pinnacle of the Whitehall pyramid through which conflict among government departments might be contained. Significantly both the European and the devolution issues have eroded these efforts with rather public divergencies of view among Ministers in government, particular under Labour administrations. The open agreement to disagree between the pro- and anti-Market Ministers in the 1975 referendum was perhaps the most spectacular example, but similar dissent had been a factor in the 1966–67 Cabinet discussions of the Labour government's application for British membership of the Community.[7] In the devolution case considerable divergences of view have emerged on the desirability and the extent of devolution among Cabinet members, only a minority endorsing the proposals with any enthusiasm.[8] Disagreement did not erupt as conspicuously on devolution as was the case over Europe. However, the complications and tensions of devolution have crept into Cabinet decisions on other problems. The most striking example was the public conflict in Cabinet over the plan to bail out Chrysler in December 1975, with the preservation of the Linwood plant in Scotland a key issue.

A parallel development has been an attempt to ensure that the management of awkward issues remains clearly at the centre of government and subject to active Prime Ministerial guidance. While it is perhaps a truism to state that Prime Ministers are likely to keep a close watch on the management of critical problems, two particular devices have been utilised to facilitate this: first, a steady expansion in the Cabinet Office; second, the increasingly frequent appointment of special Ministers working directly to the Prime Minister and Cabinet rather than based in the departments of Whitehall. The expansion of the Cabinet Office over the last decade has been startling, in terms of numbers and in terms of increased functions. The staffing of administrative-grade officials quadrupled between 1964 and 1974, with the appointment in late 1969 of a second Permanent Secretary to take particular responsibility for co-ordinating policy towards the European Communities, and a third Permanent Secretary in 1974 to assist in preparing the devolution legislation.[9] The expansion began in the latter years of the 1964–70 Wilson administration and gathered momentum under the Heath government. It reflects an increase in the number of policy areas that were either so complex or so controversial that reinforced co-ordination at the centre seemed necessary to service the Cabinet as a whole and to provide extra advice to the Prime Minister independent of or additional to that from executive departments.

While it remains one of the myths of Whitehall that the Cabinet Office still consists first and foremost of a secretariat to service Cabinet committees at both ministerial and official level, this masks the underlying trend towards a more active role for the Cabinet Office vis-à-vis the rest of Whitehall.[10] Its co-ordinating function began to shift from the modest role of organising interdepartmental consultations towards the more interventionist role of orchestrating compromises among departments. This extension of scope has been marked by the creation of a series of special units to handle particular areas of policy. Again Europe and devolution were motors of this trend, with the creation of the European Unit in 1966 and of the Constitution Unit in 1974, both by Harold Wilson.[11] Other special units have included the Assessments Staff (1968) to assess the significance of international development, the Social Services Co-ordinating Unit (1968), the Central Policy Review Staff (1970) and the Referendum Unit which had a brief existence in 1975.

The appointment of non-departmental Ministers is an important facet of this accretion of resources at the centre. Basically they have served four different aims: the one-off special task, such as Geoffrey Rippon's appointment to run the negotiations for British entry into the European Communities; the general oversight of policy that straddles different departments – R. Crossman's and A. Crosland's roles in the late '60s, or John Davies's as Minister for Europe from 1972 to 1974; the preparation of new policy initiatives – the appointment of successive Ministers since 1974 to help in shaping the devolution programme (Lord Crowther-Hunt, G. Fowler and J. Smith); and finally the troubleshooter role which has characterised Harold Lever's appointment since 1974 as Chancellor of the Duchy of Lancaster. The constraints that have led to such appointments all reflect a determination on the part of Prime Ministers to allocate responsibilities to Ministers freed of regular executive responsibilities and departmental loyalties, working closely to the Cabinet and serviced directly by the Cabinet Office staff. In managing European policy and devolution there has been the further complication that there was no obvious lead department. Community commitments cut across the boundaries of foreign and domestic policy and involve prior negotiations in Whitehall to agree a concerted British posture for bargaining in Brussels. The prospect of devolution similarly bites into the responsibilities of almost every Ministry. There is therefore an administrative rationale for conserving policy management within the central core of government. However, the decision to locate and maintain responsibility there stems at least as much from an awareness of the political significance and controversiality of the issues.

THE MANAGEMENT OF EUROPEAN POLICY

The management of Community policy in Whitehall has basically been handled by a pattern of Cabinet committees.[12] At ministerial level the regular committee meets at least weekly, and an extra and a more senior ministerial tier has occasionally been introduced to formulate strategy on major issues such as the Labour government's renegotiation of the terms of membership in 1974–75. At the official level there are two important forums: the regular co-ordinating committee for on-going Community business that drafts instructions for the Council of Ministers and the Committee of Permanent

Representatives, and an inner group of Permanent Secretaries from the main departments (FCO, Treasury, MAFF, Trade and Industry and the Cabinet Office) which looks at the major and more long-term issues. The membership of these various committees (apart from the last) includes representatives from all departments in Whitehall affected by Community policies, including the Scottish, Welsh and Northern Ireland Offices, though the departments more peripherally involved may only occasionally send representatives to meetings. Officials from the UK Representation in Brussels also regularly take part in co-ordinating meetings in London. This rather heavy structure is further supplemented by the convening of *ad hoc* groups on particular problems to thrash out British policy in a smaller circle. The European Unit in the Cabinet Office services the committees and has a responsibility for ensuring that departments both prepare briefs in time and carry through agreed decisions. This unit worked directly to Edward Heath and John Davies under the Conservative administration, but since March 1974 has worked to the Foreign Secretary. Part of the servicing and co-ordinating work is in practice undertaken by the two European Integration Departments in the FCO, which historically have played a significant part in formulating Community policy and in monitoring the involvement of home departments in Community discussions. In addition the running of the UK Representation in Brussels and of communication between it and Whitehall is the responsibility of the FCO.

This complex pattern of policy formulation incorporates directly the representation of Scottish, Welsh and Northern Irish interests through their respective Offices. Initially this derived from the general reflex of Whitehall co-ordination to involve every conceivable department in order that Whitehall as a whole should learn to 'think European'. Latterly this has taken on a more symbolic importance in the endeavours of central government to demonstrate an awareness of the different geographical dimensions of the UK's European policy. In some areas of policy, such as fisheries, hill farming and regional development, the considerable expertise of the Scottish Office has meant that its involvement has been influential rather than token. By contrast the varying interests of different English regions are only fed into the policy process to the extent that they are embraced by particular functional departments. One of the ironies of the situation is that officials from the Scottish and Welsh Offices occasionally argue that their closeness to the grass roots enables them to feed into Cabinet discussions an appraisal of public opinion that might otherwise be neglected, even on occasion to the extent of defending local English interests affected by Community developments. The involvement of the Scottish, Welsh and Northern Ireland Offices in European policy goes back to the mid-'60s and has continued on a regular basis since accession. The UK Representation in Brussels has recruited officials from these offices, though strictly speaking on the basis of specific skills rather than a representational role. Similarly the British contingent of staff in the Commission includes personnel from different areas of the UK.

As the clamours for devolution have grown stronger there has been a more active attempt on the part of central government to demonstrate its awareness of Scottish, Welsh and Northern Irish interests. This began to be evident in the first year of British membership and gathered momentum in the run-up to the 1975 referendum, when it looked as if Northern Ireland, Scotland and Wales would vote against continued membership. At a superficial level there have been a continuing public relations exercise of including Scottish, Welsh and Northern Irish Ministers on occasion in the British negotiating team in the Council of Ministers, and well publicised information visits to Brussels. Commissioners and their officials have visited Scotland and Wales in particular and the Commission has now opened information offices in Edinburgh and Cardiff. Moreover it was a fortuitous coincidence that George Thomson, one of the first British Commissioners, was Scots and that his *chef de cabinet*, Gwyn Morgan, was Welsh.

THE INFLUENCE OF DEVOLUTION ON EUROPEAN POLICY

More important, however, the devolution pressures have had a significant influence on the priorities attached by the British government to particular aspects of Community policies. This has been a striking feature of British positions on the allocation of Community funds, regional development, hill farming, fisheries and energy. The consequences have been twofold. First, the British government has endeavoured to use the Community arena as a resource in domestic politics by demonstrating that Community policies and Community money have catered adequately for demands from Scotland, Wales and Northern Ireland. Second, an awareness of Scottish sensitivities in particular has hardened the resistance of British negotiators to accepting certain Community proposals, notably on energy policy and on inshore fisheries. Devolution has thus added considerable complexity and significant constraints to the management of Britain's European policy in terms of bargaining in Brussels and in terms of domestic expectations.

The British interest in the creation by the European Communities of a Regional Development Fund (RDF) illustrates particularly vividly the interaction of devolution and Community politics. From 1972 onwards the then Conservative government attached top priority to winning acceptance by Britain's partners of the case for channelling Community funds into the deprived regions of the UK. Edward Heath insisted on a pledge being included in the declaration at the 1972 Paris summit, and the British fought hard for George Thomson to be given the regional policy portfolio in the new Commission in 1973. Several factors conspired to endow the RDF with such importance: the concern of the British government to expand the Community budget to transfer resources to the UK to compensate for the anticipated high British contribution to the CAP; the perceived need to provide tangible benefits to the UK to offset the growing public disenchantment with British membership; and a preoccupation with offering particular incentives to Scotland and Wales to prove that they would gain from accession. These factors combined to make the government argue very hard for the RDF, on which agreement was eventually reached in principle in December 1974 and in detail in March 1975, after some acrimonious exchanges between Britain and Germany.

However, the British approach was Janus-like in that while it advocated the RDF enthusiastically it resisted Community interference in the way the British share was allocated inside the UK. This caution on the procedures for implementation derived from two concerns; first, pressures from the Treasury to view the RDF primarily, if not solely, as a budgetary mechanism across the exchanges rather than as a source of 'additional' public expenditure; second, a Whitehall-wide determination to keep firm control on the decisions as to which regions should benefit and over what sort of claims would be put forward. The consequence was a widespread misunderstanding within the UK on the nature of the RDF and the mechanism for its distribution. In practice the Department of Industry was directly responsible for making claims against the RDF under the watchful eye of the Treasury, though both the

Scottish and Welsh Offices carried out the detailed work of preparing submissions for Scotland and Wales.

There were further complications at the Community level. At the time of the establishment of the RDF two committees were set up in Brussels: the Fund Committee, to approve the various national claims, and the Regional Policy Committee, to look at the more long-term problems of co-ordinating national policies. The UK was in principle given two places on each committee, like other member governments, but in practice as many as six British officials regularly attend meetings to represent the full range of Whitehall's functional departments and geographical offices. This bending over backwards to satisfy Scots, Welsh and Northern Irish needs has been striking in terms of procedures and in terms of the actual allocation of RDF monies. A similar reflex was evident during the 1975 referendum campaign, when mammoth efforts were made in Scotland and Wales in particular to demonstrate how much money they had received from the RDF and other Community funds.[13]

Not surprisingly, several English regions have complained vocally that their interests have been prejudiced as a result. The argument has been put forward repeatedly that the Scots especially seem to be winning out in the allocations, and also that English regions lack direct access to government decisions comparable to that of the Scottish or Welsh Offices. This has interacted with other rumblings of discontent among the English Economic Development Councils and the larger local authorities over devolution and what they perceive as disproportionate shares of public expenditure for Scotland, Wales and Northern Ireland. Interestingly, British government attitudes to the RDF have been modified since accession, since officials and Ministers now feel that it is an unsatisfactory method of transferring resources both across national frontiers and within the UK. How hard the government argues for the renewal of the RDF after 1977 will depend in part on whether it continues to be perceived as a useful instrument in the domestic debate over devolution and resource distribution.

The regional dimension to Community policies is most obvious in the RDF case, but is also significant in a variety of other policy sectors in which the European Communities already have or are moving towards common policies. Awareness of this has already produced pressures for direct access to Community decision-making and Community decision-makers. Though the standard response of the British government has been that it can express regional interests adequately, this has not been accepted in all quarters. Most of the running on this issue has been made by the nationalists and by non-governmental bodies, but there have also been pressures within government. In September 1973 the Northern Ireland Ministry of Commerce opened a small office in Brussels for 'promotional and commercial activities' largely designed to give Northern Ireland the chance to compete with the Republic for European investment.[14] This was accepted only with great reluctance by Whitehall after a tough exchange between William Whitelaw, then Secretary for Northern Ireland, and Sir Alec Douglas-Home, the Foreign Secretary. A similar proposal was floated within the Scottish Office, but in this case ruled out of court. The Commission's reaction to these pressures has been rather tentative. In principle officials in the Commission have been fairly open to establishing contacts as widely as possible within the member states, though most governments (including both the German and the French) have been suspicious of any direct links that by-pass central government. In the British case the Commission has been especially cautious because of its awareness of divergent trends in British opinion and of the need not to offend the British government openly. The decision to open information offices in Cardiff and Edinburgh was a significant innovation – Berlin is the only other place apart from capital cities where such an office exists. Apart from that the Commission has preferred to keep the door open to informal contacts, but to accept central government definitions of regional interests on specific issues such as the RDF, fisheries and hill farming.

THE IMPLICATIONS OF THE DEVOLUTION PROPOSALS

The fragile balancing of regional interests that characterised British management of European policy between 1973 and 1976 has, however, been thrown into question by the commitment of the government to introduce devolved assemblies and executives in Scotland and Wales. When the Constitution Unit was set up in the Cabinet Office in 1974 one of the questions on the agenda was what impact devolution might have on European policy, and vice versa. The rapidly reached official consensus was that the two areas did not interrelate except in one important respect, namely that the Community dimension of certain policy sectors made it undesirable, even impossible, to devolve executive responsibilities to Edinburgh and Cardiff. In other words, though the name of the game is constitutional change, the distribution of powers among different tiers of government has not been considered as part of a grand design in any sense. Nor was the Crowther-Hunt argument for taking advantage of devolution to lighten the load on the centre embraced. On the contrary, various Whitehall departments used Community membership as a lever to strengthen their cases for retaining power over specific policy sectors in London.[15]

The White Paper *Our Changing Democracy* made this explicit in paras. 87–92 on Scotland and paras. 219–21 on Wales. Basically this stated the following points:

(i) Only central government could represent the UK in Community negotiations.

(ii) The views of the Scottish and Welsh administrations would be taken into account but without formal statutory machinery for consultation.

(iii) The UK government would maintain the responsibility for implementing Community commitments, though in devolved fields of policy this responsibility might on occasion be delegated, subject to UK supervision.

Running through the rest of the document are passing references, occasionally explicit, more often implicit, to Community policies. Paragraph 280, for example, argued that Community obligations made devolution to the Scottish and Welsh executives impossible in areas such as agriculture and fishing. Paragraph 281 argued on different grounds that economic planning and industrial development could not be devolved, nor the powers for selective regional industrial assistance under section 7 of the Industry Act, 1972. These various functions would therefore have to be the responsibility of the Secretaries of State, who would also acquire responsibility for the Manpower Services Commission, the Training Services Agency and the Employment Service Agency. They were not, however, to acquire a direct influence over the main nationalised industries, which include steel and coal. Thus not only was devolution in these sectors ruled out by Community commitments reinforcing centralist pressures in Whitehall, they were also used to bolster the case for preserving the Scottish and Welsh Offices with their Secretaries of State as Cabinet members. The intention was clearly to facilitate the direct use of reserve powers and political control over the new executives, though the survival of the Scottish and Welsh Offices could on other administrative and political grounds be regarded as anomalous.

A supplementary White Paper published in August 1976 summarised additional government proposals. Those relevant to the Community dimension included a provision for judicial review of the competences of the new executives (para. 14), a modification of UK reserve powers (para. 15), and the transfer of the Scottish and Welsh Development Agencies to Edinburgh and Cardiff, though the government reiterated its refusal to devolve section 7 of the Industry Act. The Scotland and Wales Bill (November 1976) followed the proposals outlined in the two White Papers and firmly emphasised in clause 25 that matters relating to Community or international obligations should not as of right be devolved powers, though central government might, if it wished, devolve some such matters, subject to whatever conditions it chose to impose. Clause 48 empowered the Secretaries of State to intervene to reserve powers in respect of Community obligations without recourse to Parliament. Clause 49 devolves the industrial investment functions of the Scottish and Welsh Development Agencies, subject to 'guidelines' approved by Parliament; similar provisions apply to the Highlands and Islands Development Board and the Development Board for Rural Wales. References to agriculture and fisheries are few and explicitly define only those few and marginal powers regarded as transferable to the new executives (Schedule 6, Part I, Group 11, and Schedule 7, Group 10).

The proposals leave open all kinds of problems over relations between the new executives and central government in the management of Community policy. First, some areas to be devolved in the field of employment and industrial policy will raise awkward issues in terms of access to the Communities and their funds. Second, it is more than probable that the new executives will attempt to assert greater influence over areas such as agriculture, fisheries, regional development and steel and coal. Such an expansion of authority could complicate the management of European policy on the CAP, the CFP, RDF and ECSC matters. Third, the pattern of consultation between the new executives and Whitehall has been left entirely to informal channels which will no doubt revolve around the Secretaries of State and the Scottish and Welsh Offices as intermediaries. There must be doubt as to whether this will prove either administratively viable or politically acceptable.[16] The new executives may well establish their own monitoring units on European matters, and similarly the new assemblies could well create European scrutiny committees. Such developments would increase pressures for more public evidence that Scottish and Welsh interests were being adequately defended in Whitehall and in Brussels on Community issues. Fourth, there would probably be a fairly rapid move on the part of the new executives to set up listening posts in Brussels and to argue for systematic access to negotiations at the Community level. Finally, there are likely to be particularly acute difficulties in the allocation within the UK of Community funds. The new executives have so far been promised only an annually negotiated block grant, though there are strong pressures to allow at least modest revenue-raising powers. They are likely too to press for explicit guarantees on their proportionate shares of Community funds, which would be anathema to Whitehall but might be unavoidable. This would in turn strengthen the demands of English regions for what they would regard as fair shares of both the British and the Community cakes.

The management of the interface between Whitehall and the new executives will initially at least be full of pitfalls. How well it works will depend on the degree of mutual trust or suspicion that emerges. Other member states have had similar problems – notably West Germany, Italy and Belgium. In the latter two cases the resolution of conflicts has been handled by *ad hoc* and intra-governmental compromise.[17] The German experience has been very different. From the early years of membership the German *Länder* have had a right of access to the Council of Ministers through a collective observer, *Länder* officials occasionally participate in formal Commission consultations, and the *Länder* governments are responsible for implementing Community policies in a variety of sectors, including agriculture.[18] In the RDF case what little money West Germany is entitled to is allocated to the *Länder* on the same quota basis as the national funding arrangements for regional development. There are instructive lessons from the German experience that could be applied to the British context, with two big *caveats*; first, that the German system has worked because both the federal government and the *Länder* have made it work; and second, that the *Länder* have co-operated with each other rather than been in open competition. It is less easy to envisage a collective approach on the part of Scotland, Wales, Northern Ireland and even the English regions, unless their suspicions of Whitehall were clearly stronger than their jealousies of each other.

We must therefore conclude that the twin issues of Community membership and devolution are likely to continue to set constraints upon each other and to produce pressures that will be awkward to meet. In both areas the attitudes of Ministers and officials have been cautious and circumscribed by inhibitions as to their wider implications and their mutual interaction. Yet both areas have a momentum of their own which make it difficult for central government to escape their reverberations.

NOTES

1 *Report of the Royal Commission on Local Government in England*, Cmnd 4040, HMSO, 1969. Volume II contained the memorandum of dissent by Derek Senior which argued for five provincial councils as against the majority proposals for eight indirectly elected provincial councils.

2 *Royal Commission on the Constitution*, Cmnd 5460, HMSO, 1973.

3 See Helen Wallace, *National Governments and the European Communities*, Chatham House/PEP European Series, 1973, pp. 97–8.

4 See James Kellas, *Modern Scotland*, Pall Mall Press, 1969, ch. 7, and Michael J. Keating, 'Administrative devolution in practice: the Secretary of State for Scotland and the Scottish Office', *Public Administration*, summer 1976.

5 See T. Rowlands, 'The politics of regional administration: the establishment of the Welsh Office', and P. J. Randall, 'Wales in the structure of central government', both in *Public Administration*, autumn 1972, and J. A. Cross, 'The regional decentralisation of British government departments', *Public Administration*, winter 1970.

6 See Gavin McCrone, *Regional Policy in Britain*, Allen & Unwin, London, 1968.

7 For some of the background on this see Uwe Kitzinger, *Diplomacy and Persuasion*, Thames & Hudson, 1973, p. 287. See also Richard Crossman, *The Diaries of a Cabinet Minister*, vol. II, Hamilton and Cape, 1976, pp. 332–7.

8 Rumblings of controversy within the Cabinet have been reflected in the press. See, for example, *The Times*, 23 June 1976, and *Sunday Times*, 28 November 1976. Interestingly the Conservative Shadow Cabinet was openly divided on the issue. When formulating its attitude to the Scotland and Wales Bill disagreement led to Edward Taylor replacing Alick Buchanan-Smith as shadow Scottish Secretary in November 1976.

9 The staff of the Cabinet Office secretariat in 1964 was twenty and in 1973 eighty-seven, including the special co-ordinating units. (Source: the annual *Civil Service Year Book*.)

10 On the general role of the Cabinet Office see G. W. Jones, 'The Prime Minister's advisers', *Political Studies*, September 1973; G. W. Jones (ed.), *From Policy to Administration: Essays in Honour of William A. Robson*, London, 1976; Harold Wilson, *The Governance of Britain*, Weidenfeld &

Nicolson, 1976, chs III and IV, and Sir Richard Clarke, *New Trends in Government*, HMSO, 1971, ch. II.

11   On the creation of the European Unit see Harold Wilson, *The Labour Government*, Weidenfeld & Nicolson, 1971, p. 387, and of the Constitution Unit see Harold Wilson, *The Governance of Britain*, p. 96. (On p. 95 Wilson disagrees with his earlier claim to parentage of the European Unit.)

12   See Helen Wallace, 'The European Community and British government', in the *European Economic Community National and International Impact*, Open University Press, 1974. Much of the detailed comment that follows is based on information gleaned in interviews with civil servants, although they are in no way responsible for the views expressed in this chapter.

13   For details on the allocations of RDF funds see the *Background Notes* published by the Press and Information Office of the European Commission in London. By the end of 1976 England had received 98·69 million units of account (of which the northern region accounted for 62·49 million), Scotland 58·68 million, Wales 34·94 million and Northern Ireland 35·89 million, a total of 228·02 million units of account.

14   Northern Ireland Office, press notice, 24 September 1973.

15   The other key argument used for the retention of responsibilities at the UK level is that devolution of major economic powers would make it impossible to formulate coherent national policies within a unified economy.

16   For criticism of the government's approach see T. St J. N. Bates, 'Devolution and the European Communities', *Scots Law Times*, 9 January 1975.

17   See, for example, Donald J. Puchala, 'Domestic politics and regional harmonisation in the European Communities', *World Politics*, July 1975.

18   For more detail see Christopher J. Hull, *The Federal Dimension of the Making of European Policy in West Germany*, paper presented to a ASGP/UACES conference on 19 May 1976.

MARTIN KOLINSKY[1]

6 The changing contexts of parliamentary activity

The difficulty is not on the merits of the wretched skimmed milk powder. It is a major constitutional issue as to how the Government should behave in these circumstances, and what the powers of the House are to ensure that no Government should do anything ultimately that the House would not accept. [Geoffrey Rippon, Hexham, C., Official Report, House of Commons, 19 May 1976, col. 1584.]

The danger the Minister must face is that it has become more and more undesirable for the House to be in a position where it is just being used to take off a safety catch to allow him to do what he wants. [John Davies, Knutsford, C., then chairman of the House of Commons Select Committee on European Secondary Legislation, etc, ibid., col. 1575.]

The quotations are from a debate on the procedure for consideration of EC documents in the House of Commons. The debate arose from accumulated dissatisfactions which reached a certain peak of anger at the conclusion of a debate, on 12 April 1976, on two Commission documents attempting to reduce the surplus of skimmed milk powder. An amendment disapproving the documents was agreed without dissent, and with the Minister's endorsement. But one of the measures had been adopted some weeks earlier by the Council of Ministers and remained in legal effect, despite the Commons' disapproval.[2]

Membership of the EC, unlike membership of NATO, IMF, and the International Energy Authority, has special implications for Parliament. In contrast with the international organisations concerned with the specific issues of defence, finance or energy, the EC involves a wide range of policies and claims to represent a higher legal authority and political order than its member states. In practice this means that Parliament has to adjust to a new source of legislation, flowing in uninterruptedly. On accession to the EC there was widespread agreement among both pro- and anti-Marketeers that it was necessary to establish procedures for scrutinising this legislation and for influencing the government's actions in the

Council of Ministers. The result was the establishment of select committees on European legislation in both Houses. One of their prime activities is to determine which legislative proposals and policy documents from the Commission should be debated before the Council of Ministers reaches final decisions on them. This is discussed in the next section.

In addition to the problem of scrutinising legislation agreed in secret negotiation among the nine governments in the Council of Ministers, membership of the Community raises the question of relations with the European Parliament, a body seen by some as a potential rival. The Parliamentary Labour Party refused to send a delegation to the European Parliament until after the referendum, which underlined the tentativeness of Britain's commitment to membership at the time. In contrast, the Conservative delegation, under the leadership of Peter Kirk, made an initial impact on the European Parliament by pressing for the introduction of certain Westminster procedures. The reciprocal influence on Westminster is less evident, but participation in the European Parliament has given a certain number of MPs extensive experience of the permanent committee system, and the opportunity to be involved in pre-legislative discussion of policy with members of the Commission. These are very different experiences from those available at Westminster, and to a certain extent they are reflected in discussions about changes of Parliament's procedures.[3] The most important development, however, is the agreement to proceed with direct elections to the European Parliament, despite opposition within the Labour Party, and in France among Gaullists and Communists. Direct elections will strengthen the legitimacy of the European Parliament, and may be expected to lead eventually to demands for increased powers. At the same time the organic relationship with national parliaments created by the dual mandate system will come to an end. Direct elections therefore raise certain questions. What type of relationship, if any, should be established with national parliaments? To what extent will the European Parliament be able to acquire new powers? How long will it take, and what are the consequences for Westminster likely to be? These problems are considered later in the section on inter-parliamentary relations.

Other changes could be set in motion by devolution. Although legislation attempts to define the distribution of powers, the practical implications are open-ended. How will the political and institutional relations between the proposed assemblies and

Westminster develop? How effective could an assembly be in the specific areas allotted to it (roads, schools, aspects of regional development, etc) if it has no influence on fundamental economic policy? Will the influence of the House of Commons on economic and financial policies become greater, or more uncertain, as the government asserts its key co-ordination function in relation to both devolved matters and European affairs?

These sets of changes will affect the relations .between the executive and legislature at Westminster in many respects, although the fundamental basis of the relationship is unchanged. That is, the political life of a government rests on its ability to retain the support of a working majority in the House of Commons, and the possibility remains that a back-bench revolt on the government side could stop a Cabinet in its tracks. There were two dramatic instances in connection with the Scotland and Wales Bill. During the second reading the government conceded referenda to avoid the possibility of defeat, and loss of the Bill, should the Speaker have selected an amendment signed by 151 MPs. Then during the committee stage in February 1977 the guillotine motion was lost by twenty-nine votes, and the government's main item of legislation for the session was seriously jeopardised. Forty-three Labour MPs either voted against the motion or abstained.

But short of such exceptional situations when a significant body of back-bench opinion on both sides of the government–opposition divide is unequivocally hostile to a government policy or Bill, the new systems of decision-making could diminish the role of MPs who do not hold office. This would exacerbate the underlying tendencies of a much wider decline in the relevance of parliamentary activity and its potential for control of executive action. The tendencies derive from several factors: the vast expansion in the role of the state during this century; the powerful influence exerted by the major interest groups; the complexity and diversity of legislation and administrative decision-making; the voluminous growth of delegated legislation which allows the executive virtually unchecked freedom of action; and the weaknesses inherent in the position of individual MPs.[4] These problems have been discussed by the proponents of parliamentary reform, and by recent analysts of the neo-corporative tendencies of the modern state. A decade after the Crossman reforms, the innovation of select committees is still under discussion, and the confrontation between reformers and defenders of the traditional debating role of Parliament continues. But most of the evidence suggests that the reforms have had limited impact on departments of central government, that they have not greatly increased back-bench leverage on the Ministers, nor have they enabled Parliament to exert a significant degree of control over public expenditure.[5] The problem is part of a wide-ranging discussion of procedural changes in which Parliament periodically engages.[6] There was a new departure in June 1976 when a committee for a fundamental review of procedure was appointed. A parallel body was established in the House of Lords. However, the chances of radical changes being produced seems to be limited because these committees are confined to procedural matters, and are not able to consider constitutional changes such as reform of the House of Lords. It is to be noted that this matter was also ignored in the consultative document on *Devolution: the English Dimension* (December 1976). It is difficult to imagine how such a piecemeal approach to institutional change can be effective, and it is doubtful whether fundamental procedural reform should be separated from wider political and constitutional reforms.[7] Nevertheless the desirability of change is stated with clarity in the brief terms of reference of the special committee on procedure: 'to consider the practice and procedure of the House of Commons in relation to Public Business and to make recommendations for the *more effective performance of its functions*'.

WESTMINSTER AND EUROPE

The strength of anti-Market feeling within the Labour Party was a special impediment in the development of relations between Westminster and the European Community. Labour refused to send a delegation to the European Parliament until after the referendum, and the polarisation of attitudes on matters arising from participation in the EC made it necessary for the Heath and Wilson governments to be circumspect in their handling of issues. But the underlying problem is that, while the governments of the member states play an active role in the Community, parliaments do not. In the Treaty of Rome the place of national parliaments is confined to ratification of direct elections, amendment of the treaty itself, the implementation of Community obligations by subordinate legislation, the ratification of association and trade agreements, and admission of new member states. However, there is nothing to prevent national parliaments from establishing procedures for keeping track of their government's conduct of Community affairs. In Britain the desire for parliamentary oversight of European legislation was strong, and a select committee was appointed in each House to make recommendations on the matter.[8] Established less than a fortnight before accession, the select committees worked effectively and with some despatch. The practices in other national parliaments were closely studied, providing a useful comparative perspective. But an important contrast with most other member states is the lack of a permanent committee system which could be utilised for these purposes, as in the *Bundestag*, or with more bite on Ministers, as in the Danish Committee on Market Relations. However, there was basic agreement, transcending the pro- and anti-Market division within the Foster Committee, on the need to provide information on Commission proposals for legislation, on ordering and scrutinising the chaotic flow of material, and on developing means of influencing ministerial actions in Brussels.

In May 1974 the new Labour government implemented the recommendations of the two select committees. The measures to keep the House of Commons in touch with European affairs included monthly forecasts of Council business, accompanied by oral statements from Ministers, twice-yearly government surveys of EC affairs and six additional days of debates, as well as a special place for Community questions in the Question rota. Moreover there was an assurance that any Commission proposal which the scrutiny committee thought of 'extreme urgency and importance' would be debated before a final decision was taken at the Council. This was later (November 1975) extended further to include reconsideration, or two-stage scrutiny, of Community documents of major importance, which undergo substantial amendment in the course of Council discussions. The committees began to issue reports, and the first two debates, on economic guidelines and regional policy, were held in the Commons on 3 July. After the summer recess debates were held quite regularly in the Commons until the following spring, when the frequency declined notably. Consequently the backlog of unexamined documents which had been piling up since accession was being transformed into a backlog of issues which were singled out by the committee as requiring debate on the floor of the House.

The situation in the House of Lords was different. In its calmer atmosphere a pro-Market consensus reigned, and the scrutiny committee, with a wider order of reference, organised itself to investigate the merits of Community documents. Sub-committees were established, and specialist consideration of documents was enhanced by the co-option of peers with relevant knowledge and experience in the areas under investigation, and by the employment of *ad hoc* specialist advisers. The latter provided the sub-committees with access to the advice of independent experts, outside government departments and major interest groups. The specialised investigations of the sub-committees have turned the committee, under the chairmanship of Baroness Tweedsmuir of Belhelvie, a former Conservative Minister in the Foreign and Commonwealth Office, into one of the most effective bodies in the Lords. With over eighty members and co-opted members (i.e. more than a quarter of those who attend regularly), it has become a beehive of activity, drawing on the many available talents, and no doubt re-invigorating them. There have been thorough investigations into a number of issues – the environment, energy, water pollution, aviation, the CAP, company law, direct elections to the European Parliament, etc. The investigations are based on formal and informal evidence from department officials, experts, Ministers, occasionally from members of the Commission, and from a great number of interest groups and organisations. The committee has been eager to establish contacts and to exchange papers with all relevant bodies, including members of the delegations to the European Parliament and the committees of that assembly. Baroness Tweedsmuir has stated, 'The Select Committee appreciated enormously the way that Members of the European Assembly have tried their best to attend our Committees, take part and let us know the feeling in the European Assembly.' And in the same speech she underlined the direction in which her committee is developing: 'The seven sub-committees . . . with power of co-option roughly match the twelve specialised committees of the European Assembly, because we have amalgamated some of the functions and we already exchange documents.'[9]

The committee, then, has developed as an important source of information on current EEC issues. About three-quarters of its reports are published for information purposes, and about one-quarter are published for debate. It is difficult to gauge how influential are the debates. But there has been some pressure for more than perfunctory attention from the government to the reports and debates, especially since several of the peers involved are acknowledged authorities in their field. Their personal contacts with

Ministers and civil servants, perhaps more so than the reports and debates, may have some effect. This is more likely to occur if the government has not already fully determined its position on an issue, and if the committee is an appropriate channel of influence, as it was in the cases of pollution and company law directives, but is not on agriculture and energy proposals.

By contrast the impact of the scrutiny committee in the Commons has been much more muted. It has not attempted to divide into a series of specialised sub-committees,[10] partly because of the sharp political divisions over the EC, and partly because by its order of reference it is concerned only with recommending issues for debate, not with in-depth investigations of the merits for information purposes. The committee has no power to co-opt members, it does not employ independent specialist advisers (though it does have four clerk advisers seconded from civil service departments), and its contacts with members of the European Parliament delegations are irregular, and to some extent determined by the pro/anti-Market division, even well past the referendum. However, the committee is performing its prime task well – that of selecting politically relevant Commission legislative proposals for debate. The cascading flood of documents from Brussels are being competently sorted and classified in accordance with their relative importance. This provides a great service for the government and for MPs, although the number of them interested is limited.

The main difference between the scrutiny committees of the two Houses is the Commons' concern to select documents for debate on the floor of the House, rather than to prepare reports for information purposes. Hence dissatisfaction with the debating of issues has been pronounced, and has resulted in much discussion of procedure. The first report from the Select Committee on Procedure (294, session 1974–75) was concerned with European secondary legislation, and was debated on 3 November 1975. There was widespread unhappiness with the government's solution of treating some European legislation in the same manner as domestic subordinate legislation, and with the limitations placed on debate in standing committee. The chairman of the scrutiny committee, John Davies, took the lead in expressing the discontent. His early day motion at the beginning of 1976 had the support of the committee, and collected a total of fifty-eight signatures: 'That this House deplores the inadequacy of consideration of important EEC measures, both in Standing Committee and on the Floor of the House; and calls upon the Government, as a matter of urgency, to improve the timing, form and nature of such debates.' These problems were carried into the general debate on procedure, 2 February 1976,[11] which the government saw as the first step in 'a radical review of the procedures and practice of Parliament itself'. (The Committee of Review was set up in June 1976.) As noted earlier, it was followed by another debate on procedure in May, as a result of the debate on skimmed milk powder. All to little avail. The backlog of items awaiting debate grew: well over fifty in July and over seventy by November 1976. There was continual dissatisfaction with the timing, duration and late hour of debates, and with other problems of procedure. Matters were not improved when on 17 June 1976, a day for debate on the EC, the government tried to reduce the backlog by taking twenty-two documents in two motions. The committee's report the following week protested about the wholesale bunching of documents on overseas aid and textiles, and on company law, and reiterated its recommendation that the documents be debated in proper context.[12]

Since debates are held in government time, they have control over the scheduling and the form of debate, generally on a 'take note' motion. Debates seem to be held more for the sake of 'airing' opinions than for creating a genuine possibility of influencing a Minister on issues which are of a certain importance but do not involve basic political passions. In general, there is little evidence one way or the other, of debate as such having a direct influence on Ministers, which does not deny the importance of occasional back-bench revolts, nor the fact that Ministers may manage difficult situations by making concessions in advance. But in the scrutiny of European legislative proposals the means of achieving a direct relationship with the government was created because it involved a new source of legislation. This was the object of the Foster Committee recommendations, which were implemented in the late spring of 1974. It was reaffirmed in a debate on Europe on 11 June 1974, during the renegotiation process, when the government gave an undertaking not to allow legislative instruments to proceed at the Council until they had been examined in the House, if the scrutiny committee recommended debate.[13] The undertaking is important, but it may seem to be more than it really is. In the first place, it is morally binding on the government that gave it, but it is not legally binding, and there is little pressure to make it so. Secondly, it does not mean that Parliament is in a strong position to influence the government for the reasons stated above.[14] In fact neither the Wilson nor the Callaghan governments, both bound by the undertaking, has allowed itself to be more directly influenced than was the Heath government, whose freedom of action in Brussels was unchecked by scrutiny procedures.

The asymmetry derives from the executive's dominant position, as well as from the attitudes of MPs. Those who are hopeful of the success of the EC do not define the role of the committee in the same way as the anti-Marketeers. The former tend to see scrutiny as a function which will eventually be undertaken primarily in the European Parliament. They also tend to accept a fairly traditional view of executive–legislative relations, and are content to leave the initiative with the government. In contrast, the anti-Marketeers do not wish to see the European Parliament develop a major role, and they want to exert as much control as possible over Ministers' actions in the Council.

The result is that such influence as is generated is primarily of an indirect nature, arising in the main from party concerns. An issue may cause much annoyance within a party, such as the Common Agricultural Policy within the Labour Party, and the Minister has to act as a broker between his Community colleagues and his party. The solution may be a double-edged approach, such as frequent statements of a desire to reform CAP while making concessions at Brussels in order to gain short-term benefits. Nevertheless if pressures in the parliamentary party build up too much it may be felt necessary to give way occasionally on specific matters. The implications are that Labour governments have used the activities of the scrutiny committee as a means of monitoring sensitive political issues, and that governments of any complexion may be expected to continue to be the prime beneficiaries of scrutiny committee work.

It would be premature, however, to draw the conclusion that the Commons has irrevocably lost power. The situation is still in flux. To the vast majority of MPs very few European issues have seemed of compelling importance, and they are preoccupied with other matters. The lack of interest gives the government a much freer hand than would be the case if the issues had higher salience. Moreover the achievements of the scrutiny committee should not be undervalued. It has become part of a well established circuit which involves the Cabinet Office, liaison officers in departments, and Ministers. The latter are required to sign the explanatory memoranda on the Commission's proposals prepared by their departments, and they may be asked by the committee to give further information in oral evidence. These sources of information, supplemented by the collection of other evidence, enable the committee to provide concise statements of reasons for its views in its reports. In this way a consistent effort is made to alert MPs, and to clarify areas of ministerial responsibility. The committee also exerts pressure to further its 'aim of ensuring that the House is given the opportunity to debate instruments at the earlier and more formative stage of the Community's law-making process'.[15] In certain areas, notably the agricultural price review and consideration of the draft budget, progress is being made, and it is not unreasonable to expect that the list may be increased in time.

The experience of the first years of membership of the EC, then, seems to indicate that Parliament has adapted reasonably well to the inflow of European legislation, though it has not been able to exert as direct an influence as may be considered desirable.

WESTMINSTER AND DEVOLVED ASSEMBLIES

In principle, the sovereignty of Parliament, and the economic unity of the UK, would have been unaffected by the Bills providing for changes in the government of Scotland and Wales which the Labour government attempted to enact in the 1976–78 sessions. Nor would they be affected by any of the changes set out in the consultative paper on Devolution: the English Dimension. The first clause of the Scotland and Wales Bill, explaining the intended effect of the Act, stated that the provisions 'do not affect the unity of the United Kingdom or the supreme authority of Parliament to make laws for the United Kingdom or any part of it'. This has been constantly reiterated in government publications on devolution, in ministerial statements, and in the Kilbrandon report and the Memorandum of Dissent.

However, apart from the spectre of separation which haunts the issue, the terms on which unity is to be maintained and Westminster authority exercised are problematic. The constitutional question of the intermediate or regional level of government was posed, not solved, by the proposed legislation. How will the relationship between the Scottish executive and the Secretary of State for Scotland work in practice? How much friction and confusion will there be? How will Parliament assert its supremacy? Why should a

Welsh Assembly have less power than a Scottish Assembly? What of English regional assemblies?

The impact on Parliament of these problems is potentially considerable. The accountability of the Secretary of State for Scotland may be taken as a prime example. Formally he is a member of the Cabinet and is therefore responsible to Parliament. But if his role is to be other than the kind of colonial Governor General envisaged in the original Scotland and Wales Bill, then his relationship with the Assembly will require the exercise of the utmost skill and tact. Attempts to prevent or require action of the Assembly could lead to intense conflict, especially as there is no indication as to where the Secretary of State should look for 'the public interest'. Parliament could be placed in a difficult situation, because to refuse to support the Secretary of State would be seen as undermining his authority in favour of a subordinate executive and assembly; or if Parliament was to support the Secretary of State, it would then participate in what might be seen in Scotland as an unfair decision. Although the number of situations where the consent or acquiescence of the Secretary of State to Assembly decisions is required[16] has been reduced in the revised legislation, and although the Judicial Committee of the Privy Council is to be the final court of reference on the *vires* of assembly legislation, the possibilities for serious conflict requiring political solutions are manifold. Among the most important of these are the questions concerning the development of the Assembly's economic and financial powers, which include the issues of oil revenues and power of independent taxation. It will be as difficult for Parliament not to become involved as it may be for it to decide judiciously on matters not readily in its grasp. The awkwardness of Parliament's position is also underlined by the problem of the over-representation, in terms of population, of Scottish and Welsh MPs. Is it unfair to England in the sense that they have a say on matters such as housing and schools affecting England alone, whereas the reverse will no longer apply? Should limitations be placed on the voting rights of Scottish and Welsh MPs on these topics? Or does it greatly matter, because there will remain a UK dimension to both Scottish and English affairs? Although the government defeated an amendment calling for a Speaker's Conference on the post-devolution representation of Scotland and Wales (1 February 1977), the issue, as well as the problem of the usefulness of regional committees in Parliament, may be settled only when (or if) there are legislative proposals for devolution within England itself. In general, then, the problems raised by devolution are not likely to be resolved for years to come. Essentially the conflict is whether devolution, if necessary at all, should be kept minimal, or whether the scope of change should lead in the direction of a federal-type arrangement.

The minimalism in at least some governmental circles was expressed in the consultative paper on the 'English dimension', which appeared shortly after the devolution Bill was published. It emphasised the extent of central government authority retained, and rejected the notion of an English Assembly or devolved assemblies with legislative powers in the English regions. It seemed to suggest that limited forms of change – administrative decentralisation (i.e. more regional offices of central government departments), improved interdepartmental liaison within central government, and tinkering with local government – would be sufficient ('practicable') in England, though the problem was formally left open to a further consultative process. It is interesting to note that the paper was originally expected in February 1976, but did not appear until the following December. Wilson's resignation had led to changes in the ministerial team preparing devolution, with Michael Foot and John Smith succeeding Edward Short and Gerry Fowler, who had replaced Lord Crowther-Hunt.[17] The latter, who was formerly special constitutional adviser, wrote an acid criticism (*The Times*, 21–22 December 1976) of the consultative paper, which had in effect rejected the proposals of his Memorandum of Dissent. He and his co-author had advocated the creation of five[18] English regional assemblies, extensive redistribution of legislative and administrative powers, and had emphasised the need for 'interlocking' procedures 'whereby elected representatives and officials at one level of government are able directly to participate in the decision-making process of the immediately superior level'.[19] Moreover he had placed the whole question of devolution in the context of changes anticipated by membership of the EC.

Apart from such full-blooded devolution schemes, federalism has been consistently advocated by an articulate minority, notably the Liberal Party and *The Scotsman*. Although this constitutional principle has proved to be reasonably successful in several Western democracies, it is axiomatically ruled out by the major parties and by the government. But there is little evidence that the matter has been given sufficient consideration in governmental circles. A great deal more research could be usefully devoted to it, because if devolution as such proves unworkable in practice, then fresh, urgent and much more objective consideration will have to be given to federalism as an alternative to separatism.[20]

This line of thought is undoubtedly frustrating to the anti-devolutionist, who sees the whole issue as a false problem threatening to run away with itself. Against the expectation that devolution will enhance democratic participation by 'bringing government closer to the people', and that it will 'lighten the burden on central government and on Parliament', the anti-devolutionist is alarmed at the costs, the illusions, the interference with existing local–national links in education, housing and the personal social services,[21] and the sheer waste of time and energy. The estimated financial effects of the Scotland and Wales Bill, together with its public service manpower requirements, were made to seem trifling by the estimate in the consultative paper on the 'English dimension' of 'thousands of additional staff and additional costs probably running into hundreds of millions of pounds' for English regional authorities on the model of the Welsh Assembly. It could be replied that the sums seem grossly exaggerated, and that the essential point is that expenditure on the innovation would be justified if greater efficiency and democratic participation could be attained. But this is uncertain, and it is equally possible that the outcome could be excessive conflicts with central government and local authorities. The possibility cannot be minimised, for the following reasons: (a) regional elections would often result in political differences with the national government, as indicated by the experiences of other countries; (b) the subsequent conflicts over jurisdiction, especially in the many areas of partly devolved powers, could create legal and administrative problems; (c) there are no mechanisms for administrative co-ordination and legislative implementation, such as exist in federal systems. The assumption (or hope), in effect, is that the central government will have its way without too much fuss. This is more likely to happen in a traditionally unitary state than in a federal state, such as West Germany, where the federal government relies extensively on the *Land* governments to implement its legislation. But reactions against the centralisation of authority may be stronger than anticipated.[22]

John Mackintosh has suggested a neat solution, at least for the relations of the Scottish Assembly and Westminster. He advocates a great deal of autonomy for the former, on the principle that 'if something can be run separately for Scotland as an administrative package, then it makes sense for this to be transferred to the Assembly'.[23] He suggests further that there is no need for a disallowance power because of the superiority of UK law over any Scottish law, and that the position of the Secretary of State for Scotland should be eliminated.[24] Mackintosh's concept seeks to minimise potential conflicts and to avoid overlapping responsibilities which could divide civil servant loyalties and confuse the public. Unlike the emphasis on 'interlocking' mechanisms in the Memorandum of Dissent, his stress is on the relative autonomy of the Scottish Assembly.

It may be objected, however, that if devolution extends to English regional assemblies it is most unlikely that such a clear division of policy-making and legislative competence could be made. The problems of overlapping jurisdiction and administrative co-ordination would have to be met. This in turn would pose a further problem, to judge from the West German situation: that such co-ordination takes place through the executives of the *Länder*, and the position of the elected bodies, as such, the *Landtage*, is correspondingly weak. So there is the possibility of reproducing on the regional level the same imbalance of executive–legislative relations found at national level. The possibility is increased when the question of links between spheres of *government* are considered in the context of the European Community: the most active regional exchanges with the Community are likely to take place on the executive level.

The formal position regarding regional relations with the Community is unequivocal: national governments jealously guard their exclusive representational status in the Community, whether they are unitary or federal states. This means that no direct, formal relations between regional bodies and the Community institutions can be envisaged. Therefore, as suggested in the Introduction, the concept of a 'Europe of Regions', in which the mediation of national governments is minimal, seems totally utopian. Nevertheless, pressure for informal contacts is likely to grow, for many reasons: the desire for loans from the European Investment Bank, the need for consultation on regional, transport, agricultural, social and technical policy areas, and the need for quick and accurate information on legislative proposals and instruments.[25] Moreover the introduction of direct elections to the European Parliament will bring the Community–regional/local dimension into sharper focus: groups of regionally elected MEPs may be expected to be in close touch with the regional and local bodies in their areas, and to transmit those concerns to the European Parliament and to the Commission.[26] A further aspect is that the regional assemblies would probably want to scrutinise the European legislative instruments relevant to them, and should be able to influence implementation in their own particular circumstances. In several respects, then, a certain by-passing of central government and of national parliaments may develop. But it is unlikely to affect seriously the central strategic position of national governments in the Community and in relation to the sub-national units of government.

INTER-PARLIAMENTARY RELATIONS

It may be considered that in the contemporary political environment three major tiers of government, each with appropriate spheres of competence, may be relatively more efficient and more democratic than the concentration of powers in central government.[27] But the realisation of this potential depends, in part, on the capacity of parliaments at each level to function in a viable manner, and to interrelate with each other. There are two basic types of problem. One is that the question of which policy areas should be devolved, and which are best treated at national or European level, is difficult to resolve. There is likely to be overlapping of interests in a great many policy areas, so that conflicts and perhaps some confusion of responsibilities may be inevitable. But this is far less intractable than the other type of problem, which concerns the gaps in parliamentary competence.

The discontinuities are there from the start. The European Parliament has a potential for development as a political body which greatly exceeds its formal role as a consultative assembly. There is pressure to extend its budgetary and financial control, its influence on the legislative process, and its political impact. Although the introduction of direct elections does not immediately enlarge the powers of the Parliament, it will gain in significance as an institution, as a parliament-in-the-making. Even so, the limits of its powers, and the meagreness of its influence, are well known. Referring to both the Consultative Assembly of the Council of Europe and to the European Parliament, Giuseppe Vedovato, then president of the former, warned: 'The danger is of becoming engrossed in a game which is parliamentary in appearance but is often without any political impact and of seeing this game in isolation as an end in itself; of succumbing to the illusion that they are playing an authentic parliamentary role on a European scale while in fact they lack the means either to exercise power or to check its exercise . . .'.[28] The powers exercised in the European Community largely escape the control of the European Parliament and may be expected to do so for some time after the introduction of direct · elections. Another aspect of discontinuity exists on the emergent level of regional government. Regional assemblies could not be expected to gather momentum from the start. But how long would it take? In the meantime the changes are set out and managed by central government on the basis of its executive powers. And, beyond the transitional stages, it is to be recognised that in the absence of federal co-ordinating procedures the central administration alone will possess the capacity and information necessary to oversee the entire scope of the governmental process.

Direct elections provide new opportunities for bridging some of the gaps. There is broad agreement, with few exceptions,[29] at Westminster on the need to establish a new form of institutional link after the ending of the compulsory dual mandate (that is, the nomination of members of the European Parliament from national parliamentarians). The view that national parliaments are rivals of the European Parliament, or that decision-making in the Community would be hindered if national parliaments played a more active role, has declined steadily among proponents of European integration. Instead the emphasis in debate on direct elections and in the evidence collected by the Select Committee on Direct Elections strongly favoured close ties because the democratic functions of the two bodies were seen as complementary and mutually reinforcing. The recommendations of the third report of that select committee reflected the agreement, albeit in a cautious manner. Its emphasis was on such informal links as would be established through the participation of directly elected MEPs in their own party activities at parliamentary and constituency levels. It is therefore left to the parties to consider the most appropriate methods of participation, and to the Select Committee on Services to consider the amenities Parliament could provide to facilitate joint meetings and other informal contacts. The third report urged that informal contacts be established as quickly as possible after direct elections, but recommended that the question of formal arrangements be deferred until the informal links had time to develop. If a need for formal links was then strongly felt, it could be discussed 'in connection with any proposals for the reform of the Upper House'.[30]

The parties in any case will have to face the problems of attempting to co-ordinate the activities of elected representatives in various parliamentary assemblies. The perception that inter-parliamentary links could be most vitally created through the political parties was expressed by Michael Stewart, then leader of the Labour delegation to the European Parliament: the MEP will have ample time to spend in his constituency, 'and his political party ought to see to it that he is there at meetings on the same platform with members of this House and with members of local authorities and that he is knit into the real political life of the country'.[31] This link has not been forged to any great extent under the existing system of the compulsory dual mandate. The most important feedback is the participation of delegates in debates on European issues, which has substantially contributed to the discussions, though it has not had perceptible influence on decisions. The informal connections have been rather haphazard and of little consequence. In the Lords, there is some participation by delegates in the work of the sub-committees of the scrutiny committee. There is nothing similar in the Commons, though the scrutiny committee has made some efforts to establish closer ties.

The European Parliament has also considered the matter of its relations with national parliaments. It initiated conferences of national and European parliaments in 1963 and, after a lapse of ten years, in 1973. The stimulus for reintroducing them may have derived, at least in part, from the Vedel report, which contained a section on inter-parliamentary relations. Since 1975 these conferences of presiding officers have become an annual event, with the aims of improving the two-way flow of information, and of establishing procedures for co-operation between committees, officials, and political groups. The conference in Rome, September 1975, recommended the creation of a committee within the European Parliament for developing relations with national parliaments, as well as a committee or working group in each national parliament to be concerned with the co-ordination of European affairs. It also advocated the creation of a European institute for parliamentary research and documentation. One of the moving spirits was Georges Spénale, president of the European Parliament, whose speech emphasised the importance of inter-parliamentary relations. However, the political affairs committee of the European Parliament adopted a cautious approach in its deliberations after the Rome conference, taking more of a wait-and-see attitude, while concentrating on the issue of direct elections, then reaching the decisive stages in the Council of Ministers. Nevertheless a working group on the question was set up, and Spénale continued his preparations for the next conference, in July 1976 at Bonn. This discussed, among other matters, current problems of parliamentary democracy in Europe, and the urgency of closer co-operation between the parliaments of the member states and the European Parliament. Spénale's contribution consisted of an interesting analysis of responses from the national parliaments to a questionnaire. A variety of arrangements to ensure the participation of MEPs in national parliaments, after the ending of the dual mandate, was envisaged. These include the entitlement of MEPs to participation in committees and plenary sessions of their national parliaments, and permanent contacts between representatives of the political groups in each parliament.

There is a growing awareness of the possibilities for close ties and co-operation between the two bodies. If some of the measures under consideration are established, at least a sense of the political currents and political atmosphere will be conveyed from one place to the other. Undoubtedly contacts with the national parliaments will provide an essential basis of support for the European Parliament without risk of blurring the respective spheres of competence. Conversely, if these links are established and maintained, the development of the European Parliament as a full-blooded institution might reinforce the democratic functions of the national parliaments.

But such an optimistic conclusion may not be warranted. Parliament is caught up in new legal and administrative frameworks. It has to exercise its functions in relation to more complex systems of decision-making in which responsibility is much more elusive than the traditional doctrine of ministerial responsibility would suggest. The emergent triad of decision-making (European–national–regional) is essentially on an executive-to-executive basis, and the parliamentary processes may become more than ever marginal to it. The implications for Westminster concern its 'sovereignty' in several respects: the sharing and transfer of some of its powers; the lack of an active role in the Community; the question of its relations with the emergent parliamentary assemblies; and, most fundamental of all, its relationship with the executive authority of central government – which is strongly reinforced by a strategic position in the new systems of decision-making. In view of these changes, the problem of establishing and maintaining effective methods of democratic control over governmental activity is becoming increasingly urgent.

NOTES

1   I wish to express my thanks for granting interviews, and for help in obtaining information, to members and officials of the Select Committee of the House of Lords on the European Communities and the House of Commons Select Committee on European Community Secondary Legislation, etc, sessions 1974–76; to members and officials of the Select Committee on Procedure, session 1974–75; to members and officials of the delegation to the European Parliament, session 1975–76; to officials of the European Parliament and four Whitehall officials; to the London Information Office of the European Parliament for a study trip to Luxembourg, and to its staff; to Professor L. Neville Brown, Faculty of Law, University of Birmingham, and to Mr H. A. Howes, Official Publications, University of Birmingham Library.

2   The Minister of Agriculture, Fred Peart, had not used his veto in the Council of Ministers because he thought that the package deal (of which the skimmed milk measures were a part) was advantageous. (Official Reports, HC, 12 April and 19 May 1976.) See also leader in The Times, 'Skimmed milk and sovereignty', 15 April 1976.

3   See, for example, the speeches of Sir Derek Walker-Smith and John Osborn in the 2 February 1976 debate, and of Hugh Dykes in the 3 November 1975 debate.

4   See Eric Moonman, 'How the MP's profession is being eroded', The Times, 29 November 1976.

5   Members of the Study of Parliament Group, Specialist Committees in the British Parliament: the Experience of a Decade, PEP, June 1976; Edward Du Cann, 'Some reflections upon the control of public expenditure in the UK', The Parliamentarian, July 1976.

6   See First Report from the Select Committee on Procedure, session 1968–69 and session 1974–75.

7   See S. A. Walkland, 'The politics of parliamentary reform', Parliamentary Affairs, spring 1976.

8   The HL Select Committee on Procedures for Scrutiny of Proposals for European Instruments (L. Maybray-King), and the HC Select Committee on European Community Secondary Legislation (Foster).

9   Official Report, HL, 29 March 1976, cols. 877 and 878–9 respectively.

10 Two sub-committees were formed in January 1976 with some concern for the merits of instruments. This has taken the form of concurrent

meetings with HL sub-committees. See HL twenty-ninth report (157) and sixty-first report (388).

11 There were several interesting speeches in this connection, including Short, Davies, Nigel Spearing, John Osborn, and Sir Derek Walker-Smith, the last two being members of the European Parliament.

12 Twenty-fifth Report (8–xxv), pp. 6–7.

13 The undertaking was reaffirmed on two occasions, 4 and 27 November 1974.

14 It is easy to be misled by the undertaking into thinking that Ministers are under closer parliamentary control than they actually are. Morand, for example, overlooked the extent of the government's control over the situation in terms of the scheduling of debates, the form of motion, and the selection of amendments. (Charles-Albert Morand, 'Le contrôle démocratique dans les Communautés Européennes', VIIIème Colloque, Liège, March 1976, p. 25.)

15 First Special Report from the SC on European Secondary Legislation, etc., session 1975–76, para. 3.

16 John P. Mackintosh, 'Weaknesses of the devolution Bill', *The Scotsman*, 6 December 1976.

17 See *The Times*, 23 June 1976, for an interesting account of Cabinet views and strategy.

18 See Derek Senior's comments on the geography of regional units in Edward Craven (ed.), *Regional Devolution and Social Policy*, Macmillan, 1975, pp. 163–5.

19 Memorandum of Dissent, p. xv.

20 See D. G. T. Williams, 'Wales and legislative devolution', in Harry Calvert (ed.), *Devolution*, 1975; and James Kellas, 'The application of federalism to the UK', ECPR Workshop, Louvain, April 1976.

21 See Craven, p. 17, and the chapters by D. Eversley, T. Raison, K. Urwin and A. R. Isserlis.

22 See the report of the Association of District Councils' annual conference in *The Times*, 26 June 1976, where there was support for a regional tier of government in England, particularly in the light of the Layfield report on local government finance. See also the article by Trevor Fishlock on the desire to loosen central government control, 'Envy the first fuel of an English move to regionalism', *The Times*, 26 October 1976.

23 'The power of the Secretary of State', Edinburgh University Unit for the Study of Scottish Government, 1976, p. 23.

24 *Ibid.*, and in *A Parliament for Scotland*, Berwick and East Lothian Labour Party, 1975. The idea of eliminating the Secretary of State for Scotland was rejected in the Memorandum of Dissent, which proposed that a third non-departmental Minister should be added to the Cabinet 'to become specifically responsible for the interests of the different English regions' (para. 22, p. xviii).

25 See Christopher Hull and Rod Rhodes, 'Intergovernmental relations in the European Community: the case of sub-national government',

Preprint Series, International Institute of Management, Berlin, 1976.. See also James G. Kellas, 'The effect of membership of the European Community on representative institutions in Scotland', Report for the Hansard Society, 1976.

26 The SNP 'suggests strongly that MEPs from constituencies in Scotland should have temporary membership of the Scottish Assembly. They should have power to initiate debates and to speak, but not to vote.' Memorandum submitted to the Select Committee on Direct Elections to the European Assembly, Second Report, HC 515-I, Session 1975–76, p. 13. See also the memoranda submitted by Plaid Cymru and the Farmers' Union of Wales. See also 'Gwyn Morgan: enthusiasm unbounded for a Wales-in-Europe', *The Times*, 22 June 1976.

27 Memorandum of Dissent.

28 Rome conference, September 1975, p. 2.

29 Maudling and Roper speeches in the HC debate on direct elections, 29 March 1976.

30 Third Report, HC 715, para. 40. This seems to favour the suggestions that have been forwarded for granting directly elected MEPs temporary membership of the House of Lords. Other proposals advocated associate membership of the House of Commons, which would provide informal access to Ministers.

31 Official Report, HC 29 March 1976, col. 933.

PETER BYRD

7   The Labour Party and the trade unions

A major disagreement about membership of the European Community dominated the Labour Party after the election of 1970. The climax of this conflict during the referendum campaign led some observers to predict permanent changes, possibly including a final schism in the party and a consequent realignment of the left and centre of British politics.[1] Almost simultaneously the party had to come to terms with the growth of nationalism within the United Kingdom. The response, in the form of proposals for devolution, precipitated another major disagreement within the party.

This chapter aims to do three things: to analyse attitudes within the party to the European Community and to describe the evolution of the party's policies towards the Community; to assess the impact of this issue on the party; to describe the party's reaction to the questions of nationalism and devolution, and to try to assess the political interconnections between the European and United Kingdom axes of change. It also seeks to serve a more general purpose, namely to link the discussion of interest group activity with the discussion of political parties. It therefore pays particular attention to the role of the trades unions in the Labour party.

1.   THE LABOUR PARTY AND THE EUROPEAN COMMUNITY

(a) Attitudes in the Labour Party about membership

The Labour Party's division over Europe can be seen largely, though not entirely, in terms of the historic conflict within the party which has usually been portrayed in terms of left-wing socialism versus right-wing reformism.

The *case for membership* has seen the European Community, in terms of external policy, as the logical outcome of a foreign policy based on an integrated Western European defence strategy. The pro-Marketeers are the heirs to the policy of 'realism' which supported the formation of NATO in 1949, the rearmament of West Germany in the mid-1950s and the retention of British nuclear weapons in the late 1950s and 1960s. The right wing of the party had conflicted bitterly with sections of the left on all these issues. But whereas in these previous intra-party conflicts the right had argued in terms of regrettable but realistic necessities, deploring the existence of an unreformed international system which made the traditional instruments of power necessary, membership of the Community offered a *positive* cause. The Community was represented as a successful, imaginative and radical solution to the quagmire of West European national rivalries, and British membership of it was not merely a defensive reactionary move. In addition, membership offered the possibility of a new and constructive world role, in conjunction with like-minded nations, to replace the other two failed circles of British interests, the special relationship and the multi-racial Commonwealth.

Domestically, the members of the Community, and the Community itself, offered working examples of the sort of liberal mixed economy or social democracy which the right wing had earlier attempted to articulate as a replacement for the socialist fundamentalism of clause 4. The German SPD's Godesberg programme of 1959 and its electoral successes of the 1960s and 1970s offered the most attractive model. Pro-Europeans saw the Community as a new political environment in which the intractable zero-sum conflicts of British politics – capital versus labour, management versus trade unions – could be transformed into a positive-sum game in which moderate solutions would secure a wide consensus including capital and labour. The increase in prosperity which would follow from membership would diffuse arguments about the division of the economic cake, modernise attitudes and thereby reinforce the values of a mixed economy. The unquestioned success of the Community and its members, as viewed by the pro-Marketeers, gave their version of social democracy an ideological respectability which lifted it out of the defensive and tentative plane which had characterised much 'revisionist' thinking on foreign and domestic policies in the 1950s. The predominance of social democratic values in the social democrat and socialist parties of the Community made the left wing unsympathetic to the pro-Marketeers' argument that 'comrades' in Europe wanted the Labour Party to join them.

The left wing *case against membership* was, to a large extent, a mirror image of the pro-Market case. In foreign policy, the left argued that membership would tie Britain's hands too closely and prevent the development of an independent (and socialist) foreign policy. The pro-Marketeers' response that membership could offer a secure foundation from which to adopt a more discriminating attitude towards the American connection was rejected on the grounds that the Community increasingly froze the division of Europe into two antagonistic blocks and stifled dialogue with Eastern Europe. Excluding pacifist and pro-Soviet sections of the party, opposition to the community did not entail outright opposition to NATO. By the 1970s the left no longer fought for unilateralism with any vigour, and whilst votes at Conference could still regularly be won against possession of nuclear weapons and American bases in Britain (this even got into the 1974 election manifestos), the heat had gone out of the issue. The left wing paid increasing attention to the Community's relationship with the Third World, invoking the new left analysis to describe the relationship as 'neo-imperialist'. In this area the pro-Marketeers argued more narrowly about the level of development aid offered by the Community members, and pointed out the changing nature of the economic relationship revealed in the Lomé Convention in 1975.[2]

The core of the left-wing case against membership concerned domestic policy. The Rome Treaty and the practices of the Community placed, it was argued, an intolerable constraint on a Labour government's management of the economy. The detailed objections relating to regional policy, competition policy, agricultural policy, capital movements policy, harmonisation policy, etc, amounted to the general charge that membership rendered impossible the achievement of the goal of socialism. Objection to external interference focused on the maintenance of parliamentary sovereignty, which would be surrendered. Parliament could no longer determine Britain's fate, which would be decided by bureaucrats in Brussels applying legal rules, irrespective of the wishes of Parliament. The issue of parliamentary sovereignty not only reopened the old, and to some observers curious, alliance between Michael Foot and Enoch Powell, it also led some of the left wing into a paradoxical situation. Within the party the right wing had traditionally upheld the sovereignty of Parliament. The left wing, with some notable exceptions, had argued that, for the party, Conference was sovereign and the role of the PLP was to implement the will of Conference. The Common Market virtually reversed these positions. The right wing quietly dropped the argument about the sovereignty of Parliament, though in order to share power with the reasonable men of Brussels, not with the wild men from the constituencies. The left wing discovered the virtues of parliamentary sovereignty, although in the comforting knowledge that whilst Conference was hostile towards the Community, no conflict of obligation between their views and Conference was likely to arise. The left wing reconciled espousal of parliamentary sovereignty with advocacy of a referendum to overturn the parliamentary verdict on the Community by arguing that the issue was 'unique' and that the electorate should rescue Parliament from the impropriety of committing suicide.

Throughout the debate the pro-Marketeers and the press also taunted the left as isolationist and nationalistic. The left responded by pointing to its 'genuine internationalism', based on support for the United Nations, development aid, etc.

This characterisation of the arguments for and against membership as right-wing and left-wing is an oversimplification. The use of the right–left spectrum at all may be misleading, though it certainly has significance, even if lacking an agreed definition, for those *within* the Labour Party. More important, much of the PLP, perhaps half, belongs to neither Tribune nor Manifesto group and sees itself as part of neither wing but of the 'solid centre'. Part of this centre bloc followed the leadership's policy of evaluating the issue pragmatically and in terms of its impact on party unity. However, after 1974 the leadership failed to hold all this centre and a majority of the PLP and the conference turned from support for the leadership's policy to outright opposition to membership.

The left-wing characterisation is misleading in another way. In the 1960s there had been a small but vocal left-wing pro-Market group led by Eric Heffer. But Heffer switched position, and from 1970 onwards the committed pro-Marketeers were confined to the right wing of the party. Opposition to membership became a touchstone for membership of the left wing. But the right wing was not monolithically pro-Market. Some MPs, most notably Brian Walden, rejected membership because of its threat to parliamentary sovereignty. Reg Prentice rejected membership because of the Community's economic relationship with the Third World. In fact in 1976 both became public advocates of continued membership. Prentice was undoubtedly influenced by the conclusion of the Lomé Convention. But both he and Walden appear to have been convinced of the benefits of membership primarily as part of their militant reaction to the left wing's strident opposition to membership and its increasingly dominant position in the party generally. In other words, they decided to support membership because the crucial issue was not the question of membership itself but the more fundamental question of the survival of social democratic values within the party in the struggle against the left wing.

The most important and persistent opposition to membership, apart from the left wing, came not from these political mavericks but from those who argued against membership because of its effects on Britain's international position. Douglas Jay in the 1960s and Peter Shore in the 1970s stated the 'Atlanticist' case that Britain's economic position was best maintained by pursuing an open economic policy towards the Commonwealth, the United States and the rest of the world, rejecting the Community as an inward-looking and exclusive economic bloc. Jay had been the leading political advocate in the 1960s of a 'North Atlantic Free Trade Area', and both he and Shore feared the consequences of membership for economic relations with the United States, Britain's largest trading partner. In security terms also, Atlanticists feared that European union might be bought at the cost of damaging American support for European defence. These arguments, the recognisable descendants of the imperialist ideal of a 'blue waters' policy and isolation from entangling alliances in Europe, fitted uneasily alongside the left-wing case against membership. Atlanticists favoured an open economy; the left was turning towards a highly managed economy protected by tariffs from the world economy.

The importance of the Atlanticist case declined, however, both relatively and absolutely. Relatively, the left wing united in opposition to membership and provided the largest share of the opposition. The left wing also made the issue the central plank of its general challenge to the parliamentary leadership's strategy of reliance on moderate 'consensus' policies, in a way which Jay and Shore did not attempt to emulate. In absolute terms the case declined because in the early 1960s the centre and right of the party had been undecided and divided about Europe. Hugh Gaitskell finally committed himself to the Atlanticist position just before his death in 1963. But the failure of the Commonwealth to transform itself into an effective grouping, the atrophying of the special relationship – quite apart from the economic failures of the 1964–70 Labour government – led most of the right wing to favour membership as the only promising road towards social democracy.

(b)   The evolution of party policy, 1970–74

The Labour government had applied for membership of the Community in 1967, and was frustrated by de Gaulle's veto. The subsequent deterioration of Britain's international situation, including the devaluation of the pound and the abandonment of the East of Suez strategy, maintained the government's interest in membership, and in 1970 a further application was made. The commitment extended only to negotiation of the terms of membership, not necessarily of course their acceptance. However, supporters of the general principle of membership were well entrenched in the Cabinet and outnumbered Ministers known to be unsympathetic (Tony Crosland, Denis Healey, Cledwyn Hughes, Roy Jenkins, Harold Lever, Roy Mason, Michael Stewart, George Thomson and, perhaps surprisingly, Tony Benn in favour; Barbara Castle, Fred Peart, Willie Ross, Peter Shore, George Thomas against). Between these two groups a third group led by Harold Wilson held the balance. Its members took a more pragmatic view and saw the merits of membership primarily in the bargain which the negotiators could strike. In other words, the principle of membership was tacitly accepted but buried deep beneath more immediate considerations. In addition, it could be argued that Wilson's debacle over *In Place of Strife* in 1969, when the government had been forced to withdraw its policy proposals as a result of opposition from within the party and trade unions, placed the reaction of the party to the issue of membership, and the maintenance of party unity, as a high priority in the evaluation of the overall advantages of membership. Divisions within the party may have helped persuade the committee drafting the election manifesto to obscure these differences with a rather vague anodyne formula tucked away at the end of the statement.[3]

The defeat of the party in the election increased the difficulty of maintaining a consensus on the issue. The new Conservative government enthusiastically supported membership, and in reaction the Labour Party adopted a more critical view. The government's pursuit of radical (or reactionary) objectives in other policy areas tended to condemn, in Labour's eyes, their support of Community membership which appeared as part and parcel of the same general strategy. The Labour Party's electoral defeat also stimulated the anti-Marketeers, and especially the left wing, to adopt a more aggressive strategy. Party activists and left-wing MPs attributed their defeat to reliance on orthodox and centrist policies during the period 1966–70, when, the argument ran, the opportunity existed for a socialist programme. The leadership, if not convinced by this explanation, appreciated its political significance and accepted the need for more radical policies and the re-establishment of a close alliance with the trade unions after the conflicts of 1966–70.

The result was a dramatic reassertion of the role of the party conference as the repository of socialist ideology and source of party policy. The conference demanded new socialist policies. The NEC responded by establishing a series of committees, dominated by representatives of the left, which in 1972 and 1973 produced a whole range of new policies. These proposals were adopted by Conference in the policy statement *Labour's Programme for Britain*.[4] Traditionally the party conference and the NEC have played a more active role in formulating policy during periods of opposition. After 1970 this assertiveness was directed at an apparently vulnerable and submissive parliamentary leadership.

This shift of balance between Conference and the PLP included policy towards the Community. In 1969 Conference had approved a T&GWU resolution demanding virtually unattainable terms of membership. In 1970 the NEC proposed a compromise resolution supporting membership on undefined 'acceptable terms' which barely maintained a consensus and only just ensured the rejection on a card vote of a resolution demanding impossible conditions for membership.[5] The TUC moved similarly. The General Council's report *Britain and the EEC* was sceptical about the 'dynamic' effects of entry and generally adopted a bleak tone – 'a very arduous negotiation is in prospect'.[6] At Congress two outspoken anti-Marketeers, Dan McGarvey of the Boilermakers' Union and Clive Jenkins of the Association of Scientific, Technical and Managerial Staffs, rejected the General Council's report in favour of outright opposition to membership. Vic Feather, the General Secretary, who personally strongly favoured membership, won the day for the General Council by arguing that Congress was only being asked to note the report. But only one speaker, Tom Bradley of the Transport Salaried Staffs' Association, also a Labour MP and member of the NEC, spoke positively in favour of membership of the Community.

A potential conflict thus emerged between Party Conference, together with Congress, and the PLP, where a large bloc of pro-Marketeers remained entrenched. Nevertheless Wilson's emphasis on the terms rather than the principle of membership kept this conflict mainly covert whilst the terms themselves remained hypothetical. The government's conclusion of the negotiations in July 1971 made the conflict overt. While the government enthusiastically approved the terms, the NEC and the General Council rejected them. At the TUC congress the General Council's verdict was accepted without a card vote. Only two union leaders, Roy Grantham of the Clerical and Administrative Workers' Union and Sir Fred Hayday of the National Union of General and Municipal Workers, spoke in favour of membership. By large majorities the Labour Party conference came to the same conclusion. Congress and Conference passed resolutions calling for a general election on the issue.

When Parliament considered the issue the pro-Marketeers within the PLP tried to obtain a free vote on the government's motion approving membership on the terms negotiated. Their defeat and the imposition of a three-line whip forced them to choose between their own views and the maintenance of party unity. Sixty-nine MPs supported the government's motion and twenty deliberately abstained out of the total of 110 who had voted for a free vote and 117 who were either members of the Labour Committee for Europe or had signed an earlier advertisement in the *Guardian* supporting membership.[7] The Labour revolt, though diminished to a committed hard core, carried the government's motion despite the thirty-nine conservative MPs who voted against the government.

The Labour rebellion was seen as directly challenging the authority of Conference, notwithstanding the rebels' claims that this was a unique issue coming after, in many cases, years of loyal service to the whips. The rebellion was even more unacceptable to many anti-Marketeers because of the 'reactionary' policies in other areas of the Conservative government which had increased the general level of inter-party conflict. The reassertion of the role of the Labour Party conference, combined with the nature of the Conservative government, made the Labour rebellion particularly damaging within the party. Undeclared warfare erupted between the NEC, supported by local parties, which expressed their anger to Transport House, and the pro-Marketeers within the PLP. In Lincoln it precipitated a final breach between the party and the MP, Dick Taverne, and also dominated the selection of the new General Secretary of the party in succession to Sir Harry Nicholas. Most crucially the NEC turned to the idea of a referendum on British membership of the Community, in direct challenge to the decision of Parliament, the policy of Labour pro-Marketeers and their use of personal discretion on voting. A referendum had been rejected by the previous conference, but the chairman of the NEC, Tony Benn, who had only recently entered the anti-Market camp, championed the proposal as the means to achieve Conference's aim that the electorate should be consulted. This populist challenge was condemned by pro-Marketeers, and also by some anti-Marketeers (most fiercely by Brian Walden), on political and constitutional grounds. It was approved by the shadow Cabinet at the cost of the resignations of Jenkins, Lever and Thomson, and narrowly endorsed by the PLP with a plurality of votes (129 to 96, with 50 abstentions). Wilson, Callaghan and Jenkins were all absent from the crucial NEC meeting. But for Wilson, who had in government opposed referendum, the device now also offered the opportunity to resolve the intra-party dispute by removing a final decision on membership from the party and entrusting it to a less difficult constituency, namely the electorate as a whole.

The referendum decision, and growing hostility to the Common Market in the party, made the position of the pro-Marketeers in the PLP increasingly uncomfortable. Wilson had moved far to the left to appease the anti-Marketeers, and he now attempted an accommodation with the pro-Marketeers, whose role in the PLP was of more immediate concern than the agitation of party activists and the NEC. This accommodation was sought in the policy of 'renegotiation' of the terms of membership. During the debate in October 1971 on the principle of membership Wilson had raised the possibility of a Labour government going back to the Community and re-opening the terms of membership.[8] In July the NEC, with Wilson present, articulated the policy of renegotiating six areas of the terms of membership considered to be unsatisfactory. Following renegotiation, whether successful or unsuccessful, the Labour government would consult the electorate about continued membership by means of a general election or 'consultative referendum'. This policy only partially succeeded in postponing further conflict, because anti-Marketeers now felt aggrieved at this appeasement of the right wing. At Conference the NEC succeeded, barely, in defeating a resolution expressing 'complete opposition' to membership.[9]

The TUC had also concentrated its opposition to membership on the terms and conducted a campaign against them. At Congress the

General Council faced a similar problem as the NEC in finding a compromise policy to prevent the expression of outright opposition which would divide the movement. But, unlike the NEC, the General Council failed. A resolution sponsored by the two biggest unions, the TGWU and the AUEW, urging opposition 'in principle' to membership was passed (4,892,000 to 3,516,000). Congress then approved, without a card vote, the General Council's policy of support for the policy of renegotiation.

When Britain became a member of the Community on 1 January 1973 the TUC and the Labour Party abstained from participating in the institutions of the Community. Neither the TUC nor the PLP took up its places in the European Assembly and on the Economic and Social Committee. The support for these policies was extremely fragile. Wilson's attempts to maintain party unity had in fact revealed the tensions between the institutions of the party. The policy of renegotiation was ambiguous, for instance, about whether a Labour government or the Labour Party, or both, would decide success or failure. However, the salience of the issue now tended to decline. In 1973 the party conference concentrated on debating the domestic policies outlined in *Labour's Programme for Britain*. Jenkins was re-elected to the parliamentary committee in November. In preparation for a possible election, the party publicity united around the commitment to renegotiation and consultation with the electorate.

British membership of the Community posed different problems for the TUC. Opposition to membership remained unaltered and overwhelming. On the other hand British membership affected the interests of the unions. Employers were represented and were being consulted. This gave a strong impetus to participation. The TUC found itself under pressure to participate from the European Trades Union Conference (ETUC). The TUC had taken a leading role in forming this body of trade union confederations in EFTA and the EEC, which, after preparatory meetings in 1971 and 1972, held its constituent assembly at Brussels in February 1973. Feather and Jack Jones were the TUC representatives on the executive committee. At its meetings in March, May and June the executive committee urged the TUC to participate in the Community institutions to which it was entitled to make nominations, particularly the Economic and Social Committee.

The International Committee and the General Council discussed the issue at every meeting and found themselves badly divided. Vic

Feather and Alf Allen of the Union of Shop, Distributive and Allied
Workers, the chairman of the International Committee, strongly
favoured participation. In addition some unions participated
directly in Community affairs, by-passing the TUC boycott. The
National Union of Mineworkers and the Iron and Steel Trades'
Confederation immediately became members of the consultative
committee of the Coal and Steel Community. The Merchant Navy
and Airline Officers' Association nominated members to a
Community committee on transport policy at the request of their
international trade secretariat, the International Transport
Workers' Federation. Opponents of participation attempted to hold
the position by distinguishing between participation by individual
unions and by the TUC itself. They also pointed out that TUC views
could be transmitted to the Community through the ETUC and the
Conservative government! This failed to satisfy those favouring
TUC participation, and the matter was handed over for resolution to
Congress.

    At Congress Vic Feather introduced the long report of the General
Council, which could not conceal the differences and, implicitly
rather than explicitly, made the case for participation. Allen argued
that the issue of *participation* was quite distinct from the principle of
membership. He was supported by Roy Grantham of APEX, a pro-
Marketeer, and by two anti-Marketeers, Joe Gormley of the NUM
and J. Vickers of the civil service union, who argued that their
members' interests were directly involved. The leading anti-Market
unions, the TGWU, AUEW, ASTMS and the Boilermakers,
rejected Allen's distinction and argued that participation would give
legitimacy to the Community. The majority of industrial unions
remained committed to outright opposition, against a majority of
the white-collar and public sector unions, whose members' jobs were
now affected by the Community. The hard-liners maintained the
boycott by 4,922,000 votes to 4,452,000.[10]

(c) The Labour Party in office

The Community hardly figured as an issue in the election of
February 1974, despite Enoch Powell's advice to all anti-Marketeers
to vote Labour. Wilson's handling of the matter appeared to match
the public mood. Gallup found that 18 per cent of their sample
supported membership, 31 per cent supported withdrawal, 43 per
cent supported renegotiation. This support for renegotiation over
the two other options represented a considerable triumph for

Wilson. It meant, given the complexities of the issue and the uncertainties of the electorate, that Wilson's own final verdict on membership might well be decisive. On the other hand he had to carry through renegotiation with the PLP divided and the party conference deeply suspicious. He appointed as Foreign Secretary and chief renegotiator James Callaghan, who was closely identified with Wilson's 'agnostic' position. Wilson appointed as assistants to Callaghan Roy Hattersley and Peter Shore, leading members of the two committed groups, demonstrating to the party and the electorate his open-mindedness about the final outcome.

The government's position was insecurely based in Parliament, but within the party the change from opposition to government was important in a number of ways. In opposition the role of the conference, and thereby of the left wing, whose power base is located in Conference, is greater than when the party is in government, and the parliamentary leadership enjoys the influence which comes from electoral success and political office. In opposition, the conference and NEC are important sources of policy; in government, the civil service becomes an important alternative source, and the contingencies of the situation also influence policy. Wilson's reputation in the party had fallen after the defeat of 1970 but the successes in 1974 helped to restore his prestige in the party. The constraints on the new government's freedom of manoeuvre, including its attitude towards the Community, were drawn tighter than in 1970. Then, the government had considered membership from a relatively secure economic position – particularly in terms of the payments surplus – whereas in 1974 it inherited a serious deficit, a depreciating pound and an explosion in oil prices. The government would not take the step of withdrawal at all lightly. By 1975 the government was distinguishing between the unfettered choice of joining in 1973 and the momentous step of leaving which Callaghan portrayed as a dangerous move into an unknown future.

During the period of renegotiation two trends emerged within the party. The first was the increasing suspicion of the anti-Marketeers that the government had secretly decided to remain in the Community. Anti-Marketeers had in fact strengthened the commitment in the October election manifesto to consult the electorate. But when the party conference met in November the deputy leader, Edward Short, failed to assuage fears that the government would in fact recommend continued membership, and failed to dissuade Conference from calling for absolute safeguards for parliamentary sovereignty and a special conference at which the party's verdict on the renegotiated terms could be given before the referendum.[11] The second was the growing readiness of the government to meet a challenge from the party. Since 1971 various formulae had enabled a vestige of unity to be maintained, but the policy of postponement had now exhausted itself. After the general election victory Wilson confronted the challenge of the left wing. On 7 December he stated that, if he found the renegotiated terms acceptable, he would put his own personal authority behind remaining in the Community. Benn countered with a personal statement against membership, bringing a rebuke from Wilson, who declared that an adverse decision by the party conference would not deter him from commending membership to the electorate.[12]

On 23 January the government formally announced the holding of a referendum. The government would pronounce its view on the new terms, but individual Ministers who dissented from that view would be free to campaign in the country for or against membership. Wilson was ambivalent about whether the government view meant any majority in the Cabinet or any majority which *also* included Wilson himself. 'We shall state – I shall state – the outcome . . .'[13] The relaxation did not extend, however, to Ministers' conduct of departmental or parliamentary business. The serious distinction between official government business and the public campaign was in practice virtually impossible to enforce, but it did enable a facade of collective responsibility to be maintained in Westminster and Whitehall, despite the disagreement of Ministers in the country.

After the Dublin summit meeting in March, Wilson claimed that most of the British negotiating objectives had been met, and he endorsed continued British membership. He failed to carry all of his government with him. Seven Cabinet Ministers dissented from the official government policy (the left-wing group of Benn, Castle, Foot and Silkin; Ross, the Scottish Secretary; Shore, and Eric Varley, the Energy Secretary). Wilson also failed to carry the PLP with him, and in Parliament the government's policy was thus carried, like Heath's in 1971, only with the support of opposition MPs.

	For	Against	Did not vote
Cabinet Ministers	14	7	0
Other Ministers	31	31	9
Other MPs	92	107	24
315 MPs were entitled to vote	137	145	33

230 of these 315 had voted in the vote of principle of October 1971, when sixty-five had either voted for membership or abstained, and 165 had voted against. In April 1975 the sixty-five all voted for membership, plus fifty-one of those who had previously voted against, some of whom were covert pro-Marketeers who had reluctantly obeyed the whip in 1971. Thus the 230 voted 116 for membership, 101 against, and thirteen did not vote. Twenty-five MPs who lost their seats in 1970 and returned to Parliament after October 1971 divided thirteen for membership, eleven against; one did not vote. The group of sixty MPs who had entered Parliament for the first time in 1974 was markedly more opposed to membership. Only thirteen voted for membership, thirty-eight against; nine did not vote.[14]

These figures reveal the influence over the policies of the PLP exerted by the constituency parties through the selection of candidates. After 1970 many local parties opposed to membership had not only voted in Conference but also adopted anti-Market (and often left-wing) parliamentary candidates.

The strength of the pro-Marketeers had remained nevertheless much stronger within the PLP than in Conference. The rejection of the terms by the special party conference was entirely predictable. The NEC condemned the terms, even after Wilson had forbidden Ministers from voting against government policy. The NEC opposed the circulation to the conference of the government's White Paper recommending acceptance of the terms, but was finally persuaded to allow circulation of the paper by the government (not Transport House) at government expense. The NEC circulated to Conference its own paper rejecting the terms, despite Callaghan's denunciation of it as completely inadequate and misleading.

The majority at Conference in favour of withdrawal was rather less than anticipated and did not reach the two-thirds vote necessary for adoption as part of the party programme. Constituency parties voted about four to one for withdrawal, the trade unions about six to four. The pro-Market group consisted primarily of white-collar and public-sector unions, particularly unions with strong individual leadership favouring membership (for instance, Allen of USDAW, Jackson of the UPOW, Sirs of the Iron and Steel Trades Confederation). Ten unions made up 1,889,000 of the 1,986,000 votes cast for membership, including 350,000 of the electricians' union, whose official union policy opposed membership. The major industrial unions, led by the TGWU, AUEW, Boilermakers and

Mineworkers, together with unions with strong left-wing and anti-Market leadership (for instance, Jenkins of ASTMS and Fisher of NUPE) made up the bulk of the total vote of 3,724,000 against membership.[15] Thus the government entered the referendum campaign opposed by the TUC, party conference and a majority of the PLP. The whole issue had, then, been taken outside the party for resolution at the cost of either the government or the party being defeated by the electorate.

(d) The referendum campaign

It is not the intention here to analyse the referendum campaign in detail.[16] The Labour Party's involvement is difficult to define. The NEC and Conference approved a statement produced by the General Secretary calling for a campaign, backed by the resources of Transport House, in favour of withdrawal. The NEC then decided, prompted by the General Secretary and perhaps by the Prime Minister, against an official campaign. Transport House did produce for sale at cost price referendum publicity material, including leaflets, posters, broadsheets, pamphlets, all of which was hostile to continued membership and thus to the government's policy. *Labour Weekly*, the official party newspaper, had presented a rough balance in its news coverage of the issue and pursued a neutral though overtly suspicious editorial policy before the special conference. After Conference its editorial policy firmly opposed membership and its news columns gave greater coverage to the anti-Marketeers. Its edition preceding the referendum had a massive 'Vote NO' covering the whole of the front page. *Tribune*, of course, was hostile throughout to membership.

The conflict between the government and the party was partially contained by the mutual realisation of the delicacy of the situation. Only 452 constituency parties bothered to attend the special conference. The remainder decided to keep out, and many parties who sent a delegate to the conference did not participate further. Many Labour MPs remained silent and generally maintained a low profile. Labour politicians, trade union leaders and grass-roots activists were, of course, prominent at all levels of the campaign, but the Labour Party itself was not involved. In this sense the referendum succeeded in taking the issue outside the Labour Party. This may have contributed to the partial recovery of party morale after the referendum. Loyalty to 'the party' offered a sort of refuge from the storm within which both sides, including government

Ministers who spent the campaign criticising, more or less openly, the views of their colleagues, could shelter after the referendum. It was in practice impossible to pretend that the difference over membership did not extend, particularly in the case of the prominent left-wing Ministers led by Benn and Foot, to a much more general unhappiness about the relationship between party policy and government policy. Personality conflicts were, with the notable exception of an attack on Tony Benn by Roy Jenkins, avoided.

The most striking aspect of the campaign was the much greater cohesion and efficacy of the 'Britain in Europe' campaign than of the National Referendum Campaign. The pro-Marketeers of all three major parties formed an effective coalition and argued the case for membership on similar, though not identical, terms. Although Wilson and Callaghan kept aloof from the *Britain in Europe campaign*, they delivered magisterial judgements on the theme that whilst membership was indeed best for the country, the country could make up its own mind. Wilson's apparent conversion to membership on the pragmatic grounds of the improved terms appeared to fit the national mood much better than the obviously biased and evangelising efforts of Britain in Europe.

The result of the referendum was, of course, an overwhelming victory for the government, which gained not only the vast bulk of Conservative and Liberal votes but also a majority of Labour votes. The percentage of Labour voters who supported membership and the government was estimated at about 56 per cent by Gallup (a result confirmed by a careful analysis in *Labour Weekly* on 13 June). The *Economist* concluded that the percentage of working-class and trade union Labour voters was rather less, but still more than 50 per cent.[17] The majority for membership and the turn-out were lower in industrialised than in rural or suburban areas but the differences, were not great. Even in South Yorkshire, where Arthur Scargill's NUM campaigned actively, 63·4 per cent voted yes. Industrial mid-Glamorgan voted 56·9 per cent yes and industrial Fife 56·3 per cent yes. Labour voting appears to have been a more important correlate than social class in determining the referendum choice.[18]

The Labour vote in the campaign can be divided into three distinct levels. At the *elite* level the parliamentary party was almost evenly divided, but the majority of the government and the official policy favoured membership. At the *party activist* level in local parties and trade union branches, the overwhelming majority appears to have been against membership. They conducted the campaigns, and their failure perhaps reflects the decline of the local parties. At the level of the *mass electorate* labour voters were divided but a majority supported the government. Labour voters, torn between support of their government and support of the party against their government, could not vote for a consistent 'image' of their party, but had to choose between conflicting policies. The Labour government won the contest either for possessing the better policy or, alternatively, for representing to its supporters the authentic image of the party. This is hardly surprising. The focus of the media on the government naturally correlates in the electorate's mind the government and the party. Labour voters could thus express traditional loyalty by supporting their government. The media also portrayed the anti-Marketeers as representative of the worst side of the Labour Party. Perhaps, then, the anti-Marketeers did well to obtain so large a share of the labour vote.

(e)   The European issue after the referendum

The division over Europe, publicly declared during the referendum campaign, did not disappear. But the issue had been resolved and the government's general position *vis-à-vis* the left wing and, by extension, Conference had been strengthened. Wilson removed Benn from the Department of Industry to the less important post of Energy, and dismissed Judith Hart from the government. One result of the reshuffle, together with the dismissal of Eric Heffer during the referendum campaign, was that the four Ministers most closely associated with the left-wing industrial strategy and the National Enterprise Board (the fourth being Michael Meacher) had all been removed from the government or from crucial posts in the Department of Industry. The left-wing anti-Marketeers also found their close alliance with the trade unions dissolving. In August the TUC accepted an incomes policy (the £6 limit) which the left denounced as marking a return to the bad old days of statutory limitation.

The anti-Marketeers retained a loose organisation, reorganised late in 1975, as the 'Labour Common Market Safeguards Committee'. Ron Leighton, a veteran of anti-Common Market propaganda, was chairman and over eighty MPs supported it. This organisation consisted mostly of the left wing but included Jay, Shore and a few from the old centre and right-wing groups. The existence of the group was not disadvantageous to the government, which continued to pursue a cautious, pragmatic policy towards Brussels and doubtless used the strength of the anti-Marketeers as a negotiating lever. The government moved particularly circumspectly in approaching the question of direct elections to the European Parliament. In February 1976 a Green Paper was produced, setting out the various problems involved, including the question of proportional representation.[19] On 29 March Callaghan announced the government's agreement in principle to direct elections, without great enthusiasm, and the anti-Marketeers expressed their objections to this step towards European union.[20] On 1 April and again on 13 July the European Council resolved some of the problems, and on 20 September the Council of Ministers decided to hold elections in the period May–June 1978.

The NEC opposed direct elections in response to the government's Green Paper. Although it agreed to affiliate to the Confederation of European Social Democratic Parties within the Community in April, it did not join the working party of the Confederation responsible for preparing a common election programme. The NEC took its case to Conference, where it presented a paper giving, in a very balanced way, the arguments for and against direct elections. The NEC case rejected direct elections primarily on the grounds that they would further undermine parliamentary sovereignty and also introduce into the political system proportional representation. The Labour Committee for Europe strongly supported direct elections, but Conference supported the NEC. Nevertheless on 28 September Tony Crosland, the Foreign Secretary, anticipated the decision of Conference by committing the government to introduce the legislation necessary to give effect to the European Council's decision.[21] The House of Commons select committee which the government had set up to examine electoral methods came down in favour of the 'first past the post' system, at least for the first election.

Anti-Marketeers within the PLP and the NEC sustained their opposition to direct elections, and this appeared to be echoed within the Cabinet, which delayed the introduction of the necessary legislation. In February the government again postponed the issue by deciding to publish its own proposals on alternative electoral methods. In the same month Crosland died and was succeeded as Foreign Secretary by Dr David Owen, a strongly committed pro-Marketeer who had in 1972 resigned from a junior post in the shadow administration along with Jenkins in protest against the party's commitment to hold a referendum. While the government's proposals were being prepared the NEC intensified its rearguard action against direct elections, threatening the possibility of a special party conference. Anti-Marketeers argued that using the 'first past the post' system with large constituencies (the United Kingdom had been allocated eighty-one seats in the new Assembly) would result in a tiny Labour representation in the Assembly, whilst using a form of proportional representation would be a dangerous precedent for parliamentary elections.

In March the government's pact with the Liberal Party in the House of Commons involved agreement to consider Liberal proposals for proportional representation for elections to the Assembly. The government's proposals (*Direct Elections to the European Assembly*, Cmnd 6768, April 1977) did not go beyond describing the advantages and disadvantages of alternative methods but was noticeably milder in describing methods of proportional representation than earlier pronouncements. The familiar advantages of the 'first past the post' system were listed along with the disadvantages – very great swings in the proportion of seats held by the parties, and the real possibility of a government holding a minority of the Assembly seats. Proportional representation would avoid some problems and, because the Assembly's role was different to that of the Commons, need not be a precedent for parliamentary elections, 'A different institution might warrant a different form of election.' The government considered that a regional list system or the single transferable vote might be alternatives to 'first past the post'.

Indeed, it seemed clear that, were the government to honour its commitment to hold direct elections, then the only way to obtain a reasonable degree of representation in the Assembly would be to grasp the nettle of proportional representation. However, after the referendum in June 1975, attention within the party shifted away from Europe and back towards domestic matters, primarily the government's management of the economy and the development of a policy on devolution. It is with this second issue that the rest of the chapter is concerned.

2 THE CRISIS OF DEVOLUTION

Although the SNP increased its representation in the October 1974 elections so that the issue of devolution became more urgent, as discussed in the early chapters of this book, the government did not give immediate priority to introducing its devolution proposals after the elections. First it had to complete renegotiation of the terms of Community membership and carry through the referendum. During this period the anti-devolution coalition had yet to emerge from the two opposing sides on Europe.

After the referendum the government turned to the economic and financial crisis. In August it introduced a wages policy (the £6 limit) backed by the threat of legislation, and a policy of reducing government expenditure – mostly planned capital expenditure – was pushed through. The left wing opposed the wages policy, and in 1976 criticised the budget proposals. It attacked the government's expenditure reductions of March (when the hard-line Tribunites voted with the Conservatives to defeat the government) and July. In July Tony Benn led a deputation from his home policy committee of the NEC to confront the Chancellor. The NEC members of the TUC–Labour Party liaison committee attacked the new statement of the social contract,[22] which was passed by the full NEC by only thirteen votes to eleven, with Benn diplomatically absent.

The economic crisis prevented any healing of the breach between the government and the left wing of the party, but it shattered the left-wing alliance with the trade unions. The TUC supported the £6 limit despite the opposition of the left wing (leading to the confrontation during the party conference in September 1975 between Mikardo and Foot) and continued to support the social contract despite great unhappiness about the public expenditure reductions. The government was thus able to rebuild the social contract, which indeed the differences over Europe had *not* fundamentally shaken, and effectively isolate the left wing.

During this tempestuous period the party had continued to do badly in Scotland in local elections, but little progress was made on devolution. However, in April 1976 the situation changed following Callaghan's election as leader in place of Wilson.

The politics of the leadership struggle do not concern us directly here. Despite the divisions over Europe and the economy there was a degree of 'cross-voting' in the three stages of the contest. Foot's performance in March–April, and again in October in the deputy leadership election following Short's resignation, should be interpreted partly in terms of the strength of the left wing and partly in terms of support for his personal role as Minister in charge of wages policy and hence of relations with the trade unions. Here, indeed, the content of Foot's policy pleased the right wing, even if the manner of presentation revealed its left-wing sympathies.

Contest for leader, March–April 1976

	Round 1	Round 2	Round 3
Foot	90	133	137
Callaghan	84	141	176
Jenkins	56 (withdrew)		
Benn	37 (withdrew)		
Healey	30	38 (eliminated)	
Crosland	17 (eliminated)		

Contest for deputy leader, October 1976

Foot	166
Mrs Williams	128

In April Foot, already *de facto* deputy leader, was placed in charge of devolution. Whatever his personal views – and he had no record as a devolutionist – his appointment indicated that Callaghan was taking the issue seriously. Indeed, Callaghan challenged the anti-devolutionists that, without a Bill enacted, the party could not win the next election. Foot's defence of the proposals was, from the very beginning, that they were essential to ensure the survival of the United Kingdom. He quickly abolished the politically suicidal role anticipated for the Secretary of State by transferring responsibility for deciding the *ultra vires* of assembly legislation away from the politicians to the judiciary. He made concessions to the Scottish TUC case for greater control of the Scottish economy, and he abandoned the unpopular proposal for a levy on the rates.[23] Foot and John Smith, his deputy Minister, appeared sympathetic to the demand for revenue-raising powers but argued that no practical scheme had emerged for managing this.

By the summer of 1976 the party had not yet begun to push back the nationalists and there was clearly no alternative but to attempt to implement the devolution proposals, however unenthusiastically Ministers might regard them. The defection of two pro-devolution MPs, Jim Sillars and John Robertson, who formed their own party in Scotland, served to emphasise the urgency of the issue. But the party, particularly the PLP, remained divided.

The party in Wales had fought two general elections on a manifesto including the elected council, but about seven MPs continued to oppose the policy. In Scotland the conference at Troon in March supported the government's measures – indeed, went beyond them in the economic sector – without a vote. But the whole thrust of the policy was still purely tactical – to outmanoeuvre the nationalists – and few speakers supported the principle of a devolved system. A resolution supporting a referendum on the whole question to confront the separatist case (similar to the strategy pursued in February 1974) was remitted to the executive. In a fringe meeting Eric Heffer addressed a packed audience on the merits of a referendum and disclosed also the continuing doubts about devolution within the Scottish executive.[24]

Opposition to the proposals came from the traditional sources in Scotland on the left and the right of the party, which saw devolution as the first step towards the end of the Union. In England members of the left wing, led by Heffer, and the right wing, led by Eric Moonman and Colin Phipps, united in opposition just months after their conflict during the referendum. They also argued devolution might threaten the Union (and thus deprive England of the oil revenues), particularly if the assemblies came into conflict with Westminster. The assemblies might be controlled by the nationalists, but in any case their financial dependence on Westminster would make them pursue irresponsible policies in which they would blame Westminster for their failings. The only way to make the assemblies, particularly the Scottish Assembly, responsible would be to make it responsible for raising revenues. This meant perhaps handing over control of oil revenues, and it would certainly undermine the economic unity of the Union.

The English opponents of devolution added a further objection. They argued that to be meaningful devolution would necessarily involve conceding advantages to the Celtic periphery that were denied to the English regions. The party in north-west and north-east England argued that devolution might involve additional regional development incentives which they were denied. In any case the assemblies themselves would offer a potent device for exerting leverage on Westminster and Whitehall which the English regions lacked – unless and until the government took seriously devolution of government within England.[25]

During 1976 the anti-devolutionists canvassed a referendum as a means to delay the government's measure and to defeat the nationalists. But in Scotland the referendum was a double-edged sword, because although the separatist option would doubtless be defeated it might reveal a level of support high enough to encourage rather than deflate the nationalists. Thus enthusiasm amongst the *Scottish* anti-devolutionists for a referendum waned, although in Wales the anti-devolutionists regarded a referendum as a *sine qua non* for abstention on a second reading of the Bill.

The anti-devolutionists in both Scotland and Wales were weakened by their isolation from the trade unions. The Scottish TUC in 1976 unanimously supported an assembly with strong economic powers and a referendum was rejected as a mere delaying tactic. The trade unions were thus in advance of the Labour Party, but electoral survival had now driven the party into the devolution camp. In July a joint Scottish TUC–Scottish executive delegation pressed their case on the PLP and in September a joint demand for devolution was addressed to the national conference.[26]

At the party conference the issue was debated for the first time, with Foot putting the executive case before a short debate of only half an hour. The executive position was supported, though *The Times* noted that the anti-devolutionists won most of the cheers. However, the government had by now obtained TUC support for its policy and could invoke both the trade unions and party conference against the diehards of the PLP. The TUC had shown little interest in devolution, allowing its organisations in Scotland and Wales to take the lead. In 1974 the General Council had decided not to respond at all to the government's Green Paper. In 1976 a resolution supporting the government's proposals was passed by over eight million votes, after a short debate in which the preservation of the United Kingdom and the defeat of the nationalists were the chief themes.[27]

The Government had brought Conference and the trade unions behind its policy, but opposition within the PLP had not decreased. During the summer three right-wing opponents of devolution, Tam Dalyell, Eric Moonman and Colin Phipps, formed 'Labour against Assemblies in Edinburgh and Cardiff' and claimed the support of 100 MPs from left and right of the party. Moonman and Phipps claimed that thirty of their group would oppose a second reading of a Bill and the government considered that fifteen might go this far. More serious was the signature of seventy-one MPs on a letter to Foot stating that they would oppose any guillotine for the Bill's committee stage,[28] and the signature of seventy-six MPs (sixty-eight English) demanding agreement to a referendum before the committee stage.[29] These lists included prominent left-wing and right-wing MPs.

The government suffered also from evident lack of enthusiasm for its proposals. The party's only consistent advocate of devolution had been John Mackintosh, who has favoured greater Scottish autonomy since the 1960s. David Owen from the right wing and Robin Cook from the left argued that devolution was part of a wider movement towards decentralisation, power-sharing and participation – including industrial democracy – but few followed them. Roy Jenkins, for instance, declared his conversion to the course only two and a half years after the government began pursuing the devolutionist path. The *New Statesman* criticised the proposals as a compromise designed for electoral advantage which satisfied neither centralists nor nationalists.[30] *Tribune* was slightly more sympathetic but saw the whole strategy as diverting energy away from socialist objectives – a view increasingly argued by *Labour Weekly*.[31] Outside the party the serious press was unsympathetic, questioning in particular the sincerity of the government's policy.

The anti-devolutionists within and without the party all favoured a referendum to give the Bill a solid popular base and to head off the separatist case. The government refused to concede it, though Foot held out the possibility of a referendum after the Bill had been enacted and when it could not delay the proposals.[32] The government was thus in a weak position, introducing a Bill which could dominate the whole session and without a guarantee of success. During the second reading the government was forced to concede the referendum, to be held before the Bill was implemented. A potential trump card had thus been played very early, and its value spent, before the difficult problem of the guillotine, necessary for success at the committee stage, was reached. The concession did at least ensure a successful second reading. Ten Labour MPs voted against – Dalyell, Moonman and Phipps, plus the opponents from the north-east and the north-west. But the other Scottish MPs, with the exception of Harry Selby – the victor of Govan – supported the government, and the Welsh opponents – Don Anderson, Fred Evans, Ioan Evans, Leo Abse, Neil Kinnock, Ivor Davies, Jeff Thomas – agreed to abstain. In all thirty Labour MPs abstained. The support of the nationalists, Liberals and dissident Conservatives enabled the Bill to reach the committee stage, but then sustained opposition jeopardised its progress and created severe difficulties for the government.

In February the government was forced to resort to a guillotine motion to establish a timetable for the committee stage. This failed when twenty-two Labour MPs voted against the three-line whip with the Conservatives and Liberals, and twenty-one abstained. Of the forty-three Labour rebels, nine were from the north-west, nine from the north-east, seven from Wales, and three from Scotland. Fourteen of the rebels were members of the Safeguards Committee, most of them belonging to the Tribune Group (see note 34 for the overlapping membership between opposition to devolution and Community membership).

The government promised to salvage the Bill, but its future appeared bleak. However, in March the government concluded a pact with the Liberal MPs as the only means of avoiding defeat in a vote of no confidence moved by Mrs Thatcher. As part of the arrangement the government agreed both to consider Liberal plans for proportional representation for the European Assembly and to allow Labour MPs a free vote on the method, though not the principle, of conducting elections for devolved assemblies. The prospect of devolution was thus kept alive.

3 CONCLUSION

The leadership of the Labour Party has been constrained by the conflicts within the party over Europe and devolution. The leadership sought various compromise solutions, but none of these really produced a consensus. The problems were particularly difficult to manage because of a new spirit of independence within the conference and the PLP. Indeed, it is the splits within the PLP which have made the assertiveness of Conference so serious. After the party returned to government in 1974 the frustration of Conference with the failure of the government to implement firm socialist policies came very much quicker than in 1964–70, when there was a long honeymoon period. The reaction of the left was particularly bitter because it thought it had grasped a degree of control in the leadership after 1970; this was shown, particularly in economic and financial policy, to be misplaced. The habit of defiance extended moreover to the centre and right of the PLP, which in 1975–76 made the early running in the fight against devolution.

Three major cleavages developed. On *Europe* the division consisted of all the left wing and most of the trade unions, together controlling Conference, versus the right wing of the party, with its centre of power located in the PLP. The government itself was divided, a fact

which helped prevent any permanent schism in the party. The
referendum also limited the damage that this conflict could pose by
resolving the question outside the party. In the conflict over *economic
and financial policy* (a subject merely touched upon in this chapter) the
left wing of the PLP and Conference has opposed government. But
the trade unions have supported the government's incomes policies
and, despite union support at the 1976 party conference for left-wing
opposition to public expenditure cuts, they have continued to give
priority to the social contract and a close relationship with the
government. The left wing has been effectively isolated and its
attacks on the government made from a position of weakness.[33] On
devolution the conflict has been yet more complicated. A coalition of
left and right has attacked the government's plans. Of the seventy-
one MPs who signed the letter to Foot opposing a guillotine on the
devolution Bill, thirty-three are also members of the Labour
Common Market Safeguards Committee, which has a total
membership of eighty-three MPs.[34] A rather smaller proportion of
the opponents of Community membership (which includes some
right-wingers) are also anti-devolution. In the devolution issue there
is also a degree of conflict between England and the Celtic
periphery. Scots MPs have mostly resigned themselves to
devolution; a higher proportion of Welsh MPs continue to oppose it.
There is also marked opposition from the north-east and north-west
to devolution.

The two questions have provoked an exceptional degree of
disagreement and conflict within the Labour Party. However, one
should not lose sight of the adversary nature of the political system,
which reinforces party cohesion and moderates intra-party conflict.
Certain other issues, which have re-emerged with urgency, such as
unemployment, might also be expected to reduce the sense of
disunity. Both the Labour government and the TUC have
consistently pressed the Community to give unemployment a very
high priority, not least because it affects the deprived regions.
However, even here cohesion is strained by the general disagreement
about the government's economic strategy. Therefore it remains to
be seen whether over the longer term such traditional issues as
unemployment and the cost of living will partially displace the
conflicts over membership of the Community and devolution.

NOTES

1 See, for instance, the special edition of *Political Quarterly*, 46, 4, 1975, with articles by Peter Jenkins, Eric Heffer, David Marquand.

2 An agreement giving developing states in Africa, the Pacific and the Caribbean preferential access to the Community.

3 *Now Britain is strong, let's make it Great to Live in*, 27 May 1970.

4 *Labour's Programme for Britain*, 1972 and 1973, in *Report of the Annual Conference*, 1972, 1973.

5 Debate of 30 September 1970, *Report of the Annual Conference*, 1970, pp. 188 ff. See also Peter Byrd, 'The Labour Party and the European Community', *Journal of Common Market Studies*, 13, 4, 1975.

6 *TUC Annual Report, 1970*, p. 742.

7 See the analysis in U. Kitzinger, *Diplomacy and Persuasion*, 1973, Appendix 1, p. 100.

8 *Hansard*, 823, col. 2103.

9 Debate of 4 October 1972, *Report of the Annual Conference*, 1972, pp. 175 ff.

10 Debate of 6 September 1973 in *TUC Annual Report, 1973*, pp. 566 ff. For the earlier discussions see report of the General Council and the International Committee.

11 Debate of 29 November 1974: see the *Guardian*, 30 November 1974.

12 *Guardian*, 30 December 1974.

13 *Hansard*, 884, col. 1745.

14 Vote of 9 April 1975, *Hansard*, 889, col. 1365.

15 See *Report of the Annual Conference* 1975, p. 344 (party constitution) and *Labour and the Common Market*, report of the special conference, 26th April 1975.

16 See D. Butler and U. Kitzinger, *The Referendum of 1975*.

17 *Economist*, 14 June 1975.

18 See Stephen L. Bristow, 'Partisanship, participation and legitimacy in Britain's EEC referendum', *Journal of Common Market Studies*, 14, 4, 1976.

19 *Direct Elections to the European Assembly*, Cmnd 6399.

20 Debate of 29–30 March. Callaghan statement in *Hansard*, 408, cols. 900–18.

21 Statement by Crosland to 'Friends of *Socialist Commentary*', reported in *The Times*, 29 September 1976. The NEC paper is entitled *Direct Elections: Arguments for and Against* (no date), and the report of the conference debate of 29 September 1976 in the *Guardian*, 30 September 1976. The vote in support of the NEC statement was 4,016,000 to 2,264,000.

22 *The next three years and the problem of priorities*. See report in the *Guardian*, 26 July 1976, for the confrontation between TUC and NEC representatives.

23 *Devolution to Scotland and Wales. Supplementary Statement*, Cmnd 6585, 3 August 1976.

24 *Guardian*, 27 March 1976.

25 See articles by Moonman in *The Times*, 16 August 1976, and *Labour Weekly*, 15 October 1976.
26 *The Times*, 12 September 1976.
27 Debate of 9 September 1976, in the *Guardian*, 10 September 1976.
28 List of names printed in the *Sunday Times*, 5 February 1977.
29 *Labour Weekly*, 19 November 1976.
30 Editorials of 21 and 28 November 1975.
31 *Tribune*, 5 December 1975; *Labour Weekly*, 3 December 1976.
32 See, for instance, his statement to the party conference; *Guardian* 29 September 1976.
33 Closely connected with this conflict, the party has also had to grapple with other problems associated with its 'socialist consciousness'. These have included the readoption problems of right-wing MPs, including one Cabinet Minister, Reg Prentice, who subsequently resigned from the party, and the extent of 'entryism' by far left groups. The latter problem has been highlighted by the role of the so-called *Militant* tendency, the employment of Andy Bevan as Transport House youth officer, and the reports of the chief agent, Reg Underhill, on party organisation.
34 The Safeguards Committee includes government Ministers, the list of seventy-one obviously does not. The figures can be very crudely represented as follows:

European Community

	Indifferent or in favour	Member of Safeguards Committee	
Indifferent or in favour	194	50	
Devolution			PLP
Member of group of 71	38	33	315

The 'level of association' between membership of the two groups, using Yule's Q, is 0·54 – a moderate level of association.

JOHN R. GREENWOOD and DAVID J. WILSON

8   *The Conservative and Liberal parties*

The problems raised by regional assertion and European integration have necessitated adjustments by all the main political parties. This has been least evident in the case of the Liberal Party, which has consistently advocated devolution and British membership of Europe, although there has been some internal division over both fundamentals and details. Within the Conservative Party differences have been far more deep-seated. As the predominantly English party within the British political system (all but twenty-four of the 276 Conservative MPs elected in October 1974 sat for English constituencies), and as the traditional party of Empire, the Union, and the *status quo*, basic Conservative attitudes have been seriously challenged.

Over a century ago, in his Crystal Palace speech, Disraeli informed his audience that 'the Tory Party has three great objects . . . to maintain the institutions of the country . . . to uphold the Empire of England . . . to elevate the condition of the people'. The first two of these 'three great objects' have been threatened, and to some extent jettisoned, as successive Conservative leaders have sought to adjust to the changed political role of England within the United Kingdom, and Britain within a wider world. The traditional party of Union has found itself advocating a Scottish Assembly; and the traditional party of Empire has taken Britain into the EEC, an act seen by many Conservatives as confirmation of the end of the Empire, and as an alternative to Empire.

It can, of course, be argued that the British Conservative Party cares little for theories and principles, and that its approach to policy-making is largely pragmatic. Certainly the Conservative response to regional assertion and European integration bears signs of pragmatic adjustment. But there has also been some evidence of a commitment to principle, with the result that open division has at times appeared in a party long characterised by internal unity and loyalty to its leadership. After a preliminary section on the Liberal

Party, therefore, this chapter will concentrate upon the Conservative Party. In particular two important questions will be posed: (1) How has the Conservative Party reacted to its break from traditional principles? (2) How were the issues handled within the Conservative Party?

THE LIBERAL PARTY

A commitment to both devolution and European integration has long characterised the Liberal Party. In 1945 the Liberal Party Assembly declared that it should be the aim of British foreign policy to strengthen the bonds between Britain and Western Europe. Three years later the assembly called for 'the establishment in Western Europe of a political and economic association conceived on broad imaginative lines . . . a political union strong enough to save democracy and the values of Western civilisation'.

In 1959 the Parliamentary Liberal Party urged the government 'to start consultations with a view to the entry of the United Kingdom into the European Economic Community', and in 1971 the Liberal Party Assembly asserted that 'only by the creation of an effective political community in Europe which supersedes the existing sovereign nation states can we ensure the continuance of peace for our own and for succeeding generations'.[1] The party has pushed consistently in the post-war years for Britain to fulfil a much more important part in a united Europe. In contrast with the Conservative Party there have been no overt tensions resulting from the questioning of deeply rooted philosophical tenets.

Likewise on the issue of devolution the Liberal position is relatively clear cut. This issue is invariably dealt with in the context of the democratisation of all levels of government within a federal structure. For example, the Scottish Liberal manifesto for October 1974 observed, 'Our proposals . . . are based on a consistent policy extending over more than sixty years. A Liberal government will establish a Federal System with Parliaments for Scotland, Wales and Ulster and Regional Assemblies in the main Regions of England.' In recognition of the practical difficulties involved in the introduction of a federal system of government a contingency was offered: 'If Liberals cannot get the full Federal-type Scottish Parliament they want, they will support any proposals for an effective Scottish Parliament.'

The importance of this commitment on devolution has been

underlined in the party's general election manifesto of February 1974:

The Liberal Party believes in devolution. . . . We favour the immediate implementation of the Kilbrandon recommendations to establish elected Parliaments in Scotland and Wales and to this effect a Bill has already been introduced into the House of Commons by Liberal MP, Jo Grimond. In the long term we would establish a federal system of Government for the United Kingdom with power in domestic matters transferred to Parliaments in Scotland, Wales and Northern Ireland and Provincial Assemblies in England. The Westminster Parliament would then become a Federal Parliament with a reformed second chamber in which the majority of members would be elected on a regional basis.

There have been occasional dissenters within the Liberal Party on fundamental issues such as British membership of the EEC, but for the most part differences have manifested themselves over details. The party has long stood 'four-square' on both these issues, and has consequently experienced few of the tensions evident in the response of either the Labour or Conservative parties to these issues.

THE CONSERVATIVE PARTY

(a) Party reaction

Unlike the Liberal Party, the Conservatives, more often than not the party of government, have laboured long and hard looking for a formula which will hold together the traditional party of 'The Union' and of 'Empire'.

(i) *European integration.* For an issue which has dominated British and Conservative politics for so long, which has caused open division within the party, which came within eight votes of bringing down the Heath government, and which finally brought the Powell split, the opposition within the party is less than might have been expected. In large part this can be explained by Macmillan's efforts to 'educate' the Conservative Party on Europe in the early 1960s, a process which also helped to isolate the party's anti-Europe minority. While 'going into Europe' was rapidly becoming an economic necessity, it was also an issue calculated to provide a challenge to the party leadership. It was in November 1959 that Reginald Maudling, President of the Board of Trade, concluded a tariff agreement (EFTA) with Switzerland, Austria, Portugal and the three Scandinavian countries. After a great deal of negotiation Macmillan announced in July 1961 that the government had decided to apply formally for British entry into the European Economic Community. This reorientation of policy inevitably produced opposition within the Conservative Party, notably from the right wing, led in these early years by Sir Derek Walker-Smith and Robin Turton, both ex-Ministers. But at the 1962 party conference these dissidents were overwhelmingly defeated, and Macmillan's message was endorsed. A month before the 1962 party conference, for example, Macmillan warned in a broadcast of the consequences for Britain of remaining outside Europe: 'Supposing we stand outside, of course we shall go on, but we shall be relatively weak, and we shan't find the true strength that we have and ought to have. We shan't be able to exercise it in a world of giants.' It is in this context of 'educating' the party for Europe, begun by Harold Macmillan in the wake of the decline of Empire, that the events of the 1970s are to be seen.

In this light it is perhaps not so surprising that the 1971 annual party conference saw a ten-to-one majority of resolutions on Europe welcoming the successful outcome of entry negotiations. Moreover in the six years 1970–75 only 28 out of 250 motions put forward for debate at annual party conferences where overtly hostile to British entry into Europe (about one in nine). Indeed, even when those motions calling for a referendum are added in, the proportion is still relatively low, at one in six.

In the House of Commons, only 39 out of 330 Conservative Members voted against entry in the free vote on 28 October 1971. Only thirty constituencies were identified as definitely 'anti' by Central Office, although another seventy were described as 'wishy-washy'.[2]

Opposition within the party was therefore fairly evenly, if thinly, spread. No one *section* of the party was particularly identified with opposition, nor was any single *area* or region. Not even in *Scotland*, where demands for devolution have been most marked, was the European issue viewed in a specifically 'national' or Scottish way. Within the Conservative Party the distinctiveness of Scotland was rarely emphasised in the European debate. At Scottish Party conferences a succession of pro-European resolutions were passed in the 1970s by large majorities and, moreover, these stressed a *British* rather than a Scottish orientation. In *Wales* the issue of European entry assumed a relatively low profile. Few resolutions at the annual party conference in the 1970s dealt with the EEC, and none of these was debated.

(ii) *Devolution.*   The Conservative response to regional assertion,
unlike the response to European integration, has been largely
influenced by electoral considerations, with regional attitudes being
more pronounced. Most important has been the reaction in
Scotland, where nationalism, traditionally of peripheral importance
in Scottish politics, enjoyed an upsurge from the late 1960s. In 1966
the SNP captured 5 per cent of Scottish votes (14·5 per cent in seats
contested) and in 1967 spectacularly won the Hamilton by-election.
This Nationalist advance, moreover, coincided with a decline in
Conservative support: from 50·1 per cent votes and thirty-six seats in
1955 to 37·7 per cent votes and twenty seats in 1966. Against this
Scottish background the first major Conservative commitment to
devolution was conceived, and it is, therefore, within a mainly
Scottish context that the Conservative response to regional assertion
is here considered.

In 1968 a policy committee established by the Scottish
Conservative and Unionist Central Council recommended the
formation of a Scottish Assembly. This recommendation was
subsequently endorsed by Edward Heath in his 'Declaration of
Perth', and considered by a specially convened 'independent'
Constitutional Committee chaired by Sir Alec Douglas-Home. It
reported in March 1970, recommending a directly elected Scottish
'Convention' to take the second reading and committee stages of
Scottish Bills.[3] These findings were overwhelmingly approved by the
Scottish Conservative Conference, and the 1970 Conservative
manifesto promised that 'these would form the basis of the proposals
which we will place before Parliament'.

From the outset some Conservatives regarded devolution as
incompatible with their traditions as the 'Unionist' party in
Scotland.[4] Many were reportedly 'taken aback' by the proposals,
about one quarter of Scottish Conservative MPs were openly hostile,
and the feeling persisted that Scottish Tories 'might not have
considered the subject but for the challenge of the SNP'.[5] After the
1970 election, when opinion again polarised between Conservative
and Labour, the anti-devolutionists' influence increased, and,
following back-bench pressure, the new Conservative government
agreed to await the report of the Royal Commission on the
Constitution before implementing its manifesto pledge. When
Kilbrandon reported in 1973 Prime Minister Heath again promised
to 'produce proposals for Scotland' but pledged 'the widest possible
public discussion' before any decision.[6] By now Scottish

Conservatives had hardened against devolution. Fifty-three per çent of resolutions submitted to the 1973 conference opposed an Assembly, the conference itself 'reneged on the proposal',[7] and the February 1974 Conservative manifesto merely promised further study of the Kilbrandon report.

The loss in February 1974 of four Conservative seats to the SNP, who overall won seven seats and 21·9 per cent of Scottish votes, revived devolution as an issue. After the election Scottish Conservative MPs themselves presented proposals for an Assembly, and in May the Scottish conference voted for an Assembly indirectly elected from local authorities. In October the manifesto promised administrative decentralisation and an Assembly with a say in 'how to spend Scotland's share of the UK budget'. This represented a compromise between the *status quo* and Heath's original proposal for a direct Assembly. The outcome was electorally disastrous. The SNP won eleven seats and 30·4 per cent votes. All four gains were from Conservatives, who won fewer votes than the Nationalists and only sixteen seats.

Following the October election the Conservative leadership in Scotland endorsed Labour's proposed Assembly, and the 1975 Scottish Conservative Conference almost unanimously supported devolution. When Labour's White Paper was published the Conservatives rejected the proposed Scottish Executive, but accepted a directly elected Assembly. As after 1968, however, many Scottish Tories felt that this threatened 'Unionist' principles. Others accepted direct elections, but expressed opposition to any further concessions towards devolution. Among Scottish Conservatives open divisions appeared. In January 1976 Alick Buchanan-Smith (shadow Scottish Secretary) was attacked by back-benchers for advocating a direct Assembly, and the Scottish Central Council divided 100 to 60 in favour. In April Scottish Young Conservatives supported an Assembly by only forty-three to thirty-nine. The direct Assembly faction claimed support from eleven of the sixteen Scottish Conservative MPs, while opponents claimed five firm 'antis' and two or three 'uncertain devolutionists'. Many Scottish constituency officials were reportedly 'anti', and almost one-third of 1976 conference resolutions submitted to the Scottish Conference rejected devolution.

Both factions now openly appealed to the 1976 Scottish Conservative Conference for support. Both Buchanan-Smith and Russell Fairgrieve, MP (Scottish party chairman) threatened to support Labour's Bill if the conference rejected an Assembly, while opponents, only days before the conference, launched 'Keep Britain United', an anti-devolution group. Supported by leading Scottish Conservatives, the group was described 'as an umbrella movement rather like . . . Scotland in Europe'.[8] In the event the conference approved 'a directly elected Assembly' but totally rejected Labour's proposals. The voting, however, was disputed. The conference chairman declared a 'show of hands' majority of three to one, but anti-devolutionists, who raised not only hands but union jacks, claimed it was nearer to six to four.

By this time, however, the issue had taken on a British dimension. Until February 1974 both major parties regarded devolution as a non-issue outside Wales and Scotland. Between 1968 and 1973 English and Welsh constituencies submitted only eight resolutions on devolution to the (UK) party conference, no fewer than six of which were pro-devolution in sympathy. Thereafter the situation changed dramatically, with fifty English and Welsh resolutions – twenty-three of which were anti-devolution and eleven pro-referendum – being submitted between 1974 and 1976. By 1976 division was reported within the Shadow Cabinet, and also among Conservative back-benchers, with claims that 'up to 90 per cent of British MPs [were] against an Assembly'. When Parliament debated the subject in January 1976 English and Welsh Conservatives overwhelmingly 'spoke against devolution, and twenty-nine back-benchers defied the Shadow Cabinet by voting against the government's White Paper. After 1974, therefore, the devolution debate acquired a British dimension, with most English and Welsh Conservatives opposing devolution. This presented the prospect, in addition to division among Scottish Conservatives, of a split between the pro-Assembly majority in Scotland and the overwhelmingly anti-devolutionist majority south of the border.

This confused situation culminated with the Shadow Cabinet's decision to vote against Labour's devolution Bill in December 1976. While the overwhelming majority of Welsh and English Conservatives supported this approach, Scottish Conservatives were now more divided than ever. Three pro-devolution Scottish shadow Ministers resigned (Buchanan-Smith, Rifkind and Corrie), with Teddy Taylor, a 'hard-line' anti-devolutionist, replacing Buchanan-Smith as shadow Scottish Secretary. In the event ten of the sixteen Scottish Conservative MPs, together with a handful of non-Scottish pro-devolution MPs, including Edward Heath, defied the whip by failing to vote against the second reading. The whole party, however, voted solidly against the guillotine motion in February 1977, which, given support from Liberal and dissident Labour MPs, greatly reduced the chances of passing the Bill in the 1976–77 session.[9]

Conservative reaction to regional assertion has, therefore, been confused and divisive. Opposition to an Assembly has remained strong, not just in England and Wales, where electoral pressures were minimal, but also in Scotland, where they have been intense. Opposition has been partly tactical, on grounds that an Assembly would be predominantly non-Conservative and would provide an SNP platform; and partly policy-based, notable objections being extra costs, increased bureaucracy, conflict, and delay in decision-making. Changing circumstances also affected attitudes over time, notably British entry into Europe, which confirmed the world-wide trend towards centralisation and amalgamation into large units, the impact of oil, the reorganisation of local government, and so on. More fundamentally, however, opposition has been grounded in the principle that devolution threatened the United Kingdom and its institutions. Thus of thirty-four anti-devolution/pro-referendum resolutions before the (UK) party conference between 1974 and 1976, sixteen saw devolution threatening the unity of the Kingdom. Scottish anti-devolutionists have depicted 'two Parliaments on one island' as threatening 'the break-up of Britain' and contravening 'basic ... Conservative and Unionist ... beliefs and traditions'. Similar views have been expressed by non-Scottish Conservatives, and significantly the 1922 Committee, immediately before the 1976 Scottish Conference, reflected 'that the party should stick to its "Unionist" traditions'.

During late 1976 and early 1977, as Conservative support increased throughout Britain and as polls in Scotland showed the Conservatives gaining ground on both Labour and the SNP, Scottish Conservative opinion again hardened against devolution. According to one poll, 52 per cent of Conservatives and 32 per cent of all Scottish voters were opposed to any form of devolution, and in March 1977 Scottish Tory devolutionists were reported as accepting that 'the Party nationally was no longer on their side'.[10] Partly perhaps to conceal the divisions in their own ranks the party had publicly advocated, before the crucial guillotine motion in February 1977, all-party talks to consider the whole issue of devolution afresh. Following the guillotine defeat it was reported that 'despite the views of most of Scotland's sixteen Conservative MPs, the party's

commitment to a directly elected Scottish assembly is dead', and
Edward Taylor (shadow Scottish Secretary) suggested as an
alternative the removal of Scottish functions from Westminster to
Edinburgh. Once again, as the electoral fortunes of the party
improved so likewise the Conservative commitment to devolution
faded.

(b) How the issues were handled

(i) *European integration.*   On the issue of European integration there
was a strong degree of commitment from the Conservative Party
leadership. Given the generally pro-EEC sympathy within the party,
the lack of any regionally based opposition, and the absence of any
dominating anti-EEC elements at any level within the party
organisation, the leadership was able to commit the party to a pro-
EEC stance but at the same time allow a measure of freedom to
individual MPs and constituencies wishing to differ. Edward Taylor,
for example, a vehement anti-Common Marketeer, was taken back
into the 1970–74 Heath government after having resigned on the
European issue. While not encouraged, therefore, opposition within
the Conservative Party was at least tolerated.

The referendum.   It was shortly after the October 1974 general
election that the Conservative Party chairman, William Whitelaw,
set up a central co-ordinating committee, with Lord Fraser in the
chair, to direct party activity towards the now obviously imminent
referendum. Following its defeat in two general elections in 1974, the
party was obviously not electorally strong; it needed the support of
all pro-Europeans, not simply the votes of faithful Conservatives, if
the referendum campaign was to be won convincingly. The party's
decision to join 'Britain in Europe', and to exercise such an
influential role within it, was, therefore, largely pragmatic. It could
have been fatal for the Conservatives to have infiltrated the 'Britain
in Europe' movement too overtly. In the event Conservatives, both
nationally and locally, tended to play it cool, utilising the all-party
umbrella, thereby deliberately avoiding the possibility of further
alienation from an electorate which had already recently twice
rejected it at the polls. It is, however, important to remember that
many of the leading officials of 'Britain in Europe' were
Conservatives; even the former doorman at Central Office became
commissionaire at the Old Park Lane headquarters of the 'Britain in
Europe' organisation. Throughout, the Conservative Party's aim
was to play the campaign in such a way as to avoid accusations of

party politics. This is where the 'Britain in Europe' movement was so useful in providing such ideal cover for Conservative activity locally. To assert this is not to argue that at the local level the movement was entirely synonymous with local Conservative associations; it certainly was not. A variety of others were involved, some of them non-party, and some with Liberal/Labour sympathies. However, except in the occasional Liberal Party stronghold, or where there were a significant number of Labour pro-Europeans, grass-roots activity was largely Conservative-based. Yet the overt nature of this commitment was shielded, thanks largely to the 'Britain in Europe' organisation.

(ii) *Devolution.* This was an issue which compromised traditional party principles and where, unlike European integration, expediency rather than conviction provided a main motivating force. In spite of open opposition to a Scottish Assembly from both Scottish and, particularly, non-Scottish Conservatives, the party remained committed to devolution for most of the 1968–76 period, and the party's position in 1976 was consistent with that first proposed in the 'Declaration of Perth'. Moreover, unlike Labour, no 'break-away' Scottish Conservative Party emerged. That consistency and unity were maintained, while traditional party principles were jettisoned, was due largely to the way the issue was handled.

There are four particularly significant aspects here. Firstly, the issue was handled within an essentially Scottish context, a process aided by the constitutional autonomy of the party in Scotland. The initial demand for an Assembly came from Scotland, and devolution was frequently debated by Scottish Conferences after 1968. Outside Scotland, however, these developments went largely unnoticed, and the party leadership did little to arouse interest. The (UK) party conference never discussed devolution until 1976 and, according to one MP, 'there was virtually no consultation . . . outside of Scottish Members and organisations'.[11]

Consequently the devolution debate was initially contained in a Scottish dimension, which enabled a party commitment to devolution to be made before the mass of generally anti-devolutionist English Conservatives became interested in the issue. Only after 1974, when striking nationalist advances placed devolution in the forefront of English politics, was the scene set for an English anti-devolution backlash.

The second significant aspect is the leader's role. At crucial times, as with Heath's 'Declaration of Perth', the leadership has decisively moved the party towards an Assembly. Mrs Thatcher similarly revived consideration of a direct Assembly in 1975, despite conference votes for alternative policies in 1973 and 1974. Significantly, however, she appeared personally non-committal, officially referring the matter to a Shadow Cabinet committee. Similarly, while giving the 1976 Scottish Party Conference a clear lead, as one reporter put it, 'to adhere to the proposals of the Douglas Home committee',[12] she nevertheless gave both factions reason to claim her support. By the time the government's devolution Bill was introduced, however, the Shadow Cabinet's enthusiasm for devolution appeared to be waning. Although in public Mrs Thatcher still assumed a low profile and a somewhat ambivalent approach, under her new 'anti-devolutionist' shadow Scottish Secretary the party's tactics seemed designed to kill the devolution Bill, and to extricate the party from its commitment to a directly elected assembly 'as quickly as possible'.

In one respect, however, the leader's position has been unusually constrained. This concerns the third aspect of significance, namely the Scottish Party Conference, which normally plays little part in policy-making. The proposed Assembly conflicted so sharply with 'Unionist' principles that the leadership appears, exceptionally, to have felt the need for conference endorsement of its policy. Consequently the devolution debate within the Scottish party has been more open than with most issues, with both factions appealing publicly, particularly after 1974, for Conference support. Despite the unusual importance of its proceedings, however, Conference behaved as it has traditionally always behaved, demonstrating loyalty to the leadership by supporting whatever new initiatives on devolution have been proposed.

The final aspect concerns the handling of the issue of principle. Heath's original proposal in 1968 offered too sharp and sudden a break with 'Unionist' principles. After 1974, however, not only was the SNP – with its separatist proposals – far stronger, but a Labour government, committed to elected Scottish and Welsh Assemblies as well as a Scottish Executive, was in power. In these changed circumstances the Heath–Home proposals appeared as an alternative to more radical forms of devolution, even separation. Far from threatening the Union and its institutions, these proposals, Alick Buchanan-Smith claimed, maintained 'the integrity of the United Kingdom' and adapted its institutions 'to meet new circumstances'.[13] In this way, it was claimed, traditional 'Unionist' principles could be reconciled to the demands of an increasingly nationalistic world. Seemingly, however, by 1977 even this limited. breach with party principles was proving too much for the majority of Conservatives to accept.

By these complex manoeuvres the Conservative Party responded to the demands of regional assertion. The commitment to a directly elected Scottish Assembly was never fully supported within the party, and the level of support for it varied over time with changing political fortunes. Although the commitment still nominally remained, the party voted against Labour's devolution Bill in December 1976, and appeared to have effectively killed it off with the help of other anti-devolutionists in the guillotine motion in February 1977. In May 1977, at the Scottish Conservative Conference, this weakening commitment to a directly elected Assembly was further confirmed. Although a future Assembly was not ruled out – Mrs Thatcher herself conceded privately 'that there will eventually be an assembly in Edinburgh' – in effect the proposal was relegated to the status of an option available for consideration. The party's official position was that all-party talks should take place 'without preconditions or preconceptions', and the conference itself called 'for a searching re-examination of the entire structure of government as the basis of fresh proposals for effective devolution'. More bluntly, the party's devolution spokesman, Francis Pym, conceded after the conference that the party's commitment to a directly elected Assembly was 'in a sense inoperative'.

With the Scottish Tories in 1977 relatively free from electoral pressures, Scottish Conservative opinion again shifted sharply against an Assembly, and with the majority of the English party also strongly opposed the commitment to a Scottish Assembly was given, as one anti-devolutionist put it, a 'decent burial'. Although there was still division on the issue[14] the Conservative and Unionist Party had apparently reverted to a minimalist solution consistent with its traditional attachment to the maintenance of 'the Union' and 'the institutions of the country'.

CONCLUSION

The Conservative and Liberal responses to the demands of both regional assertion and European integration have been very different. Whereas the Liberals have been generally united and followed a consistent approach, the Conservatives have been neither united nor, on devolution at least, consistent. In part, the Conservative response has been a pragmatic one. The European commitment, geared as it was to the withdrawal from Empire, as well as to a degree of economic necessity, was partly pragmatic. The commitment to devolution, fluctuating as it has with changing political fortunes, was even more marked by pragmatism. Nevertheless, issues of principle have been at stake, for in responding to the demands of regional assertion and European integration traditional Conservative principles have to some degree been challenged.

This threat to traditional principles has led to internal opposition, which in both cases has been strong and vocal, and which had expressed itself at all levels – in the constituencies, the parliamentary party, and even among front-benchers. Both debates within the party have been unusually open and public, with particular importance being attached to Conference decisions. On Europe the opposition was thinly and evenly spread and ultimately unsuccessful. On devolution it was stronger and probably decisive, first in forcing inaction upon the Heath government and subsequently in committing the Conservatives under Mrs Thatcher to oppose Labour's Bill. Differences were perceptible between the leaders involved, with Heath clearly and enthusiastically committed to both Europe and devolution, and Mrs Thatcher – while retaining the outward semblances of support for both policies – appearing less committed if not cool. Heath's heavy involvement in the European referendum campaign, for example, contrasts sharply with Mrs Thatcher's relatively low profile; as does Heath's defiance of Mrs Thatcher's party whip on devolution. Despite these differences, however, leadership initiatives have generally been followed by the majority of the party both in Parliament and in Conference, opponents have been tolerated, and minorities have remained within the party. While the response to regional assertion and European integration has thus aroused internal opposition, the party's traditional unity and loyalty to the leader, although at times under strain, have nevertheless ultimately held firm, and fundamentally Conservative patterns of behaviour have prevailed.

NOTES

1 Quoted in *The Liberal Manifesto for Europe*, 1975, pp. 3, 4.

2 Interview with Lord Fraser of Kilmorack, 4 March 1976. The authors are very grateful to Lord Fraser for his help in the preparation of this chapter. Interpretations of data, however, remain the sole responsibilities of the authors.

3 *Scotland's Government*, Report of the Scottish Constitutional Committee, 1970, p. 9.

4 Until 1965 the party was named the Unionist Party; thereafter the Scottish Conservative and Unionist Party.

5 See J. G. Kellas, 'Scottish Nationalism', in D. Butler and M. Pinto-Duschinsky, *The British General Election of 1970*, Macmillan, 1971, p. 457.

6 Hansard, 31 October 1973, cols. 164–6.

7 J. G. Kellas, *The Scottish Political System*, 1975, pp. 110, 133.

8 The 'Keep Britain United' campaign was launched in Glasgow in May by Iain Sproat, MP. See *The Times*, 4, 10–12 May 1976.

9 During the committee stage of the devolution Bill, Conservative, Labour and Liberal opponents of the Bill tabled numerous amendments and sustained debate to the point where after eleven days and nights only three of the 115 clauses had been considered. The government lost its guillotine measure by forty-four votes. Only two Liberal MPs (Emlyn Hooson and Geraint Howells) voted for the guillotine. Officially the Liberals were in favour of a federal solution which would give 'meaningful devolution' and were also anxious to secure provision for proportional representation to the Scottish and Welsh Assemblies.

10 *The Times*, 1 February and 28 March 1977.

11 Ronald Bell, MP, Hansard, 15 January 1976, col. 623.

12 *The Times*, 11 May 1976.

13 Hansard, 14 January 1976, col. 431.

14 These continued divisions were institutionalised in the various party groupings which formed around the devolution issue. The most important of them in 1977 included the Union Flag Group, an anti-devolution group of seventy Conservative MPs, and the New Alliance for a Scottish Assembly, an inter-party group founded by Alick Buchanan-Smith to press 'for a more powerful assembly than the Conservative leadership would accept'. See *The Times*, 28 March 1977. Throughout the devolution debate powerful Conservative supporters, notably the CBI, continually emphasised the economic unity of the United Kingdom. The Scottish CBI was particularly firm in its opposition to devolution. These and similar pressures provide an important backcloth to the debate both in the country and in Parliament.

GORDON SMITH

9   *The reintegration of the state in Western Europe*

THE STATE AND THE CONTEXT OF CHANGE

There is in Europe a pervading mood of political change. It is a feeling that cuts across old party loyalties and involves a widespread disposition to accept alterations in the political ordering of society. In contrast to the dislocation brought about by violent upheaval, the changes represent a process of cumulative adjustment, secured on the basis of consent. Nevertheless, the direction to be taken appears radical enough, and the implication of a fundamental alteration exists whether we actively will it or not.

An examination of specific problems – such as the impact of regional movements in Britain or the consequences for government and administration of membership of the European Community – requires a close empirical argument. But the attempt to link the trends which may be apparent and to treat them as forming an overall pattern is a much more speculative exercise. Despite the pitfalls that obviously exist, there is a case for looking at Western Europe as a whole, making generalisations, and tracing connections which may otherwise be neglected. The question immediately arises: what perspective can best accommodate all the diverse indications of political change?

Ultimately the various contemporary pressures can be related to the powers and functions of the state. The significance of national political institutions, the distribution of popular loyalties, the location of the centres of decision-making – these are all matters which bear closely on the attributes of the state. In the prevailing climate of reappraisal it is the traditional view of the state which appears to be at risk, threatened by forces from different directions: centrifugal ones acting from within and centripetal ones from without. At the present time the possibility of an 'inner' fragmentation of the state corresponds to the extreme demands for regional autonomy, whilst the pressure to find an external cohesion – within Western Europe – reflects a more gradual process of adjustment.[1]

What is true of both types of influence is that they have received an impetus arising from the weaknesses first displayed by the state: the pressures for change should be regarded as a consequence rather than as a cause of those weaknesses. For this reason it is preferable to examine the implications of political change from the viewpoint of the contemporary state, and thus to begin by examining the reasons for its apparent vulnerability. In particular, the question is raised: why are the states of Western Europe especially affected?

Three types of general explanation can be advanced, all with a direct application to Western Europe: the nature of the regimes in these states, their external competence, and their internal responsibilities. The West European states are mainly alike in being based on the principles of liberal democracy, and there is a good case for arguing that precisely in this type of political system the state is most liable to become externally inadequate and internally overextended. There is no need to paint a dark picture of 'the inadequate and overextended liberal state': other types of political system have their own problems in coping with the stress of change, and in the end they may respond less constructively.

A salient feature of the liberal democracies is that their political institutions are geared to the relatively free expression of choice and to the open voicing of dissent. It follows that – in an immediate sense, at least – they are sensitive to the structural problems of their societies, susceptible to demands for change, and are adaptable to a degree impossible for authoritarian and illiberal systems. But the conflict and competition inherent in liberal politics, although it makes for a greater surface turbulence, need not mean a larger risk of instability than for non-liberal states. Two major tests of the adaptability and stability of liberal systems are contained in the charges of 'inadequacy' and 'overextension' levelled against them. We ought to consider first these sources of weakness before making an examination of possible modifications to the traditional state.

SYMPTOMS OF INADEQUACY

A clarification of the concept of 'inadequacy' is essential – for it presupposes agreed criteria for adequacy. The historical states of Europe could be described as 'adequate' in the sense that individually each was able to present a cohesive front to the outside world. This judgement is unaffected by the fact that some failed in practice: the point is that they acted, and were treated, according to their pretensions. The adequacy of the state in this external context was based on three leading claims: the state was the prime unit of physical security, the guarantor of economic autonomy, and the expression of national solidarity. In contrast, the inadequate state is quite unable to make these claims.

Most telling in the present era is the confessed inability of the West European states to provide for their own physical security – at least in respect of perceived and likely threats to their existence. Their armed forces individually are suited more to a policing function or to conducting residual colonial-type adventures. For the citizens of these states, fears of foreign domination have receded, and the idea of physical security from an external enemy has become quite remote – relegated perhaps to the vague comfort of a NATO exercise held somewhere off Spitzbergen.

Inadequacy of the West European states in the external economic sphere is almost as apparent, for they are all especially open to the demands of advanced industrial society and the requirements of developed capitalist systems. The interdependence of markets and currencies, the needs of production and the means of its financing – these factors help to enforce the rules of capitalist internationalism, and the conditions are most applicable to countries – such as those of Western Europe – with limited resources and restricted internal markets. As a result of these pressures, the competences and even the frontiers of the state in Western Europe have become restrictive and outmoded. One reaction to the state's inability to provide a suitable framework for economic activity is to promote its integration within a larger, more rational economic unit. The European Community is a response to economic inadequacy.

Without a continual reinforcement of the state's presence in its 'physical' and economic capacities, it loses two of its important historical functions. In so far as the expression of national attachment is derived from and depends on the performance of the state in these directions, then its decline as the highest symbol of unity is to be expected. Western Europe was the original seedbed of the national idea, and its fulfilment was accomplished by applying the formula of 'the nation state'. The powerful dynamic of this appeal has declined, and the specific identification of state and nation no longer carries a strong conviction. Although the extent of the decline may be disputed, and it is anyway an uneven process, the tendency seems indisputable.[2]

Applying the label of inadequacy to a state does not mean that it will be unable to survive. Thus there is no reason why the inadequate state should not rely on multilateral defence arrangements – although it has to avoid becoming a mere client of a dominant power. It may even cease to control its economic destiny – but it has to stop short of being totally dominated by foreign interests and multinational firms. The inadequate state may allow its citizens to develop a spirit of gentle cosmopolitanism – as long as they do not begin to cast around for new loyalties.

Nor is it the case that inadequacy necessarily entails redundancy, for in other ways the state may continue to prove successful; its deficiences in failing to present a credible external front may be more than offset by its internal achievements. If, however, in addition to a modest external showing, the state piles on a failure to meet the demands originating from within, then the prospect of a lingering impotence may actually loom.

THE LOGIC OF OVEREXTENSION

Inability to satisfy demands emanating from society is a typical feature of the overextended state. Increasingly – it can be argued – this trait is applicable to the liberal democracies of Western Europe. The state may appear to 'fail' not because it has been unwilling to entertain the wide variety of claims made upon it, but simply because it could be overwhelmed by them.[3] Indeed, there is a central paradox of failure: that feelings of disillusion and thwarted expectation should be so rife in an age during which the state has become almost hypersensitive to the expressed needs of society.

Contradiction between intention and outcome is partly explained by the nature of the commitments the state has shouldered – especially the ones with an economic content and including those in the broad band of the 'welfare function'. There are two commonplace effects which result from the aggregation of commitments to economic intervention and the provision of social welfare. Firstly, such undertakings tend to be open-ended in the sense that no obvious limit can be set on the share of resources to be absorbed under any one head of activity. A second well known consequence is that expectations continually outrun performance: demands escalate as standards of provision rise and, in the process of adjusting between competing claims, certain regions, sectors or groups become relatively underprivileged. At the same time, the reallocative nature of much government intervention arouses all kinds of expectation – negative and positive – in the redistribution of the community's wealth. The 'failure' of the state consists in its inability to satisfy all social claims, and in trying to appease a wide variety of social interests governments may sacrifice the secure base of loyalty to be found in their relationship to particular social classes. This fragmentation need not lead to a crisis of legitimacy, but it does mean that successive governments are forced to rely on wide alliances to maintain their authority, which is frequently endangered by shifting electoral support.[4]

Rapid and continuing economic growth is a palliative rather than a cure for the weakness of government. During times of economic expansion extensions of state activity can best be assumed and financed, but discontent often arises through the social dislocation accompanying an economic upsurge. In the harsher climate of an economic downturn, the state is unable simply to shrug off its additional responsibilities. The stark option of permanently reducing the load on the state is not a realistic way out of the predicament. Sharp halts have to be called, but, other than on a temporary basis, a large reduction would require the rigid ordering of an authoritarian state and would destroy the essentials of a liberal system.

This portrayal of the 'motor' of overextension is crude and necessarily abbreviated, but it is sufficient to highlight the problems of the liberal, interventionist state. They become acute in pluralist systems because of the difficulty of devising mechanisms to scale down the level of demands on the state. The 'automatic' regulator supplied by market forces can be used only sparingly, since the growth of state intervention has been dictated by a desire to counteract the effects of those forces.

An additional handicap is presented by the party system of a liberal democracy. Party competition ensures that the bids made to secure a democratic majority will shun any drastic reorientation, and the parties have to pay regard to the interests of the increasing number of people who directly or indirectly become the beneficiaries of the state's involvement. Regardless therefore of the changing party complexion of governments, the state is positioned on a rail of expanding responsibility.

To escape from this commitment would require a strategy of extrication based on a thoroughgoing philosophy of anti-statism. But this way out of the liberal state's embarrassment is not easily taken, because the political connotations of a determined anti-statist view have proved to be electorally unacceptable. A hankering for a return to the *laisser-faire* state of 'individual freedom' is associated with irresponsible right-wing views or treated as a hopeless escapism. The opposite solution of 'socialism without the state' has been equally unsuccessful, linked as the idea often is with the anarchical fringe of politics and with a preference for 'direct action' over parliamentary and constitutional forms.

Whether the slogans of the political extremes will continue to be unacceptable is another matter, but it is relevant that the parties of moderation – the ones which so far have sustained liberal democracy – have failed to generate new lines of political argument. In particular, they have been unable to promote alternatives to their own assumptions and practice – that the state is the best, even the sole, means of ensuring collective social progress.

In adding together the weaknesses of the modern liberal state, a sense of impending calamity may prevail, but the conditions for the actual disintegration of any of the stable – or even the less stable – democracies of Western Europe seem unlikely to be met: a sudden abdication of authority or its violent overthrow, the wholesale abandonment of existing political institutions, the fragmentation of a state's territory. A state also has to be considered as an entity of self-regarding interest, concerned to secure its own survival as a state. Faced with the pressures of integration, those in Western Europe are all intent to make realistic bargains and ward off threats to their existence; in adapting to new circumstances they are unlikely to fritter away the valued assets of state identity.

Rather than predict a sudden transformation or suppose that the individual states of Western Europe will gradually 'wither away', it is more reasonable to assume that they will learn to live with their overextension and inadequacy. The traditional state is still the major point of reference for political organisation and its accomplishments are too important to be discarded. Nevertheless, within the shell of its received form a number of changes are evident which point to a substantial redefinition of the state's functions.

A WORKING DEFINITION OF THE STATE

In order to show the direction of a possible evolution, it is first necessary to establish a definition of the state which is relevant to contemporary problems. Once that has been done, it will be easier to see how current – and often disparate – developments in Western

Europe can be related to changes in the structure and functions of the state – or what will later be referred to as its 'reintegration'.

The 'working definition' employed here involves some simplification and a neglect of attributes which are of importance in other contexts. But in stripping 'the state' down to a few, relevant essentials, we can best appreciate current developments on a comparative basis. There are substantial variations within Western Europe at the present time: some states seem better placed to adjust to their inadequacy or else show fewer signs of overextension. A form of definition is required that is sufficiently wide to bring out these differences.

Central to the following formulation is the idea of the state as a 'unifying apex' – a summit which unites two distinctive realms of politics: the 'territorial' and 'functional' dimensions. In treating the state as a kind of apex, we can further define it as *the authoritative point of intersection for political territory and for the functional arrangements of a society*. The two elements stand in their own right and are only brought together by the state. For 'a state' to exist at all – on this definition – there has to be an irreducible minimum of final authority over both: a state which either failed to exercise a control over territory or was unable to assume a general responsibility for the political ordering of a society would hardly qualify as a state.

As far as the state is concerned, neither territory nor function can exist in isolation. However, it is possible to examine the two 'axes' separately; by so doing it is easier to examine the major forms of political change and to see how the idea of reintegration can be applied to the states of Western Europe. Whilst the basis of the definition in terms of an 'authoritative point of intersection' has to be retained, the scope for reintegration is considerable along each of the two axes.

THE SIGNIFICANCE OF POLITICAL TERRITORY

Quite suddenly, it appears, many West European countries have been affected by the reactivation of the principle of political territory. As far as Europe was concerned, the matter seemed once to have been settled in the realisation of the nation-state. Yet although their external frontiers are now secure, there has been a steep increase in forms of territorial movement originating within the states, and these have given a sharp new cutting edge to domestic politics.[5]

A spectrum of territorial claims is represented by the various demands for local autonomy. Although only separatist movements carry a direct threat to a state's integrity, they all imply at least a restructuring of authority – whether in the form of federalism, 'home rule', or a measure of decentralisation, possibly by regional devolution. However, the content of restructuring is less important here than is the wide incidence of territorial discontent which in the first place gives rise to demands for change.

One of the most powerful movements which may beset the contemporary state is based on what may be termed a 'sub-state' nationalism. These movements – rooted in ethnic, cultural, or linguistic affinities – are evidence of a widespread rejection of the simple equation of nation and state. Had this type of protest been the only one to occur, then it would be fair to conclude that only 'old identities' were involved which had been swamped or suppressed in the rise of the nation-state. But strung along the territorial axis all kinds of localist claims signify an unrest, and often it is impossible to say that they are based on ethnic or related loyalties. Even where a recognised sub-state nationalism is concerned, the specific cause of its activation may have little to do with its original appeal.

A feature of localist movements is a common perception of grievances – often a communality of economic interest – which crystallises in opposition to the policies imposed by the centralised state. Frequently it is the regions which are remote from the metropolitan centres that first show a growing local awareness and voice a protest based on territorial interest. A 'revolt of the periphery' is a typical outcome when the clustering of economic and social issues leads to a confrontation with the authority of the centralised state.[6]

A special example of peripheral behaviour can be seen in the 'frontier regions' of Western Europe.[7] Any one frontier region may be regarded as a partial unification of the peripheries of two or more adjoining states, and the 'unification' implies a common perception of problems within the frontier region – regardless of the actual state boundaries. Their artificiality is most apparent where, for reasons of employment, there are large temporary flows of people from one country to another. All kinds of issue – economic, planning, and environmental – give the basis for a transnational consciousness and interest; in certain circumstances it may appear as a threat to the solidarity of the parent states.

The case of the frontier regions of Western Europe shows the possible causal connection between a decline of national identity and the rise of territorial politics. The example of the frontier regions is all the more important because there is scarcely any question of a *pre-existing* consciousness holding a latent challenge to the state. Thus the growth of localist loyalties can be related to a decline in the significance of the state, and the decline – with special relevance for the frontier regions – may be seen as a result of the decreasing importance of the state as the guarantor of territory and the diminished need, within Western Europe, for the state to provide physical security against an aggressor. Outside of Europe, many countries have not had the intense pressure of keeping a sharp watch on their frontiers, but the states of Western Europe largely grew up with this preoccupation. As the tensions have eased, there has been a release in other directions.

More generally, it may be preferable to regard the territorial dimension as essentially passive – in the nature of a 'receptacle' to be filled by active political elements. But this passivity can be quickly transformed: in providing a focus for several issues of an economic or social character, the territorial movement can become a factor in its own right and one which imposes an additional constraint – a framework within which a resolution of the issues has to be found. Political territory becomes a symbol of unity and thereby subsumes demands and discontents which might otherwise be given only a diffuse expression.

With the aim of providing an orderly and 'visible' outlet for social pressures – in preference to facing random and disruptive expressions of grievance – advice on the reform of the modern state could well include extensive measures of decentralisation, deliberately implemented and in advance of any marked demand. By such timely action it is possible that the intensity of demands made directly on the state would be reduced; in effect the argument is that a local autonomy which develops as a part of the existing institutional structure differs considerably from a situation which the local autonomy develops as a force against the state.

Yet there are reservations to be made about recommendations for a 'model' decentralised state. Whatever degree of refinement shown in the measures of devolution, there is no certainty that the lines of division will prove suitable – they may be irrelevant to problems arising later. There is little point in dismantling an efficient, centralised state only to find that the pressing problems of a society do not lend themselves to a territorial resolution after all. Questions affecting the whole economy or even just particular sectors involve decisions which require firm direction from a central government and policies which cut right across territorial subdivisions. It is this 'national' concern – with many aspects besides the purely economic ones – that brings us to consider the state from the second leading perspective, its functional dimension.

CORPORATISM AND THE FUNCTIONAL AXIS

It is clear that the idea of functionality bears no definite or necessary relationship to political territory, save in their final coincidence at the level of the state. As a result it is possible to consider them in isolation, but this helpful simplification still leaves the problem of the variety of constructions that can be placed on the expression 'functional arrangements' – the political ordering of society in all non-territorial aspects. There would be little point in even trying to outline all the possibilities, but there are two broad accounts which are particularly relevant to Western Europe: the conventional model of pluralism and the increasingly fashionable 'corporate' theories.

The two accounts are alike in that they both refer to substantially similar types of society: ones with an economic system based on a market economy and having a significant section in private ownership. They also relate to societies whose political systems are founded on the tenets of liberal democracy. They differ most sharply in their evaluation of the role taken by the state.

Two cardinal requirements of pluralist theory should be emphasised. Firstly, pluralism requires that a degree of competitive or co-operative equality exists for all social groups and organised interests. Secondly, a pluralist society can only be maintained if the power of the state is limited – in the degree of its intervention in society and in its ability to rise above all other social organisations.[8]

We are not so much concerned here with the pure theory of pluralism, for it is bound to be an idealised version of reality. But for the theory to allow a convincing description of the structure of West European states it has to be substantially accurate in a wide application – to include the economic as well as political aspects of society. Specific questions have to be asked. What are the furthermost limits to be ascribed to the 'restricted' state? At what point does 'competitive equality' cease to be a true account of reality? Once certain limits have been passed, there are strong arguments in favour of dropping a pluralist model which may have become misleading and substituting one that gives a better weight to the evidence of social imbalance and state involvement.

The alternative theory of corporatism certainly redresses the balance. At one time the concept appeared to have become irredeemably associated with Fascist ideology; as a result 'corporate society' is frequently understood to be the complete antithesis of the pluralist order – especially in the idea of the unification of state and society and their fusion into an organic whole. But the revival of interest in corporatism in recent years has little connection with the Fascist interpretation; it is rather an attempt to describe the present functioning of society and show the logic of its development.[9] As such, corporatism is best treated as a radical amendment to pluralism rather than as a complete alternative.

There are, however, a number of ways in which the supposed corporate structure of society can be depicted. One version places an emphasis on the existence of powerful 'corporations' which appear to have won a leading and independent place in society.[10] Another rendering concentrates on the dominant role of the state, taken by virtue of its increasing social and economic responsibilities. But the difference of emphasis does not make the two approaches incompatible, since it is rather a question of the weight of influence, and there are common elements as well: both stress the 'economic' base of corporatism and both present a challenge to the orthodox pluralist order, especially to the importance of parliamentary institutions for decision-making. To distinguish the two types, one may be called 'state corporatism' and the other a form of 'societal' or 'liberal' corporatism.[11]

A significant feature of state corporatism is the leading position assumed by the state in relation to the economy. Whilst the framework of the market and private enterprise system is preserved, the state changes from being the external regulator and supporter of the private sector to a position of effectively controlling a range of decisions that were formerly taken by the firm. The principle of private ownership is maintained, but increasingly firms become dependent on the state for their continued survival, not just their well-being.[12]

Although this development may be associated with a deliberate programme of socialisation, the current manifestations of state corporatism do not spring from a conscious doctrine; they are best regarded as a pragmatic response to economic problems. All the same, there are important values and priorities concealed in the corporatist drift, and the underlying values of collectivism and 'national purpose' may take precedence over those which typify a pluralist system.

Societal or liberal corporatism avoids the close association with state power, but at the expense of raising important economic 'corporations' to a position of great influence – the state has to co-operate and bargain with them. The autonomous corporations differ from 'normal' interest groups in two ways. Firstly, the corporations become part of the institutional structure of decision-making; their 'incorporation' implies a special recognition accorded by the state. Secondly, their position and power are such that they are brought to work with one another, not just with the government.[13] The breadth of co-operation forces them to accept a responsibility for the determination of public policy.

There is no particular need to choose between these two versions of corporatism, for to some extent they will exist side by side. One country may lean towards the statist type and another towards societal corporatism. But for either form a debate on 'where the power really lies' is not easily settled. Even if the state is apparently able to co-opt, use, and finally control social interests, its influence may still run to the benefit of powerful corporate groups. Conversely 'liberal corporatism' could not exist without the backing of the state, for the corporations depend on its partnership and on the institutional structure which the state alone can provide.

Two features are evident in corporatism, whatever judgement is made about its 'true' nature: one is the leading role taken by the state – which holds good even for societal corporatism – and the other is the decline in importance of representative institutions based on political competition.[14] Few people will actually welcome the pervasive influence of the state, and the habits of corporatism can erode pluralist politics: co-optation is usually preferred to competition.[15] At most a form of 'institutionalised pluralism' will result, with the plural elements preserved in the interstices of the corporate state.

The ubiquitous state need not be an omnipotent one as well. The entanglement of the state with society is a source of weakness as well as of strength: the co-operation required of the corporate partners ensures that compromise has to be the basis of policy. Moreover, a leading cause for the shift to corporatism is the overextension of the state – the inability to satisfy all the demands made upon it – and corporatism is an indication of the state's vulnerability just as much as it is of power.

A CONTRAST IN ADAPTATION

Some states are better able to adapt to changing circumstances than are others. In Western Europe, Britain and West Germany provide a good illustration of the range, although they are not necessarily polar types. They are sufficiently similar in important respects – in the practice of liberal democracy, in size and population, and economic development – to make a comparison realistic.

Britain has had the benefit of a continuous historical tradition and a gradual evolution of her political institutions, whilst the West German state is a relative upstart. The Federal Republic came into being only in 1949, and her political institutions were then entirely untested. The new Germany had to be built without the foundation of tradition, for the experience of the Nazi dictatorship and the utter collapse of the German state in 1945 together marked a severance from past history. Moreover the fragmentation of the Reich had the consequence for the two states which were later established that neither represented the whole German nation.

In taking account of these inauspicious beginnings, it is remarkable that the Federal Republic should have been able to cope so well with the changed situation of Germany. By contrast Britain has shown signs of evident political strain and is still in the throes of painful adjustment.[16] The change in Britain's status from being a victorious world power in 1945 to being only a modest European one now is an indication of the extent of the adaptation needed, and particularly difficult since the loss of status occurred without any immediately obvious cause. Britain's external weakness and her continuing economic malaise have had a number of repercussions. In particular, the disarray of the party system, in part directly caused by demands for regional autonomy, is symptomatic of the whole troubled political system.

With none of Britain's inherited advantages, Western Germany has much more readily accommodated to altered conditions. In fact the Federal Republic represents an almost exemplary case of the inadequate state, and indeed the republic was founded on that basis – deliberately set up in a position of external dependency. Although scarcely a puppet state, the Federal Republic was created by the Western allies and depended absolutely on the guarantees of the

NATO alliance. As the protégé of those powers, there was no question of the Federal Republic being able to pursue an independent foreign policy. These origins coloured her subsequent political development. In a similar fashion Western Germany was at the outset economically inadequate as well; her economic recovery derived from foreign aid and investment, and government policies have been based on the need to participate in wide economic groupings. Thus the Federal Republic has probably been the mainstay of the EEC since its inception.

These are two of the hallmarks of the inadequate state; a third condition relates to the inability of a state to make a strong 'national' appeal. In this respect the German development was more gradual, for at first the Federal Republic laid claim to represent the entire German nation as the sole legitimate successor to the former Reich. This pretension long remained a cornerstone of West German policy, but as a result of Brandt's *Ostpolitik* and especially following the conclusion of the Basic Treaty with the German Democratic Republic in 1972, the 'national claim' lost substantial meaning. Instead it appears that West Germany has developed a more limited 'state consciousness' – a modest loyalty, but most fitting for the inadequate state.[17]

Without the bond of a powerful national appeal, it might be expected that West Germany would suffer from the divisive effects of centrifugal forces, but territorial movements have been notably absent. Part of the explanation for the cohesion lies in the federal nature of the republic. Two points of comment are relevant. One is that the West German system accords precisely with an argument advanced earlier: a decentralised structure introduced in advance of active pressure serves to rob potentially disintegrative movements of a territorial nexus. The second comment is that federal systems are often uncritically regarded as a means of dividing power, but the 'obverse' is also true: a sensible territorial dispersion of authority can strengthen the integrative ability of the state.[18]

With the exception of Bavaria and the Hanseatic states, the *Länder* of the Federal Republic lack historical justification. In this sense the federal system is 'artificial'; it was devised as a barrier against undue centralisation, with the peril of totalitarian rule still fresh in mind. German federalism is also 'weak' in character; unlike the customary version of federalism as consisting of a sharp demarcation between central and state powers – the so-called 'co-ordinate' type – the West German system depends for its effectiveness on the high degree of co-operation enforced on the federal authorities and the *Länder*. The close working relationship is maintained by a dispersion of executive authority: the *Länder* act as the administrative agents of the federation, and in so doing they achieve a substantial parity in many respects, at least an enhanced bargaining capacity.[19] The administrative form of federalism reaches its effect through a 'horizontal' division of powers, as opposed to the 'vertical' split according to the conventional model. Possibly the combination of a 'passive' decentralisation with an emphasis on co-operation between the units has – fortuitously – helped West Germany avoid territorial discontents.

Signs of innovative capacity have been absent in Britain, and until the pressures of regional assertion became too acute to ignore the political structure remained entirely static. When the threat reached the level of the party system, endangering the hegemony of the Conservative and Labour parties, belated consideration was given to the devolution of power. Even so, the proposals concerned Scotland and Wales only, the immediate cause of the disruption in the party system, and failed to take the opportunity of making a radical reappraisal for the whole country. A complication exists in the imbalance favouring England within the United Kingdom; there is a parallel with Germany at the time when Prussia dominated the Reich. The parallel might be extended: only after the destruction of the Prussian state was it possible to evolve a balanced territorial structure in Germany. The likeness may be inexact, but the United Kingdom still has to resolve the problem of a dominant 'English rule', the legitimacy of which is increasingly questioned.

Besides grappling with territorial difficulties, Britain has also had to come to terms with external inadequacy. Whilst the Federal Republic reached a maturity in this condition, for Britain the realisation has been a long-drawn-out process. Her entry to the European Community was a partial admission, and the final seal was placed by the result of the referendum held in 1975. Until then the myth could be perpetuated that, in some way or other, Britain could 'go it alone', the residual hubris of a once-powerful nation state.

An extended comparison of the fortunes of Britain and West Germany would also have to take account of other differences in their political systems. These are best related to the broad 'functional' dimension, and in particular to the distinction made between state and societal corporatism. Without attempting to push either country completely into one of the two categories, it is of use to relate Britain and Germany to the alternative forms.

To say that Britain follows the line of state corporatism and that West Germany accords more with a societal type appears to be at odds with their previous historical experience. But really there is no contradiction involved: pluralism is not a bar to the development of state corporatism, and the legacy of a 'strong' state – particularly applying to Germany – is compatible with societal corporatism; for both there is even a necessary connection. The growth of an unbridled pluralism makes it inevitable that the state should become heaped with responsibilities; by default it is the only 'responsible' authority. In a contrary fashion, there has to be a tradition of the state's leading influence on society for societal corporatism to grow; in this way the exercise of a public responsibility will be enforced on the corporate interests.[20]

Social pluralism has become pronounced in Britain partly as a result of the recent decline in the authority of the conservative value system which once held together and modified the pluralist order; its decay has been accompanied by a political and social fragmentation. The burdens on the state have multiplied, and the direct pressures of overextension are felt sharply perhaps because there is an absence of a corporate 'insulation'. In Germany, it may be admissible to speak of a 'corporate pluralism' which draws attention to the fact that the public function of corporate interests had long been recognised.[21] Their participation acts in complement to the state rather than in competition, and the consequence is that the authority of the state is diffused rather than weakened.

An interpretation along corporatist lines shows that a movement away from pluralism in Western Europe can take different paths. The German development is distinguished by its reference to pre-existing social forms. Preferable as the balance may be to an undiluted state corporatism, the idea of a partnership between the corporations and the state entails a measure of inertia in the political system. The West German consensus is rooted in the principle of the 'social market economy' to which all economic interests – and governments – have to conform.[22] The restriction is not burdensome as long as the performance of the market economy can be maintained, but the partnership could inhibit policital initiative and leadership if conditions were to change fundamentally.[23] But does state corporatism really allow any greater flexibility? A party coming to power is faced with a formidable administrative apparatus and inherits long-term commitments which have to be met. The constraints of party competition, in a liberal democracy, also weaken the ability of an incoming government to impose a new direction.

The abundance of contrasts between Britain and West Germany makes it difficult to isolate any one factor as particularly significant. Taken together, they indicate how states can vary in adaptive capacity. In the West German example, various factors point in the same direction: the origins of her statehood, her dependent international position, certain constitutional considerations, the nuances of state–society relationships. Whether the Federal Republic can be treated as a prototype for other states depends on the allowance that has to be made for her special circumstances. However, if there is a common trend within Western Europe, then perhaps supporting evidence should be sought by looking at those states which have shown the greatest adaptability.

THE STATE AND EUROPEAN INTEGRATION

The argument for a 'common trend' is strengthened by the similar position of the West European states facing the impact of European integration. This especially applies to the effect of membership of the European Community, with the possible result that the national differences will be eventually overridden. Whilst 'integration' can be defined in various ways, the European form was conceived as an open-ended commitment to which different labels could be applied at successive stages, depending on the kind of policies agreed – economic, political or legal – with radical implications for the powers of the individual states. In general terms, the development of the European Community suggests a closer relationship of member states over a steadily increasing number of areas, but the obligations to the 'Community' are much more exacting in the long run than those of simple trade or defence agreements.

The flexible form of integration adopted makes it impossible to predict how the Community will finally shape or how the constituent states will be ultimately affected. There is no shortage of competing versions: a federal Europe, a 'functional' Europe, a 'Europe of States', or possibly an indefinite era of the European states acting 'in concertation'.[24] But there is little reason to prefer one to another as a model for the eventual outcome; at the present intermediate stage of evolution there are some influences which undermine the position of the states and others which act as a reinforcement.

Member states are weakened as a natural consequence of the creation of supranational authorities which serve the Community as a whole, and the same diminution of state power occurs when members accept policies which thereafter place permanent constraints on their actions. The effect of this functional mode of integration adopted by the Community is that, as the number of commitments increases, the states lose their power of unilateral action – in effect, their sovereignty – even though in a legal and formal sense they remain sovereign states.

This central drive of integration, the functional impetus, has slackened considerably, and there is an apparent preference on the part of the member states to develop policies in the form of understandings *between* governments rather than fashioning formal planks of integration. Seen in this light, the framework of the Community is used more as a means to articulate national interests than as a way leading to the supersession of the state. These reservations apply to specific aspects of the Community: for example, the permanent Commission failed to develop as an embryonic government, and institutional reforms have made little headway. It is too early to judge how the long-delayed direct elections to the European Parliament may affect the balance, but there is no imperative reason to suppose that a new 'European' party system will emerge to challenge the voices of the individual states in the Council of Ministers.

It is also the case that the states are given an enhanced importance by virtue of their membership. What they lose in individual 'sovereignty', they gain in collective strength and influence. They are encouraged, and sometimes dragged, into formulating new policies; the resulting commitments have to be implemented in their own countries, and in this respect the states are the competent executive authorities. It is unlikely that even a Europe much more integrated than at present could function without the infrastructure of the individual states: they remain the key intermediaries.

Reinforcement takes place in other ways as well. Despite the differences between them – in size, wealth, political stability, and social cohesion – the Community puts all the member states behind a common protective shield; in the first instance it is a form of economic protection which helps to ensure the viability of even the weakest countries. But the protection afforded also works in another way: although there is a margin of toleration, a degree of political conformity is implied for the members, just as it is required of aspiring candidates. The comfort offered by the Community is that of a rather civilised Procrustean bed.

There are thus diverse answers to be given to questions concerning the future of the states inside the European Community.[25] A further uncertainty is presented by the growing imbalance of economic strength as between the members. This disparity will become even more evident if the Community expands to include countries – Greece, Portugal and Spain – with weaker economies. The formal equality and weighted balance provided by Community institutions may be insufficient to prevent political leadership, even a virtual hegemony, being exercised by one or two states, or at least the emergence of opposing coalitions. The unity brought by integration could thus be combined with a fragmentation and an increasing divergence of interest within the Community system.

It is important, therefore, to avoid overemphasising the role of the European Community at the cost of neglecting the basic relationships between the states. As long as no authoritative and general power acting from the 'centre' exists over the states – the requirement of full political integration – the institutions and resources of the Community will continue to fulfil a limited ameliorative and adjustive function.

The flux may not persist, but it is too early to be sure whether European integration has yet proceeded far enough to affect the nature of the states decisively. There may, however, be a permanence in the dual and contrary effect already noticeable: a simultaneous erosion and reinforcement of a state's position. A conclusion along these lines shows that it is incorrect one-sidedly to assume that the West European state will become either 'weaker' or 'stronger' as a result of integration. It may be more satisfactory to view the process in the wider context of the development of the state, that is, as related to its 'reintegration'.

STATES OF A NEW TYPE?

As we have seen from the experience of Britain and West Germany, a range of factors affects the response of a state to its changing circumstances. We should not expect a stereotype to emerge, but the states of Western Europe face an integrative pull which puts them in a common mould. Their reputation for political stability and the inherent powers of adaptation in the liberal democratic systems makes it likely that changes will come about in the course of a prolonged and complex process of readjustment. Nonetheless, over a long period of time it may be desirable to speak of a redefinition of the state's functions.

In order to draw the various threads of the preceding discussion together, it is useful to indicate the major relationships in summary form, as shown in the diagram. The three 'responses' of the state – its corporate involvement, territorial diffusion, and wider integration – add up to a composite picture of a reintegrated state, on the assumption that all three tendencies are permanent. The path taken in the original formation of the nation state can be termed the stage of primary integration,[26] whilst a future evolution – the secondary stage of reintegration – involves a reordering of the state's characteristics to allow for internal and external changes which were not formerly in evidence.

Influences on the contemporary State

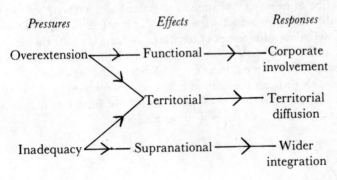

Pressures	*Effects*	*Responses*
Overextension	Functional	Corporate involvement
	Territorial	Territorial diffusion
Inadequacy	Supranational	Wider integration

Modern European states generally arose by advancing the cause of national integration, and to win the coveted badge of the 'nation state' they had to show that they exercised a complete control over national territory and to prove themselves externally adequate. Some states, it is true, were more concerned than others with the intimate regulation of society, but the nature of earlier European development – especially the limited extent to which there was a popular participation – precluded the type of overextension which is now evident.

In contrast to the traditional state, the reintegrated one loses the burden of adequacy and shoulders that of overextension. It combines the feature of a possibly pre-modern territorial diffusion with an apparent omnipresence of the state. To this compound one has to add the effect of a wider integration which, among other results, erodes the close association of the state with its historical frontiers. However we care to describe the new type of state, it is evidently different from that hitherto representative of the modern era in Europe.

It is helpful at this point to return to the definition of the state suggested earlier. The vital quality of the state was said to be its function of providing a 'unifying apex' for society: a failure in this respect would imply its dissolution. What is apparent in the movement towards reintegration is that there is an increasing disjunction between the two components of territory and function and that the unifying capacity of the state could be stretched to the limit. But it is important to keep a sense of historical perspective: the perils of reintegration are rather less than those that had to be faced in the course of primary integration.

There are too many unknown factors for it to be possible to describe a 'new type' of state. The outcome could well be a stable equilibrium in which the wide competences of the state counterbalance the forces of territorial diffusion, whilst they in turn counteract the political effects of modern corporatism. Such forecasts may turn out to be wrong. Even so, the benefit of taking an approach through the idea of reintegration remains: we can avoid treating 'the state' as one of the 'constants' of European history and instead regard it as a dependent variable.

NOTES

1   See Ghita Ionescu, *Centripetal Politics: Government and the New Centres of Power*, Hart-Davies MacGibbon, 1975. He deals with the corporate, territorial, and supranational influences which are the concern of this chapter.

2   In the present context the argument is only that there is a divorce between 'national' feelings and the state. The wider question of a decline in nationalism in Europe is likely to remain unresolved – because the concept of nationalism is itself vague: 'It does not imply a precise reference to a phenomenon in the real world.' (Godfried van den Bergh, 'Contemporary Nationalism in the Western World, *Daedalus*, vol. 95, No. 3.)

3 Additionally, 'failure' may arise because of 'the sacrifice in political values found necessary to fulfil these new obligations'. (James Cornford, in *The Failure of the State*, Croom Helm, 1975, p. 8.)

4 The problem of the parties facing 'shifting electoral support' relates to the phenomenon of 'the politics of diffusion'. See G. Smith, 'Social movements and party systems in Western Europe', in M. Kolinsky and W. Paterson (eds), *Social and Political Movements in Western Europe*, Croom Helm, 1976.

5 See George G. Hoffman, *Regional Policies and Regional Consciousness in Europe's Multinational Societies*, IPSA Congress, August 1976.

6 'Revolt' need not result in violent confrontation; 'the revolt of the periphery' in Norway refers to the referendum rejection of EEC membership in 1972 and the fragmentation of the party system.

7 For a discussion of the significance of the frontier regions see Malcolm Anderson, 'Frontier regions in Europe', in B. Chapman and A. Potter (eds), *W.J.M.M. – Political Questions*, Manchester University Press, 1974.

8 The term 'pluralism' has various meanings. See David Nicholls, *Three Varieties of Pluralism*, Macmillan, 1974. The usage here corresponds to 'English political pluralism' as related by Nicholls.

9 In particular see P. C. Schmitter, 'Still the century of corporatism?', in F. B. Pike and T. Stritch, *The New Corporatism*, Notre Dame, 1974.

10 The 'corporation' which relates to corporatism is an organised body, with a recognised public status, representing a *segment* of society. It thus approximates to a form of 'estate', not to the American business 'corporation'.

11 The distinction between state and societal corporatism follows that made by Schmitter. But he makes a sharper break than seems necessary for Western Europe in arguing that the transfer from state to societal corporatism occurs through a degeneration of state corporatism and a strong pluralist reversion. Gerhard Lehmbruch uses the expression 'liberal corporatism' in a similar sense to the societal form: *Liberal Corporatism and Party Government*, IPSA Congress, August 1976.

12 This rendering of state corporatism is based on Jack Winkler's version: 'Corporatism is defined by one particularly important qualitative change, the shift from a supportive to a directive role for the state in the economy'. He cites the Planning Agreements introduced by the British Labour government as confirming the directive principle. (J. Winkler, *Corporatism*, Centre for Environmental Studies, February 1976.)

13 This distinction between corporations and interest groups is made by Lehmbruch.

14 It is possible to take a rosier view of the compatibility of corporatism with parliamentary institutions. Thus Lehmbruch maintains that corporatism 'has entered into a sort of symbiosis with the party system which may take varying forms . . . [It] has not so much superseded but rather supplemented parliamentary government . . . [and] filled a functional gap left by parties and parliament.'

15 In connection with 'co-optation' as a mode of governing see M. O. Heisler (ed.), *Politics in Europe*, David McKay, 1974. His 'European polity model' accords with societal corporatism in many respects.

16 Britain's current stresses are examined in Ionescu's *Centripetal Politics*.

17 The conclusions reached by Gebhard Schweigler, *National Consciousness in Divided Germany*, Saxon House, 1975, point to a West German 'state-consciousness' as opposed to a national one.

18 Confirmation of the 'model' view of decentralisation as an integrative force is seen in the example of the Italian regions. Thus Martin Clark concludes: 'Paradoxically . . . the real importance of the Italian regions lies in the help they may give to the centripetal tendencies of the modern state and the modern economy.' (*The Failure of the State*, p. 73.)

19 The 'parity' depends in part on the balancing features of the federal constitution – as expressed by the role of the Federal Constitutional Court and through the direct representation of the *Länder* governments in the Bundesrat; the latter balance depends on the party composition of the *Land* governments as against that of the federal government.

20 However, Schmitter (*op. cit.*) argues that for societal corporatism to develop there has to be a 'liberal-pluralist past'. But it would be difficult to accept this contention for Germany without qualification.

21 The historical roots of German corporatism can be related to the present outlook. A study along these lines has been made by Philip Paur, '*Social theories of the industrial enterprise in Germany*', Ph.D thesis in preparation at the London School of Economics.

22 In developing his ideas on 'liberal corporatism' Lehmbruch (*op. cit.*) details the West German and Austrian techniques of economic management.

23 For the constraints affecting the Federal Republic see G. Smith, 'West Germany and the politics of centrality', *Government and Opposition*, autumn 1976.

24 Ionescu (*op. cit.*) discusses 'the politics of concertation', which he regards as typifying European development within the states as well as at the Community level.

25 The argument for the continuing importance of the states is put by Stanley Hoffman, 'Obstinate or obsolete? The fate of the nation-state in Western Europe', *Daedalus*, vol. 95, No. 3.

26 As used here, the term 'primary integration' lacks specific reference, but is used in a developmental sense. See Charles Tilly (ed.), *The Formation of National States in Western Europe*, Princeton University Press, 1975.

HUGH BERRINGTON

10 Dangerous corner?
An overview of political changes

Almost every political commentator, it seems, is tempted to ascribe a significance of an enduring character to what often turns out to be a transient event. It is easy, faced by what seems the advancing flood, to forget the regular ebb and flow of the tide. Yet even a short historical perspective should enable us to set some of the recent developments in British political life in their proper context. After the two elections of 1974, and particularly after the stalemate of the February contest, there was a tendency for analysts to write off the two-party system in Great Britain. Growing disillusionment with the two established parties, it was said, would enable parties like the Liberals in England and the Nationalists elsewhere to break through the barrier set by the electoral system. In the same way it was easy to interpret both the cruel struggle in Ulster, and the rise of new parties, as a resurgence of the periphery in British politics, a renewal destined to leave an indelible mark on British political development.

One of the greatest occupational hazards of the political commentator at times of political change and uncertainty is that of projecting the aspirations and fears voiced within the political and social elites on to the millions of relatively uninvolved and politically unsophisticated voters. It is too easy to invest the discourse of the politically active and of the politically aware with a popular support and indeed a popular commitment that is in fact lacking. Politicians and political commentators move primarily amongst those to whom politics is a matter of continuing and all-engaging concern, whose mode of discourse and manner of thinking are remote from, if not almost unintelligible to, those many electors for whom politics is a matter of intermittent interest and often of obscure importance. What seems to elite political actors and commentators to be the outcome, perhaps the inevitable outcome, of profound and deep-seated historical movements may be far from the preoccupations of ordinary citizens. In the last resort, deep-seated political changes have to be undertaken by people. Events are made by men. The historian of the late twenty-first century may well write as though British membership of the European Economic Community were a necessary, unavoidable development, given the changing economic context of, and strategic balance in, the world. British membership, nevertheless, had to pass two major tests. It had first to be espoused by elite political actors and had to win the allegiance of at least one major party in the state, whose strength itself depended on popular election; it had finally to be ratified by a referendum of the adult population. It would be easy to show that had a referendum been held before Britain entered the Common Market, what with hindsight can be regarded as an inevitable step might well not have occurred at all.

Elite political discussion, therefore, and that of the mass public often take place at two different levels – levels separated by an enormous gap in information and sophistication.[1] Moreover there will often be a striking contrast in the way elites and mass publics perceive political events. Nevertheless in a liberal democratic society where, ultimately, power resides with those who can obtain a majority of seats at an election based on universal suffrage, we have to look carefully at the popular base on which elite authority resides.

'MINOR PARTYISM'

Between 1945 and 1974 there were three waves of 'minor partyism' in Britain. The first manifestations occurred in 1957–58 with some pronounced Liberal by-election successes – as runners-up at Rochdale (the seat they were to win fourteen years later) and as winners at Torrington. The second wave occurred between 1961 and 1963 and reached its high point with the capture of what had hitherto been rightly seen as the safe Conservative seat of Orpington. The third wave occurred in 1972–74. The by-election triumph of the Independent Labour candidate Dick Taverne against the party machine at Lincoln, a sequence of Liberal by-election victories, and the simultaneous capture of Berwick by the Liberals and of Glasgow, Govan, by the Scottish Nationalists in November 1973, all seemed to indicate a new and permanent repudiation of the two-party hegemony.

At the election of February 1974 the Liberals took 19 per cent of the total vote (over 23 per cent in the constituencies they actually contested) and returned fourteen Members of Parliament, their highest figure since the election of 1935. Even more remarkably, the

Scottish Nationalists took 22 per cent of the vote in Scotland and won seven seats, a gain of six, whilst the Welsh Nationalists, though not faring as dramatically as the SNP, captured two seats from Labour in North Wales. In Northern Ireland the old connection between the Conservative Party and Ulster Unionism seemed to have finally sundered with the election of eleven Ulster Unionists MPs whose only allegiance was to their party organisations and their Protestant constituents in Northern Ireland.

Each wave of 'minor partyism' since the war has been stronger than the previous wave, but only clearly in Scotland and much more doubtfully in Wales has the rise of the minor parties posed a palpable and immediate threat to the established parties, and to the normal assumptions of British political life.[2]

After 1974, however, Liberal support seemed to wane. At nearly every by-election between October 1974 and March 1977 the Liberals have polled a smaller share, often indeed a much smaller share of the vote, than at the general election. The same message was repeated in the numerous opinion polls taken since the end of 1974. In the light of this, talk of the inevitable break-up of the two-party system in England looks, to say the least, premature. Within one year of the second election of 1974, the huge Liberal vote of that year seemed to have dissolved.

The fleeting nature of the Liberal gains in England, however, contrasts with the constancy of SNP support in Scotland. After three years the Scottish National Party has remained not merely a significant electoral force but one capable of profoundly altering the balance of political forces in the Westminster Parliament and a party whose programme introduces a new and disruptive element into British politics. Thus it is easy to show that a rise since October 1974 of 10 per cent in the SNP's share of the Scottish vote drawn equally from Conservatives and Labour would (assuming no other changes) give them forty-one seats. An increase of 20 per cent, which would give them just over half the total votes in Scotland, would bring them sixty-six of Scotland's seventy-one seats.

Electoral support for Scottish Nationalism, like the electoral support of other political parties, reflects not one but a number of different forces. First of all we may identify it as a specific manifestation of the general growth of minor parties. Secondly we may see Scottish Nationalism as growing naturally out of a specific national cultural tradition which is absent in most regions of England. More doubtfully, we may regard it and perhaps support for other minor parties as a protest against economic deprivation. Some, too, see it as born of the hopes of self-sufficient prosperity which awaits Scotland as a result of the exploitation of North Sea oil.

It is obvious enough that voters who are disillusioned with both established parties are likely to be drawn towards a minor party. Sometimes that party may exhibit clear 'anti-system' feeling, in other cases these anti-system views may be more diffuse, but in both situations a third party is likely to attract those disillusioned with the two main parties. What is more surprising, however, is that such a party can attract not merely those disenchanted with but also those who are satisfied with the two big parties. William Miller illustrated this in a graphic way in his survey of a sample of the Scottish electorate after the election of October 1974.[3] Miller wanted to find out to what extent voters trusted the two main British parties. Simplifying matters, there are four possible outcomes – some voters will trust both main parties, some will trust neither, some will trust Labour but not the Conservatives, and some trust the Conservatives but not Labour. Not surprisingly, the SNP attracted most support among those who trusted neither of the two big parties. Here, at any rate, is evidence that the SNP did appeal to those with an 'anti-system' feeling of some kind. What was remarkable, however, was the extent of SNP support among those who reposed their trust in *both* main parties. Where SNP support was weak was where there was a situation of unbalanced trust, that is to say, where voters trusted the Labour Party but not the Conservatives or the Conservatives but not Labour.

It is easy to see that there is a sense in which the two main parties depend upon each other for their strength and maintenance. Robert Lowe made a similar point, of the two established parties of his day, in a debate on one of the precursors of the second Reform Bill. In 1866 the Liberal government of Lord John Russell introduced a Bill to extend the suffrage: this Bill was strongly opposed by the Conservative Party and by a section of the Liberals – the famous Cave of Adullam. Lowe, one of the Liberal opponents of reform, argued in a remarkable speech that the two traditional parties, the Liberals and the Conservatives, depended upon each other for their own continued existence. The Liberal government had designed a Bill to strengthen its own party and to damage, and perhaps destroy, the Conservative Party, but Lowe saw the continued existence of the Conservative Party as being a condition of the continued vitality and power of the Liberals.

The annihilation of one of the aristocratic parties . . . would be a folly like that of a bird which feeling the resistance the air offers to its flight imagines how well it would fly if there was no air at all, forgetting that the very air which resists it also supports it and ministers to it the breath of life.[4]

One reason, then, for the rise of minor parties and more specifically of the SNP appears to lie in the widespread popular belief that 'there's no difference between them'. This feeling that there is little to choose between them is often expressed in a negative way; but even where it is held in positive fashion, and the voter regards both parties as being essentially benevolent, minor party support is quite high.

A parallel phenomenon can be observed in the kind of seats won by minor parties in the last few years. Paradoxically, it is the seats which are conventionally described as safe which are most vulnerable to Nationalist or Liberal attack. It is in seats like Galloway and South Angus, in Merioneth and the Isle of Wight, where one of the two big national parties is locally very weak, that the minor party threat is most acute. It is not merely the intensity of feeling each big party generates, but the severity of the competition between them, which helps to sustain their primacy in the state.

The SNP breakthrough has been the most significant manifestation of minor party strength since the second world war. Its importance lies partly in having, unlike the Liberals, an extensive geographic and cultural base. Scottish Nationalism represents a new form of minor partyism; it reflects a reawakening of the periphery, a reinstatement on the agenda of British politics of issues, once fraught with passion and danger, that seemed to have faded from public controversy after 1918. That it has a distinct geographic base gives it a strength, and may well endow its clientele with a stability, that the Liberals must envy. The SNP's electoral following consists of more than a collection of individuals giving voice to a vague discontent. Territorial concentration gives the SNP vote a psychological support and a strategic power that the much larger aggregate of Liberal voters do not have.

The SNP poses the threat it does chiefly because of the character of the electoral system. If the 'first past the post' regime inhibited the growth of the SNP in its early stages, beyond a critical threshold it affords a substantial, perhaps an immense bonus to that party. The British electoral system positively benefits those parties whose electoral following is linked to the simple fact of geographic residence. It is the nature of members of the same social class, or the same national or ethnic grouping, to live together; parties which appeal disproportionately to such groups therefore enjoy a large, if not an immense advantage, whilst those like the Liberals whose support is drawn from a cross-section and therefore dispersed evenly over the country are heavily penalised. Five and a quarter million Liberal voters in October 1974 could elect thirteen Members; 800,000 Scottish Nationalists could return nearly as many. It is ironic that the Conservative Party, which claims to be above all the party of 'the nation', should be so strongly committed to an electoral mechanism which rewards those parties whose appeal is most disruptive of what Conservatives mean by the nation.

The rise of the SNP has probably been a consequence, as it has been a manifestation, of Scottish electoral instability. In the election of December 1910 Scotland returned fifty-eight Liberals, three Labour, and nine Unionists. By 1935 the Liberals had been reduced to three; their strongholds in rural Scotland had been captured by Conservatives or held vicariously for the latter by National Liberals. In the 1960s there were signs of a renewal of Liberal strength in Scotland, and in 1964 the Liberals made three gains in northern Scotland. In an area separated from the mainstream of British national life, which fitted uneasily into the new national pattern of class-based cleavages, it is not surprising that large numbers of voters should have been 'available' to minor parties. Now, having been largely built on the rural base lost by the Liberals, the SNP faces the test of breaking into the urban, and mainly industrial, seats of Clydeside and the Lothians.

If the near-disappearance of the once dominant Liberals has imposed a discontinuity in Scottish politics which has benefited the SNP, another 'available' group of voters are the young. Commitment to a party, it is argued, increases with age; the more often we vote for one party, the more likely we are to go on voting for it. Habit grows by its exercise. Those who have never voted before, or but once or twice, are 'available' for mobilisation by a new party. So, in the American presidential election of 1968, it was found that whilst old people thought as highly of the third-party candidate George Wallace, as did the young, they were much less likely to vote for him.[5] It is not surprising that surveys show SNP electoral support to come disproportionately from the young.

The very success of the SNP prompts the question whether, leaving aside the possibility of a fourth, perhaps decisive upsurge of Liberal support, there will be any English counterpart. It is not easy

to see English regional feeling forming the mass basis of new
political parties, though it is equally not hard to perceive that feeling
being displayed at elite level through the media of local councils and
regional groups of MPs and, of course, in the behaviour of trade
unions and interest groups (see below, pp. 204–6, for example). The
last two years have seen some increase in the electoral appeal of the
extreme right, exemplified in the votes obtained at by-elections by
the National Front and, to a lesser extent, by the National Party.
The support for these parties still remains very low; nevertheless, it
remains true that fifteen years ago the Scottish National Party was
looked upon as a collection of eccentrics and romantics unable to
muster more than about five per cent of the vote in a parliamentary
election.

It is arguable, however, that major electoral realignments are as
likely· to be precipitated by the elites as by the mass public.
Economic catastrophe (such as might follow the abandonment of the
incomes policy) or an open split in the Labour Party might create
one of those rare opportunities for the establishment of a new
political formation. In the same way, the adoption of certain kinds of
electoral reform would undermine the dominance of the two main
parties in England. Short of such changes, disillusionment with the
traditional parties, and in particular the decline of the divisions
between them, will continue to foster support for minor parties.
What is lacking in England is the crucial additional element of a
pronounced territorial/cultural identity, reflected in a demand for
distinctive political institutions.

Economic adversity, and in the specific case of Scotland the
discovery of North Sea oil, have been advanced as explanations of
the electoral growth of nationalism. Lack of space precludes
discussion of both these explanations, but Miller[3] has argued
cogently that neither can account for the growth of SNP support.
Suffice it to say here that, whatever the precise connection between
economic experience and the rebirth of the periphery, the
relationship seems far from simple. If such a view is comforting in a
time of acute economic difficulty, by the same token it offers little
hope that prosperity, of itself, will lay the ghost of nationalism.

THE DEVOLUTION DEBATE AND THE PARTIES

Political debate occurs at the two distinct and often barely
connected levels of the political elite and the mass electorate. It

would be wrong to assume that issues which engage the one are necessarily of concern to the other. There is considerable doubt whether Senator McCarthy mobilised electorally significant popular support in his anti-Communist campaign;[6] and in turn public feeling over immigration in Britain in the late 1950s evoked few echoes among the political class until 1961. The issue of nationalism, however, can hardly fail to be a source of disturbance at both levels. In Scotland the SNP showed in October 1974 that it could mobilise thirty per cent of Scottish voters. The success of the Nationalists has been much less striking in Wales, but even here in the most Welsh parts of Wales the Plaid Cymru has been able to poll between a quarter and a third of the votes. Scottish developments, however, are obviously of greater immediate importance; given the simple crude 'first past the post' electoral formula, there is a strong possibility of the Scottish National Party winning a clear majority of Scottish seats on a minority of total votes cast. Further gains by the SNP are likely to damage Labour rather more, since there are fewer Scottish Conservative seats left to take.

Although opinion polls show that a majority of Scottish voters do not want separation, there remains the possibility that the SNP would regard victory in a majority of Scottish seats as a mandate to press for full independence. Such a situation would clearly open a new, strange and perilous chapter in the history of the United Kingdom.

The first and most obvious effect, however, would be that it would make it difficult for either of the two main parties to achieve an overall majority on their own. Given the relatively close division between Labour and Conservative at most general elections, the existence of a third party, say forty strong, plus perhaps another twenty Members unattached to either of the two main parties, could well produce a minority government or a coalition. Even here, however, the distortions of the electoral system at the United Kingdom level can help to muffle the distortions it creates on the Scottish scale. The electoral system does tend to translate relatively small leads in the aggregate vote into substantial majorities of seats. Thus the Labour Party had a margin of over 100 seats over the Conservatives in 1966, though its popular plurality was only 6 per cent. The Conservatives achieved a similar result in 1959, and the Labour Party again achieved a very large overall majority with a lead of about eight per cent over the Conservatives in 1945. Experience after 1885 is also instructive; the Irish Nationalist Party emerged with about eighty safe seats, but for most of the period one party (counting the Conservatives and Liberal Unionists as one) was sufficiently strong to govern on its own. If the electoral progress of the SNP culminated in national separation, or short of that in a near clean sweep of Scottish seats, the effect would be to weaken the Labour Party and to make it difficult but not impossible for it to obtain an overall majority. Thus in 1964 the Labour Party's overall majority of five would have disappeared but for the margin of fifteen supplied by Scotland. The same dependence is clearly visible in the election results for October 1974.

More interesting perhaps would be the effects of the establishment of assemblies with devolved powers and the creation of various executive bodies in Scotland and Wales. So far the evidence from local elections suggest that people carry their partisanship over from national elections into local elections. Labour councillors bear the brunt of public anger with a Labour government just as Conservative councillors are held responsible for failures of a Conservative administration in London. The existence of regional assemblies in both Scotland and Wales, however, may blur the sense of party identification in these two areas. Canada is notable for the extent to which parties which make little impression at national level are able to form the government at provincial level. With the apparent breakdown of traditional party loyalties in Scotland and the much more modest erosion which has been occurring in Wales it is not too far-fetched to see the development of different party allegiances corresponding to the two levels of government.

The rise of Celtic nationalism illustrates the inadequacies of the simple left–right dimension which we employ as a convenient descriptive shorthand. Centre–periphery conflicts cut across the issues of class, and economic control. At elite level the impact of the devolution debate will, in a curious sense, be to unify the Labour Party, or at any rate to inhibit the continued polarisation of the party along the left–right axis. One feature of the debate within the Labour Party in Scotland has been that the issue has tended to cut through the normal left–right divisions. Thus John Mackintosh, on the right of the Labour Party, has made common cause with Dennis Canavan and Norman Buchan on the left. In England too the devolution issue seems to be cutting through the normal divisions within the Labour Party. Thus, although Peter Byrd shows that there is some tendency for opponents of the EEC to be hostile to devolution (those critical of both constituting what can be termed a

Great Britain, Little England' group), the association, as he notes, is moderate.[7] A breakdown of the forty-three Members who either voted against or deliberately abstained on the devolution Bill guillotine in February 1977 shows that eleven of them, or 26 per cent, were members of the Tribune group – not much short of the proportion of non-ministerial Tribune MPs in the back-bench party.[8] In other words such an issue is likely to unite former enemies and to separate old allies. By that very fact it is likely to contribute to the overall unity of the party.

REGIONAL PRESSURE POLITICS[9]

However, a much more sinister danger besets British politics. Let us concede that the SNP remains an important political force and is able to wield considerable power in the British House of Commons without actually achieving its goal of independence. Let us also assume that it remains perceived as a potent electoral threat. In such a situation we are likely to see some aggravation of the present tendency for governments, particularly Labour governments, to try to buy Scottish votes by a series of concessions made ultimately at the expense of the English regions. Indeed, the more the Scottish electorate perceive that the threat of a large SNP vote is a lever with which to exort additional good things from the Westminster government, the greater the incentive to vote for the SNP. Paying danegeld rarely buys off the Danes.

The trouble with regional pressure politics is that it is a game that can be played to advantage only by one or two. An innovating businessman may for a while enjoy monopoly profits, but his very success will, by tempting new competitors into the field, undermine his monopoly. The logical consequence is that other regions will start putting pressure on governments in order to achieve what they regard as their rightful share. In some cases this may take the form of break-away splinter regional parties, but the pressure is much more likely to be exercised within the majority party by particular regional groups of MPs. Thus the concessions offered by the Labour government to Scotland and Wales have already provoked the 'English backlash'. Some critics from the English regions have emphasised the need for administrative and institutional mechanisms not unlike some of those which have been conferred on Scotland and Wales. Others have stressed the need for direct, material assistance. One north-eastern Labour Member, John Horam, introduced a Private Members' Bill, subsequently withdrawn, calling for the creation of Development Agencies for the north of England, for Merseyside and for south-west England which would have had powers similar to the Scottish and Welsh Development Agencies.[10] Some months later Labour MPs for the northern region pressed for a North East Development Agency, and were rebuffed by the Lord President of the Council, Michael Foot.[11] Tyne and Wear Council expressed unanimous opposition to the Devolution Bill on the grounds, *inter alia*, that 'this will bring about an excessive imbalance favourable to Scotland at the expense of the North East Region and other English regions'.[12] A former Labour Minister, Tom Urwin, declared that 'the Northern Region is entitled to expect at least equal treatment in industrial and infrastructure development as other similar areas . . . A far greater number of employing industries have been domiciled in Scotland since the redistribution of industry in 1945 and imbalance has developed through the presence of the Scottish Office in Edinburgh allied with the Cabinet presence of a Scottish Secretary of State.'[13]

North-eastern and north-western Labour Members have also voiced deep resentment against what they see as discriminatory economic help for Scotland. Tom Urwin complained that £14 million had been provided for Marathon on Clydeside to build a speculative oil rig, on the eve of the parliamentary recess, only months after similar aid for Laing Offshore in Hartlepool had been refused.[14] Lancashire Members, too, have added their protests. 'I am not a Merseyside Nationalist,' said Eric Heffer, 'but I certainly intend to protect the interests of the Merseyside people . . . Merseyside has the highest rate of unemployment in the whole of Great Britain . . .'[15]

North-east England's political leverage has been weakened by the party complexion of the area. The region's solid array of impregnable Labour seats is an uncertain blessing. With few constituencies vulnerable to the Conservatives on any 'normal' swing, and no third party like the SNP to bother about, Ministers have little spur to respond to the grievances of the north-east. In default of a grass-roots voter reaction, the only power the region can exert is through its contingent of usually loyal back-bench Labour MPs. Their ultimate sanction lies in acquiring a disposition to make trouble for Ministers, to deploy their votes in important legislation with an eye to tactical advantage, and even, if need be, to threaten to bring down the government. 'There is a lesson to be learned from the past ten years', said Ted Leadbitter, MP for Hartlepools.

'Reasonableness does not always win in government. . . . It is already clear in my area that Scotland is more militant in getting what it wants and somehow seems to get it.'[16] Members from the north-west have spoken in a similar tone. 'It is an illustration of the old Scots saying that a greetin' bairn gets the best attention,' said James Lamond of Oldham; '. . . the more noise one makes and the more difficulties one causes the government, the better the attention received from them.'[17]

There are signs that north-eastern Labour Members are now prepared to take their protests into the division lobbies; four voted against the guillotine on Labour's devolution Bill and five abstained. Thus nine out of twenty Labour back-benchers from the region helped to set back a major item of legislation during the 1976–77 session.

Recently, the north of England has gained some substantial benefits, though it is not yet clear how much these owe to political pressure from back-bench MPs. The survival of the scheme to construct the new 'Metro' railway service on Tyneside had been in doubt, but the government eventually agreed to the continuation of the project. Similarly the north-eastern firm of Swan Hunter Ltd received a Ministry of Defence order for a new naval carrier in 1976 which guaranteed employment for the work force for eighteen months.[18]

Underprivileged regions, however, campaign not merely against governments but against other regions. The location of the headquarters of the new Shipbuilders' and Ship Repairers' Association became a matter of keen dispute between Merseyside and the north-east.[19] The north-west's power is enhanced by the fortuitous advantage of having a large number of marginal seats.

Hitherto the visible expression of regional claims and grievances in the House has been largely confined to questions, and to pious statements on the House of Commons Order Paper. In future this expression may take a more dangerous and acrimonious form.

The impact of regionalism in Britain is likely to blur the ideological polarisation of the Labour Party and whenever Labour is in office to substitute a rather undignified kind of pork-barrel regional politics, conducted to a large extent behind the scenes at Westminster, for the simple clash of the Tribune group and the Manifesto group. When there is a Conservative government the West Midlands, the south-west, and north-west England are likely to exert similar regional pressure.

Even if the appeal of Scottish and Welsh nationalism is not primarily economic in origin, their example may well intensify the problem facing government of satisfying demands of an economic kind. The cultural nationalism of Scotland and Wales may, by the precedent they offer, open the way to a crude economic regionalism in England. Areas with little sense of distinctive identity may come to find an artificial persona in pursuit of economic well-being. The political renaissance of Celtic Britain may spell the fragmentation of the Anglo-Saxon heartland.

Thus the continuing struggle between social classes (or, perhaps more accurately, among different occupational groups) over the distribution of the national income will be partly replaced by competition among the regions for the benefits at the disposal of central government. This new kind of regional politics will afford further illustration of what Gordon Smith calls 'the overextension of the state'.[20]

THE IMPACT OF THE EEC ON BRITISH PARTIES

The impact of the EEC on British parties is much less easy to trace. Before the referendum the fear was expressed that 'things would never be the same again'. The spectacle of a national campaign cutting through each of the established parties and in particular dividing the Labour Party in such a continuously visible fashion would, it was said, so sunder political friendships and political alliances as to leave a permanent breach within the party. Yet these fears seem to have been largely dispelled. The Labour Party conducted its referendum dispute with a degree of dignity and forbearance unusual in its history, and, moreover, meeting as it did the shock of the run on the pound and the subsequent imposition of the £6-a-week pay policy soon afterwards, the issues of the referendum were soon put behind. In one sense, moreover, the referendum campaign and the whole Common Market issue was a source of party unity. It is true that about 95 per cent of the left within the Parliamentary Labour Party were opposed to continued British membership of the EEC. It is also true, however, that nearly half the remainder of the party, roughly the centre and right, were also opposed to British membership of the EEC. What the issue did was to split what can loosely be called the non-left of the party down the middle. Once again we can see the unifying function of cross-cutting conflict in helping to blur what might otherwise be a dangerous ideological polarisation.

The future impact of the European Community issue upon both the elite and the mass levels of the political parties in Britain is difficult to assess. Clearly at the elite level the issue is not completely spent. Thus the question of elections to the European Parliament, the scrutiny of EEC legislation and future moves towards a closer political union are likely to be a source of continuing argument within the parties, particularly within the Labour Party. The EEC is likely to be 'the grumbling appendix' of British politics. There are still powerful elements within the Labour Party seeking either British withdrawal or changes in its nature which would reduce the Community to a loose confederation; but, in contrast, some of those, such as Peter Shore, who have hitherto been among the most ardent opponents of British membership, have indicated at least a conditional acceptance of the referendum verdict. It is not easy, at this time, despite the pressures of the Labour left, to see the debate assuming the critical significance that the question of British membership itself did.

As the process of integration becomes more marked so the impact of EEC membership on the sense of daily well-being of the mass public will increase; presumably issues such as higher food prices will give anti-Market politicians a certain mileage.[21] Nevertheless we ought to beware of over-investing any continuing debate with too much deliberation and rationality. Objective facts are subjectively interpreted. As the referendum debate surely demonstrated, it is possible for almost any claim about British membership of the Common Market to be supported by some kind of argument with surface plausibility. It is rarely in the unanimous interest of politicians to assign responsibility where it properly belongs: a rise in the cost of living will be attributed by some to membership of the Community, by others to the misguided policies of the government in power. Again we should not underestimate the capacity of ordinary electors to misinterpret or distort events so as to fit in with some broader preconception or more general prejudice. The authors of one of the earliest studies of voting behaviour in the United States showed convincingly how Democrats who themselves were opposed to the re-enactment of price control were able to persuade themselves that their candidate, Harry Truman, was against price control – even though the re-imposition of controls was one of his chief election calls.[22] More recently we have seen in our own day how for years the Labour Party was able to escape electoral reprisals for its antipathy to controls on immigration. The chief role of British membership of the EEC at the level of the mass electorate will be to provide one further scapegoat for demagogues of both right and left. It seems unlikely, however, that this new scapegoat will succeed in displacing the government of the day as the entity held mainly responsible when things go ill and given praise when things go well.

CONSTITUTIONAL PRACTICE

It is already clear that the twin developments of integration with Europe, and territorial division within the United Kingdom, are leaving their mark upon the country's constitutional code. Thus the referendum was employed in Britain for the first time on a national scale in order to defer, and with hope to resolve, the conflict within the Labour Party on the question of EEC membership. More recently the government sought to buy off dissatisfaction over the devolution Bill by promising advisory referenda in Scotland and Wales. Having been defeated on the floor of the House over its proposal to guillotine debate on the devolution Bill, the government accepted the rebuff. A year before, a defeat arising from widespread left-wing abstentions had been followed by a call for a vote of confidence from the House.[23] The conventions governing the relationship between government and Parliament (when is a government obliged either to resign or advise a dissolution?), which were never precise, have now become even more blurred. Soon, perhaps, back-benchers will come to realise that the dagger of dissolution (or resignation) that governments flourish under challenge is a rubber knife. The threat that a parliamentary defeat may mean a general election will lose its credibility if Members find that they can vote against their government, or abstain, without exposing themselves to the risks of a new election. Labour governments, in particular, will see their authority suffer; right-wing rebels will still run the hazard of being disowned by their constituency parties but the left will be under no such constraint. The devolution issue, because it cuts across the normal lines of cleavage in the Labour Party, is likely to exacerbate the tendency, already discernible, for back-benchers to carry their disagreements into the division lobbies. A new set of conventions may develop, conducive to greater back-bench freedom.

New conventions will probably become essential if, as a result of electoral reform, no party is able to govern with an overall majority in the House. The concordat reached between Mr Steel and·Mr Callaghan whereby the thirteen Liberal MPs agreed to support the government on the vote of confidence in March 1977 in exchange for formal consultation could be the forerunner of a permanent acceptance of government by coalition. It is notable that, but for the loss of seats to the Scottish and Welsh Nationalists, the Labour government would not have been in danger. Moreover, it seems that a distinction has been drawn between supporting the government on votes of confidence and giving general support to government policy in the division lobbies. In the days leading up to the vote of confidence Mr Callaghan himself distinguished between 'governing' and 'legislating'.[24]

Moreover both the EEC and the devolution questions are likely to lend force to the movement for adopting some kind of proportional representation. Even if the British Parliament decides to keep the traditional 'first past the post' mechanism for the first direct elections to the European Parliament, it is likely that within a few years all national elections to the European Parliament will have to be conducted under proportional representation. In addition, both the proposed Scottish Assembly, and elections in Scotland to the Westminster Parliament, pose the threat of a freakish result; with three parties each commanding between a quarter and two-fifths of the votes, the outcome becomes totally unpredictable – and may well prove to be incapable of justification. Despite the patronage of the powerful vested interests which have grown up under its protection, the 'first past the post' formula may prove to be one of the first examples of our national complacency to fall to the combined pressures of internal divison and European integration.

The rise of nationalism as an electoral force represents the rebirth of issues which seemed to have died by 1922. Before the first world war the main issues dividing the parties were questions of nationality and religion. The cause of the centre was embodied in the Conservative Party (or Unionist Party, as it later came to be called); that of the periphery was expressed either through the Liberals or through the Irish Nationalist Party. With the secession of southern Ireland, and the apparent exhaustion of religious issues, class cleavages became dominant. These posed questions of a different order to those put by the cleavages of Edwardian and Victorian Britain. To many, the emergence of parties based explicitly or tacitly on class was a frightening development, portending political disintegration and social disruption. In fact, the problems raised by the 'class war' have proved to be less divisive, less fraught with danger than issues like those of Irish Home Rule and religious education. That these more modern cleavages also raise serious difficulties is shown by Britain's chronic inflation. The recent revival of nationalism, however, is likely to present policy-makers with both sets of problems at once. The passions of national identity and cultural separateness are likely to combine with the bread-and-butter questions of living standards, jobs and housing – questions now to be put not in a class framework but in a regional or cultural context.

If, as seems likely, nationalist support remains considerable, the prospect facing future British governments will be harsh. There is no guarantee that the claims of the periphery can be settled by simple process of accommodation through parliamentary means. The capture by the SNP of thirty-six Commons seats might lead to their presenting the London government with the *fait accompli* of a UDI. In the last decade or so British governments have steadily lost the will and the capacity to rule. Governments that are not prepared to vindicate the right of citizens to watch the cricket match of their choice, or to uphold the law against a handful of recalcitrant councillors, may when faced by a seemingly resolute nationalist delegation of MPs lack the confidence to insist that the unity of the kingdom can be abrogated only through the normal procedures of law. The external adequacy of the British state, its capacity to offer physical security, is now in doubt. Little by little, recent British governments have dissipated and dispersed that great store of authority their predecessors handed down to them.

Every nation, in its history, has its 'dangerous corners' to negotiate. The years just before the first world war afford one example for Britain, whilst 1940 offers another. If nothing that occurs in the next decade, apart from the risk of a world war, is likely to pose a choice as terrible as that of 1940, the hazards are visible enough. Britain's nationhood, unquestioned for so long, is now under threat, whilst the continuance of her democratic regime can no longer be assumed as complacently as it once was.

Yet there remain no inevitabilities in politics. The events of the past few years may have left an imprint on the national psychology which could free the elites from the constraints imposed by excessive public expectations. The effects of North Sea oil on the British economy, and especially on the balance of payments, will make it easier to satisfy electoral demands. The margin, with an electoral system like the British, between electoral triumph and political annihilation can be narrow. If 40 per cent of the vote would give the SNP a majority of Scottish Members 25 per cent would probably see it reduced to impotence. Nor, in contemplating the unhappy accidents that can befall a country, should we forget the role of beneficent chance. The decision to go on fighting in 1940 was vindicated, even if the grounds on which hopes of victory were built at the time were later shown to be illusory.

Decision-makers always face a twin temptation. There is the tendency to give the ephemeral a permanence it does not warrant, to lend the anxieties of the day a consequence they do not deserve; the other, equally seductive, is to regard real and lasting changes as sudden and transient incidents. Part of the skill of the decision-maker lies in his capacity to distinguish rightly between the volatile and the durable. If he must avoid interpreting 'every chance event', to use Freud's phraseology, 'as a premonition of evil' and 'exploiting every uncertainty in a bad sense . . .',[25] he must also know and take to heart General de Gaulle's warning: 'The future lasts a long time'.

NOTES

1 The higher level of political knowledge of the political elite does not necessarily mean a greater capacity for making wise political choices. The ideological sophistication of the political elite, for instance, is sometimes a severe handicap to rational political decision-making.

2 Northern Ireland might be added, but it offers a more ambiguous example.

3 W. Miller, 'The connection between SNP voting and the demand for Scottish self-government', *European Journal of Political Research* (forthcoming) and enlarged version (mimeo). The enlarged version offers a full examination, based on survey data, of the relation between demands for self-government, other attitudinal variables and SNP voting.

4 *Hansard's Parliamentary Debates*, vol. CLXXXIII (3rd series), col. 1648 (31 May 1866).

5 P. Converse *et al.*, 'Continuity and change in American politics: parties and issues in the 1968 election', *American Political Science Review*, December 1969.

6 N. Polsby, 'Towards an explanation of McCarthyism', *Political Studies*, October 1960.

7 See chapter 7.

8 Membership of Tribune Group as reported in *Political Companion*, autumn/summer 1976. For name of Labour MPs voting against, or abstaining, on the devolution guillotine see *The Times*, 24 February 1977.

9 I am particularly indebted to Roger Guthrie for much help with this section, and to Iain McLean for providing me with numerous newspaper references.

10 *H. C. Deb.*, vol. 906, cols. 1728–1811 (5 March 1976).

11 The Journal, 8 December 1976.

12 See *Is This a United Kingdom?*, published by Tyne and Wear County Council, 1977.

13 *Ibid.*

14 *Financial Times*, 7 and 8 January 1977; *Northern Echo*, 7 January 1977.

15 House of Commons Standing Committee on Regional Affairs (9 July 1975), p. 27.

16 *Ibid.* (5 November 1975), col. 36.

17 House of Commons Standing Committee on Regional Affairs, 17 November 1976, p. 7.

18 *Evening Gazetteer*, 13 June 1975. I am grateful to Roger Guthrie for drawing my attention to this reference.

19 Information supplied by R. Guthrie.

20 See chapter 9.

21 See *The Times*, 22 February 1977, report of NOP survey in which 41 per cent of the sample thought that EEC membership had contributed 'a great deal' to rising food prices.

22 See B. R. Berelson, P. F. Lazarsfeld and W. N. McPhee, *Voting*, University of Chicago Press, Phoenix edition, 1966, p. 221.

23 See *The Times*, 11 and 12 March 1976.

24 See *The Times*, 19 March, 1977.

25 See S. Freud, 'Introductory lectures on psycho-analysis', Part III, p. 398, in *The Complete Psychological Works of Sigmund Freud*, vol. XVI, Hogarth Press, 1963.

INDEX

Atlanticists, 134

Benn, A. W., 135, 138, 142, 146, 149
Britain: external inadequacy, 186, 211; nationhood, 211; sovereignty, 3 f, 29–30; state corporatism, 187
British government: attitudes to devolution, 92–3, 94–5, 96; attitudes to European Community, 92–5, 96; EC policy, 98–103, 105–6, 109, 117; organisation, 90–1, 97–8; regional policies, 57, 88, 95 f; role, 91, 96–8; special units, 90, 97–8; threat to, 211
Buchan, N., 53, 56, 59, 63, 67
Buchanan-Smith, A., 65, 67, 163 f, 168, 171 n.
bureaucratic administration, 19–20, 42, 92
Bureau of Unrepresented Nations, 85

Callaghan, J., 141, 145, 149 f
centralised government role, 4–5, 8 f, 93 f, 98, 104
Central Policy Review Staff, 90 f
civil service, 90
Common Agricultural Policy, 15, 27, 32, 35, 37, 101
Communist Party, 65
Confederation of British Industries, 56, 66, 69 n., 171 n.
Conservative Party: attitudes to devolution, 6, 162–5, 167, 170; Unionist tradition, 160, 162 f, 165, 168–9; and European integration, 7, 160 f, 166–7, 170; and EC referendum, 54, 166–7; in Scotland, 50, 64–5, 162 ff; in Wales, 77, 81–2
constitution, 91, 209; Royal Commission on, 2, 44, 90, 92, 162
Constitution Unit, 2, 97, 107
corporatism, 181, 182–4, 186–7
Council of Ireland, 39
Crowther-Hunt, Lord, 92, 104

decentralisation, 7, 86, 180, 186
devolution: Bill for Scotland and Wales, 6, 64 f, 67, 94, 105, 111, 118, 153–4, 164–5, 169, 206; English dimension, 112, 118, 120 f; government proposals, 62; impact on European policy, 100–7, 120; interdependence with national government, 95; maximal, 67; minimal, 61, 63, 120; opposition to, 151–3, 155; powers under, 110–11; White Paper, 1975, 23, 62–3, 104

economic deprivation, 13, 34 ff, 49, 68 n, 73–4, 198, 201, 206
economic regionalism, 206–7
elections, general, 1974, 2, 44, 48, 52, 64, 71, 195 ff
electoral system, 48, 202 ff
elite, political, 8, 145, 196, 201, 208
English regionalism, 7, 13, 86, 201, 204–7; assemblies, 120, 122; EC aid, 102, 106
Europe of Regions, 14–16, 122
European Commission: financial aid, 34–7, 38–9, 87; Regional Development Fund, 13, 35, 87, 101–2; Regional Policy Committee, 87
European Community: British accession, 1, 3 f, 14, 91; economic and regional planning, 37; expansion, 190; implications for Parliament, 109–10, 112–18; information offices, 42, 59, 86, 103; regional policies, 40, 122; scrutiny committees on legislation, 110, 113–18; and devolution, 100–7, 120
European integration, 1 ff, 7, 12, 14, 17 f
European Investment Bank, 35
European Parliament, 2–3, 19, 60, 110, 122, 189; elections to, 110, 124, 147–8, 210; relations with national parliaments, 123–7
European Unit, 97, 99
Evans, G., 70 f
Ewing, W., 54, 60, 85

federalism, 94, 120 f, 159 f, 185–6
Foot, M., 81, 149–50
Foster Committee (Select Committee on EC Secondary Legislation), 113, 116 f

Grimond, J., 54